Created in China

This book examines China's creative economy – and how television, animation, advertising, design, publishing and digital games are reshaping traditional understanding of culture. Since the 1950s China has endeavoured to catch up with advanced Western economies. 'Made in China' is one approach to global competitiveness. But a focus on manufacturing and productivity is impeding innovation. China imports creativity and worries about its 'cultural exports deficit'. In the cultural sector Chinese audiences are attracted to Korean, Taiwanese, and Japanese culture, as well as Hollywood cinema. This book provides a fresh look at China's move up the global value chain. It argues that while government and (most) citizens would prefer to associate with the nationalistic but unrealised 'Created in China' brand, widespread structural reforms are necessary to release creative potential. Innovation policy in China has recently acknowledged these problems. It considers how new ways of managing cultural assets can renovate largely non-competitive Chinese cultural industries. Together with a history of cultural commerce in China, the book details developments in new creative industries and provides the international context for creative cluster policy in Beijing and Shanghai.

Michael Keane is Research Fellow with the Australian Research Council Centre of Excellence for Creative Industries and Innovation (CCI) at Queensland University of Technology, Australia. His most recent book (co-authored with Anthony Fung and Albert Moran) is *New Television, Globalization and the East Asian Cultural Imagination* (2006). He is co-editor of *Television across Asia: Television Industries, Programme Formats and Globalization* (Routledge); and *Media in China: Consumption, Content and Crisis* (Routledge).

Routledge Media, Culture and Social Change in Asia
Series editor
Stephanie Hemelryk Donald,
Institute for International Studies, University of Technology, Sydney

The aim of this series is to publish original, high-quality work by both new and established scholars in the West and the East, on all aspects of media, culture and social change in Asia.

Created in China
The great new leap forward

Michael Keane

Routledge
Taylor & Francis Group

LONDON AND NEW YORK

First published 2007
by Routledge
2 Park Square, Milton Park, Abingdon, Oxon OX14 4RN

Simultaneously published in the USA and Canada
by Routledge
270 Madison Ave, New York, NY 10016

*Routledge is an imprint of the Taylor & Francis Group,
an Informa business*

© 2007 Michael Keane

Typeset in Times New Roman by Keyword Group Ltd
Printed and bound in Great Britain by Biddles Ltd, King's Lynn

British Library Cataloguing in Publication Data
A catalogue record for this book is available from the British Library

Library of Congress Cataloging in Publication Data
A catalog record for this book has been requested

ISBN10: 0-415-41614-0 (hbk)
ISBN10: 0-203-93747-3 (ebk)

ISBN13: 978-0-415-41614-6 (hbk)
ISBN13: 978-0-203-93747-1 (ebk)

Contents

Tables

Foreword

John Howkins

Hindsight can be a wonderful thing. Looking back over the past 200 years we can see how half a dozen European countries and then America engendered a new kind of capitalist dynamo, a wild spree of invention, investment, production and branding. In 1800, Asia had contributed over half the world's wealth. A mere two centuries later, its share has fallen to 20 per cent. Today, the world's dominant thinking in research, business and finance, as well as popular culture, are American and European.

The cause of the West's growth was a mix of personal freedoms, education, scientific inquiry and private capital. The exact proportions were, and remain, a mystery.

Having raised themselves to the top of the mountain, the rich countries face a quandary. Where next? Their continued success depends on ever more extensive global markets, whether for raw materials (energy, food), cheap data processing, or new consumers. But global markets can be exploited by anyone from Chicago to Shenzhen.

Meanwhile, the immense achievement of the rich West hides a major shift in what is happening at ground level in their own countries. They are losing many thousands of manufacturing jobs a year. The success of their strategies for globalisation and open markets, and the widespread availability of the Web, have increased local expertise in almost every country. So what to do? The West is looking to its undoubted strengths in R&D and innovation, and its control of global marketing chains and branding. In 2006 the British Chancellor Gordon Brown pointed out that, whereas 25 years ago the market value of Britain's top companies was based entirely on their physical assets, their market value today is five times their physical assets. This, he said, demonstrates the economic power of knowledge, ideas and innovation.

At the same time, the rest of the world, and most noticeably in Asia, have started to use their own strengths in these matters. The most remarkable developments can be seen in China. China has always been a major world presence, if in a quiet way. Through the 1960s and 1970s it continued to pay its full dues to the UN and other international organisations and to keep abreast of global R&D. In the 1960s a NASA delegation was astounded to learn that the Chinese were ahead of

America in certain key technologies. In the 1970s, I had first-hand knowledge that its prowess in optic fibres, then a key communications technology, equalled the better known work in Britain.

Today, its expertise is obvious. The owner of a Shenzhen factory recently turned up on my doorstep in London to brief a London law firm in order to raise money on the London stock market. It was a routine visit, undistinguishable from a typical London meeting except that the team included a Beijing professor of creative industries.

As well as technological and financial strengths, China also brings its own attitude to the role of culture. One company which demonstrates this symbiosis very well is Shanghai Automotive Industrial Corporation (SAIC). A few months before Gordon Brown's announcement, I told SAIC I was impressed by its investments in the city's design ventures. I contrasted SAIC with the British car manufacturers which declined because they refused to take part in the British creative community, and had literally shrunk away. The conversation switched fluently between vehicle design, the environment and the work of a little-known Shanghai photographer whom I admire.

The quality of Chinese creativity is not in doubt. The story has been wonderfully recounted in Joseph Needham's *History of Science and Civilization in China*. We are now seeing a new narrative which could be called 'The History of Art, Innovation and Civilization in China'. In this, Michael Keane is a spirited and expert guide.

The creative economy, above all, is an economy of individuals wanting to express themselves. It is based on individuals seeking to make sense of the world, and hoping to make an impact on the world. The creative economy can be defined in a thousand different ways but it always comes down to this: an individual wanting to create something that he or she believes another individual will like and perhaps want to buy.

China's future will be greatly affected by China's confidence, gained over thousands of years, and its unique approach to ideas and the ownership of ideas and the commercialisation of ideas.

Central to this is the role of government and especially its relationship with creative people. Governments like to have rules and explicit principles. Creative talent likes to play around with the rules and to trust their own judgement. Both the Western and Chinese governments are struggling with figuring out new relationships for the new economy. What is the role of government in an economy based on individuals and their search for novelty?

How will the West and how will China enable their citizens to use their imagination and integrate their ideas into the national economy?

Acknowledgements

The American playwright Lillian Hellman once wrote, 'Nothing you write, if you hope to be any good, will ever come out as you hoped'. This book has been a long journey. I have visited many places and benefited from a wide range of insights. The people I met in these travels challenged me to think and reshape my assumptions. Many people are not mentioned by name but their ideas have helped me to understand China and my relationship to my writing.

There are many people I want to thank directly.

The research was made possible by an Australian Research Council Discovery Grant, *Internationalising the Creative Industries: China, the World Trade Organisation and the Knowledge-based Economy* (2003–2005). I would like to acknowledge the important inputs of John Hartley, Stuart Cunningham, Stephanie H. Donald, Terry Flew and Christina Spurgeon into this project. This book would be intellectually poorer without the contributions of Weihong Zhang and Linda Watterson who provided invaluable help in the final stages. Jiannu Bao, Li Hui, and Vicki Chiu were also integral to the project.

I owe thanks to many people in China. First and foremost Zhang Xiaoming from the Chinese Academy of Social Sciences, who helped in raising awareness of the 'Created in China' project and put me in touch with many of my contacts. Jin Yuanpu from Renmin University Humanistic Olympics Research Centre showed great interest and supported our Beijing conference in 2005. Thanks to Hui Min at Chinese Academy of Social Sciences for providing me with industry data.

I would like to acknowledge and thank the following people in China who gave me time and their thoughts, sometimes in passing, on China's creative economy: Lillian Lee, Alex Guo, Tom Wang, Jerry Wang, Pan Jin, Su Tong, Fu Ying, Ma Chenyu, Wang Bing, Zhao Yuxin, Zhang Zhaoxia, Mao Shaoying, Tao Dongfeng, Zhou Ziyan, Vincent Hsieh, Wang Liuyi, Charles Qu, Wang Jici, Lu Xuewu, Yang Rui, Zou Yu, He Shouchang and Li Wuwei. Particular thanks are due to Zheng Hongtao, who introduced me to the heart of Chinese culture in Henan, and to Wu Xiaoyan who made the trip there more enjoyable. In Chongqing I was assisted by Sherlyn Yang and Fiona Lee. In Hong Kong Sen Lee provided precious help in getting me to Hengdian, where I was looked after by Lee Kwok Lap and

Zhang Xianchun. I would also like to thanks friends Cao Shule, (Sophie) Wang Xuechun, Fanny Liu, Ran Ruxue, Leila Wu, Liu Cheng, Wang Hongyue, Yu Le, Huang Peijian and Wu Jing.

During the course of the project I benefited greatly from face to face and email discussions with Jing Wang, Justin O'Connor, John Howkins, Lily Kong, Patrick Mok, Desmond Hui, Kate Oakley, Michael Curtin, Toby Miller, John Sinclair, Ying Zhu, Wanning Sun, Ted Tschang, Gu Xin, Han-teng Liao, Andrew Ross, Eric Ma, Anthony Fung, Harvey Dzodin, Ned Rossiter, Liu Yan, Evert Verhagen, Fritz Demopoulos, Gilbert Yang, Ryan Stokes, Terry Cutler, Reginald Little and Dagfinn Bach. I would also like to acknowledge the support of Australian government trade department and embassy personnel in China: Laurie Smith, Paul Sanda, Christopher Wright, Jennifer Sparks and Scott Sheppard. Thanks to Hong Zhang for being the facilitator of many of the meetings I had in Beijing. Nina Shen played a similar role, particularly in Shanghai. I would like to express my gratitude to Hsu Chia-Cheng, my Chinese teacher at University of Adelaide, where this journey began, and to my teachers there, Andrew Watson, Carney Fisher and Zhang Ning, and my colleague Gerry Groot who continues to send me valuable information. Many of my friends at QUT have inspired me to complete this study. Thanks to Don Lamberton, Jason Potts, Peter Higgs, Lucy Montgomery, Jaz Choi, Kim Machan, Ian Creighton, Jinna Tay, Sue Street, Greg Hearn, Carol Chow, Tingting Song, Hong Lu, Bonnie Liu, Anna Rooke and Steven Copplin. Finally, I would like to express my appreciation to the series editor Stephanie Hemelryk Donald for her enthusiastic support during this project, to Peter Sowden at Routledge for believing in the project, and to Rasika Mathur and Alison Garman at the Keyword group for their professionalism in the copyediting stage of production.

My deepest thanks, however, goes to my partner Leigh, who encouraged me to finish this work. Finally, this book is dedicated to my father, William Keane.

Introduction

Cultures in collision

In 1985, the Australian writer Frank Moorhouse published *The Cultural Delegate*, a short story about cultures meeting in unexpected ways. The delegate in the story was Francois Blasé. Before taking up an Australian diplomatic post in Beijing, Blasé conducted research on Chinese etiquette. He read that Chinese were punctual, took speech-making and banqueting seriously, and preferred to avoid displays of drunkenness and boisterous behaviour. He read guide books on protocol, which told him that Chinese were moralistic about sex, did not display affection publicly, and were embarrassed about receiving large gifts. Unbeknown to the cultural delegate, however, the Chinese hosts were conducting their own research how Australians preferred to interact with strangers. When Francois Blasé attended his first banquet in Beijing, he acted according to his acquired stock of knowledge; the Chinese responded accordingly by getting drunk, slapping him the back, throwing food at each other, kissing him on the mouth, and asking not too subtly for gifts including cars and motorbikes.

Created in China: the Great New Leap Forward is about a deepening of China's engagement with the international discourse of creativity, a signifier that operates at several levels with different inflections – the governmental, the educational, the cultural, the aesthetic, and, most significantly in this study, the sphere of industry. China has advanced in the past two decades – from impoverished developing country status to transitional economy. Change brings with it destruction of old ways. Transitions involve flows of ideas about how to manage growth, how to be more efficient, how to become sustainable, and above all, how to adapt to international norms. Change disrupts stereotypes, especially when it occurs at breathtaking pace. Many of the changes in urban centres are recent, so much so that visitors are often overwhelmed by the sheer dynamism of Shanghai, Beijing and Guangzhou. The austere architectural style of socialist city planning is now a cultural relic; former factories serve as façades for urban redevelopment; fast food franchises and shopping malls flourish. Modern entertainment complexes advertise personal transformation. Chinese architecture takes on the appearances of hyper-modernism, albeit with degrees of orientalist singularity. Large spectacular buildings and stadiums that might take two years to construct in most international cities appear in the space of several months.

No-one denies China extraordinary economic development. Productivity is seemingly assured by low-cost labour. A growing number of companies from the developed economies line up to outsource production to the Mainland. However, is China a creative nation? While scarcely a defining concern for most Western researchers and journalists, creativity has become a hot topic on the Mainland. Concepts such as creative nation, creative city and creative century are endorsed in policy statements within the Eleventh Five-Year Plans of many Chinese cities. How did 'creativity' come to China so suddenly? Why has it been embraced so enthusiastically?

The answer has much to do with accelerated internationalisation. In 2001 – the year that China joined the World Trade Organization (WTO) – the fourth session of the Ninth People's Congress ratified the concept of the cultural industries (*wenhua chanye*). A series of *Blue Books of China's Cultural Industries* were launched to evaluate, to report, and to make recommendations on cultural industry developments. By 2004, however, the cultural industries were being challenged by a new 'foreign' idea – that of the creative industries. In early 2005, the Shanghai Municipal Government launched extensive creative industries plans, including a research institute, the Shanghai Creative Industries Research Centre. Beijing eventually followed suit in December 2006 with the First International Beijing Cultural and Creative Industries Expo, opened with due ceremony in the Great Hall of the People by senior officials of the Central Propaganda Department and the Ministry of Culture. A report from the event noted that, while 2006 was the year in which the concept 'cultural created industries' (*wenhua chuangyi chanye*) entered into mainstream discourse, 2007 would be the year of rolling out further policy and securing the development of China's creative industries; and 2008 would be a year in which transnational companies – the so-called 'international cultural aircraft carriers' – would participate in the 'great ocean' of cultural creative industries with emerging Chinese national champions (Fan 2006).

For some international observers of China's stalled media reforms, this latest emergence appears like a rewriting of the WTO script. When audio-visual services were quarantined from the General Agreement of Trade in Services (GATS) component of the WTO agreement in 2001, except for minor concessions in content distribution and cinema theatre construction, it was clear that the Chinese leadership was sending out two signals: first, that media content production would remain highly sensitive, and second, further liberalisation would occur when China's cultural and media industries were ready to compete. In the interim, Chinese companies would benefit from protectionist and advantageous industry policies.[1]

However, while 2006 may be officially recognised as the year in which cultural creative industries received the green light from the national government, the momentum had been building in China's cities. Disused manufacturing factories had already transformed into so-called creative clusters (*chuangyi jiju*) or creative precincts (*chuangyi yuanqu*). This phenomenon is now accelerating: spaces like Beijing's 798 Factory, Hangzhou's Loft 49, Shanghai's Tianzifang, and Chongqing's Tank Loft provide opportunities for alternative modes of production not permitted under previous political regimes. Consumption is also a part of the revitalisation of many former industrial precincts as the new pluralism on display draws tourists.

Why is this important? Let me give an example to illustrate. During a focus group at Beijing Film Academy in 2004, I asked students for their views about the value of Chinese culture. One student was quick to offer the view that China had a large quarry of tradition to draw on, and from this perspective alone should be considered a creative nation. Another student responded, 'Yes, I agree, but they constantly dig up the same kinds of things'. The metaphor of digging provokes some interesting parallels – raw material, buried treasures, archaeology, and natural wealth. In the ancient past, what came from the ground formed the elements for the creation of Chinese material culture: low carbon wrought iron was fused with high carbon cast iron to form co-fusion steel; saltpetre formed the basis for gunpowder; high temperature clay casting produced porcelain. The Chinese were great alchemists. Now, the economy is powered by manufacturing, the World Factory model.

Herein resides a problem: how to assess the importance of creativity in relation to economic growth. As the quarry metaphor implies, for some Chinese tradition is already creative enough; for others it is resolutely static. Many theme parks currently exploit tradition to generate income. About an hour outside Zhengzhou, the capital of Henan Province is the Shaolin Temple, where Chinese Buddhism meets kung-fu (*gongfu*). The visitors to the Shaolin Temple are predominantly under 30. It is apparent that tradition generates strong demand. However, it is also apparent that traditions which can be remade into contemporary media forms (cinema, TV drama and video games) stand more chance of producing profits and luring younger visitors.

Elsewhere in Henan the Millennium Park (*Qingming shanghe yuan*) in Kaifeng, a former capital city, celebrates life in the northern Song Dynasty; performers sing, dance, and enact tales from popular novels of the period. The many visitors to this park are mostly aged over 50. Most of these sightseers were denied access to the traditional culture of China during the Cultural Revolution (1966–1976). Visiting the park is undoubtedly a cultural pilgrimage for many.

The creativity conundrum extends to urban design and the nation's modernisation project. Chinese cities abound with international brands. But Starbucks, KFC, the Body Shop and other international icons prominently displayed on big city billboards are surface manifestations of uneven transformations. Visitors to Taiyuan, the capital of Shanxi province in central north-west China, can see the ancient walled city of Pingyao, now carefully preserved and marketed as a heritage site. Once centres of Chinese cultural life, cities like Taiyuan and Kaifeng are flanked by regions offering foreign companies low-cost manufacturing. Meanwhile, industrial production pollutes the Yellow River (*huang he*).

Creative industries: the road to economic development?

Optimism is reflected in a faith in *creative industries*. The term is now widely accepted in China, most conspicuously in the large coastal cities. A problem however is that creativity has no universally agreed definition, and as Chris Bilton (2007) notes, definitions of both creativity and creative industries tend towards duality and contradiction. The term 'creative' seems to privilege the creative personality – the individual – while 'industry' conjures up organised production. It is apparent also that many products and services touted as creative by industry spokespersons are conspicuously uncreative. The UK definition of creative industries, which is most often cited, favours the exploitation of intellectual property: '[The creative industries are] those industries which have their origin in individual creativity, skill and talent and which have a potential for wealth and job creation through the generation and exploitation of intellectual property' (DCMS 1998).

Some critics argue that the focus on creative industries, which has captured the attention of governments in many nations and regions, is symptomatic of the excesses of neo-liberalism (Hesmondalgh 2007). People refashion themselves as entrepreneurs, places brand themselves as 'cool' and cosmopolitan, and culture is increasingly turned into 'content' which is distributed across national borders. Audiences become consumers and end-users. Alternatively, the term 'cultural industries' evokes a more national and ultimately more civic articulation of cultural identity. This distinction between ostensibly related cultural resources leads to an economic development paradox. Cosmopolitan Shanghai, Beijing and Hong Kong are refashioned as 'creative cities' while Kaifeng, Taiyuan and Luoyang serve as 'cultural hubs'. The latter have tradition but lack the economic capital or proximity to the eastern seaboard to exploit the creative turn.

A critical question outside the large cities remains how to use tradition as a resource. Arguments about uneven cultural development therefore need to be contextualised. In many respects China is still adhering to a developmental state model: national and local governments remain architects of progress; they welcome international capital and will amend and bend rules to favour investors as well as local players. Investors meanwhile identify service and creative content sectors as growth industries in the big cities. Low-cost production – the factory model – moves to the hinterland and the regions, where labour is plentiful and environmental concerns are often disregarded.

Despite differences of interpretation the term 'creative industries' provides a useful analytical tool. In the following discussion, I use it to describe a set of interlocking segments of the economy focused on extending and exploiting symbolic cultural products. These include the arts, films, television, and interactive games. These industries provide business-to-business symbolic or information services in areas such as architecture, advertising and marketing, design – as well as web, multimedia and software development (Higgs *et al.* 2007). The term 'creative industries' has advantages over related descriptors in that it draws attention to *creative inputs* into production, marketing and distribution. It emphasises the value of human capital in the process of creating new ideas. In comparison, 'copyright' industries are defined by the nature of asset and industry output, 'content' industries by the nature of traded output, and 'cultural' industries by public policy function and funding (CIRAC and Cutler 2004: 11).

A key element of creative industries therefore is novelty generation and diversity – as opposed to pure information delivery and propaganda functions. The desire on the part of writers, artists and producers to challenge convention and to be critical has for the past several decades been constrained by political supervision. Novelty is now more evident in design, digital content, electronic games, advertising, marketing, TV, music, and film. Globally, these industry sectors are risky businesses because ultimately they compete for audience and user attention. This risk factor of consumer mediation is a new and different kind of challenge in China where the entry and exit of firms has not been based on market characteristics. Certainly variety is a characteristic of China's massive discriminating consumer market. But to what extent are new ideas generated? Do the media and cultural industries in China generate novel ideas, embed new ideas, or reinforce existing ideas? Where are the novelty generating industries located in China?

This brings us to the issue of political economy. The link between culture and economics has seldom attracted interest from China scholars, except in the broader Weberian sense of how Chinese cultural values impact upon wealth creation. Likewise the academic bias in the humanities towards activities of transnational media corporations ultimately reflects one-way traffic. The top-down perspective on China's media control is a familiar story. Variations on imperialism are frequently rehearsed, yet they tell us little that is new. Perhaps we should ask: why has the focus been so much on multinationals and national champions? Large corporations rarely take the same kinds of risks as smaller independent players. For media moguls, the desire to protect relationships with government officials precludes flexibility and impedes innovation.

China's next 'stage of development' may see its cultural producers successfully targeting regional and international markets. In order to achieve this, however, there is a need for Chinese cultural and media industries to break free of institutional and political shackles. Currently, the 'old' mass media (television, press) remain under tight state control and are barred from foreign investment. On the other hand, periodicals, magazines, animation, video games and mobile content applications are diversifying their market scope, targeting niche markets more than mass consumption, and finding ways to respond to their most valued demographic, the urban youth market.

This book will take the reader on a different kind of journey through China. I trace the history of cultural exchange, in particular the transfer and translation of ideas about progress and innovation. I present an alternative account of China's emergence. In contrast to conventional views of policy formulation as a top-down process, dominated by central government committees and propaganda chiefs, I argue that new ideas, knowledges and technologies make their way indirectly into policy discussions through epistemic communities. These include scholars, business professionals and international scholar-consultants.

My purpose in this book is not to provide a detailed account of specific media or cultural sectors so much as examine commonalties among these sectors. These interdependent relationships, and the emergence among policy makers and investors of belief in the future centrality of the intangible creative economy, reflect my argument that Created in China will one day be as important as Made in China. The creative development of people, technologies and processes is an important 'new leap forward'. It is a challenge now confronting China.

Chapters

The book is divided into two parts. The first part, culture and commerce in China, is historical and is based on secondary sources. While I am primarily concerned with the evolution of media and cultural policy, I have shamelessly borrowed 'big ideas' from world historians and economists. I make no claims therefore to being comprehensive and where necessary have directed the reader to more detailed accounts of history.

In the second section I adopt the position of a participant observer as well as detached chronicler of what I called the *created in China project*. Since 2003, I have tracked the emergence of the rhetoric of creativity. The Chinese creative century is a popular and ultimately reassuring idea for many. It appeals to government and business as a way forward. Its acceptance and rehabilitation – creativity was formerly a bourgeois concept – has culminated in major urban renewal projects. In the process of observing these changes, I have been fortunate to discuss their implications with policy makers, small business operators, artists, consultants, publishers, journalists, scholars and advisors, both Chinese and international. While I was following my many leads, a number of disparate threads were emerging and connecting. I have tried to integrate as many of these as possible but it is not possible to document every initiative, every intervention or every policy change. There will undoubtedly be other versions of this story. As an outsider with the benefit of many good 'inside' connections, I have attempted to show how these developments have moved from the margins into the mainstream.

In Chapter 1 I set out some of the key ideas. I argue that while both culture and economy are dynamic, China analysis and news reporting conventionally reflect unchanging traditions and recalcitrant authoritarianism. A more dynamic perspective shows that the resources of the past – those materials quarried from history – can be given new life; they can be converted into sustainable cultural assets through adding value and variety. In doing this, China is moving simultaneously through five stages of development: outsourcing, imitation, franchising, market identification, and industrial clustering. In Chapter 2 I argue that *stages of development*, a term central to the Chinese lexicon, is tied to institutional change

Chapter 3 provides the reader with an historical overview of cultural commerce from 2000 BCE until 1849 CE when China was opened up to the West by the Opium wars. In Chapter 4 I look at the years from 1849 to 1978, a period in which commercial culture rose to prominence in China's coastal cities before losing ground to the political expediencies of Marxist cultural renovation and nation building. In Chapter 5 I briefly examine the culture fever period of the mid 1980s, the debates about China's failure to catch up, and subsequent moves to recognise the cultural economy and the cultural industries.

Chapter 6 begins the second section – from Made in China to Created in China. The shift to include innovation as a key element of cultural industries reform opened up a space for the import of another Western concept – the creative industries. The swift uptake of this idea in China's cities has been assisted by the political obligation to 'catch up' to the developed capitalist economies. Chapters 7 and 8 examine creative cities, clustering and new centres of production as China attempts to up-scale its innovative productivity through new forms of creative organisation and management, often in designated clusters. In effect, the science park model of industrial innovation is extended to the creative economy.

Chapter 9 examines how China's large and fragmented marketplace gives rise to ways of production and distribution that don't always conform to global benchmarks. The tendency to imitate brings advantages of speed to market without the outlay of resources in testing (research and development). In Chapter 10 I consider how co-production, joint ventures, formats, and franchises are changing the landscape of China's creative industries. These processes involve an exchange of knowledge, skills and capital. Regional initiatives are helping Chinese media and creative industries to become recognised for their original value, rather than for their low cost. With a new wave of Korean and Taiwanese culture – movies, television, games, and fashions – capturing the youth market, governments and most citizens are asking how to build the national, but yet unrealised 'created in China' label.

In Chapter 11 I turn to the question: What does creativity mean for regions outside the big cities? I travel to Badaling on the Great Wall, to the Hengdian World Studios in Zhejiang Province, and to the Shaolin Temple in Henan Province. Finally, in Chapter 12 I offer a synthesis and an assessment of China's potential to compete in the creative economy, taking into account the broader political, social and economic contexts of development. Can Created in China co-exist and complement Made in China? What will be the future of the Created in China movement as it becomes increasingly embedded in state propaganda? Will creativity lose its critical edge as it move into closer association with the spheres of business and government?

Part I
Culture and civilisation

1 The innovation ecology

In Beijing's western Shijingshan district a massive project is under way on the site of the Beijing Capital Iron and Steel factory.[1] The Capital Recreation District (CRD) will be an 'integrated services centre'. The CRD will include an animation production base, a digital entertainment and leisure centre, conference and exhibition facilities, finance and business facilities, as well as environmentally friendly living, blending traditional and contemporary design supplemented by education and training centres. The vision is ambitious and the scale of the project is massive by any international comparison. This is part of a larger plan to alleviate Beijing's urban congestion while at the same time providing a sustainable development model for future generations. The key political idea underpinning the CRD is China's transformation into an innovative nation (*chuangxin xing guojia*).

In Beijing's eastern Tongzhou District plans are well established for a 200 hectare Cultural Creative Park, again with an emphasis on animation and digital content. The Park will house a new university campus. Its mission is to nurture a creative talent base. China's largest municipality, Chongqing, is meanwhile developing a 'creative ideas incubator' on the banks of the Yangzi River. Elsewhere disused factories, warehouses and streets have been refashioned into creative clusters. Shanghai proclaimed 36 such clusters by the end of 2005; by the end of 2006, Beijing had designated 18 key projects with another 12 scheduled for commencement by 2010; Chongqing has plans for 50 by the end of 2010.

A great new leap forward is imminent. The 'world factory' is no longer the default setting for development. China aspires to be a serious contender for the spoils of the global cultural and service economies, spheres of exchange largely bound together by forms of ephemeral property. These include bundles of rights, licensing and syndication agreements, human and social capital, brand names and customer databases. Currently, a small number of production and distribution centres dominate these so-called 'weightless' economies. Hollywood, Bollywood, London, Tokyo, and New York are global centres. In addition to these media capitals, we can append a short list of transnational companies and dominant enterprises – including Dentsu, Time Warner, News Corporation, Disney, Bertelsmann, Viacom, Globo and the BBC.

The perspective on China's engagement with the global economy in this book is at odds with much academic research and journalistic accounts of China's media. I argue that China's emergence needs to be framed within a broader system of innovation that takes into account interdependent emerging relations between creativity, technology and knowledge. Whereas conventional national innovation systems approaches focus primarily on institutions and technologies (Freeman 1995), the key issues are deeper, and arguably more fundamental to systemic change. China has embraced the discourse of creativity, a much more flexible and mutable concept than innovation. Creativity is not peripheral to mainstream industrial growth but is central to the integration and diffusion of new technologies. As Potts (2006) argues, the creative industries are a *'driver'* of growth in much the same way that agriculture was a driver in the early twentieth century, elaborately transformed manufacturing in the 1950s–1960s, or information and communications technologies through the 1980s and 1990s. The distinction I propose in this study follows from this. Potts maintains that the creative industries function to coordinate the economic order in a manner analogous to the national systems of innovations approach, typified by science, education and technology.[2] These 'techno-economic' spheres of innovation have been championed by policy makers and think tanks, particularly in China.[3] However, evidence from several countries suggests that the creative industries are growing at up to twice the rate of the mainstream economy (Potts 2006; Howkins 2001). Much of this growth is fed by increasing affluence, lower costs of technology, and hence a rising demand for new products and services. However, my emphasis in this study concerns process innovation more than product innovation, and it is less about specific sector growth (for example, film, animation) and more about the systemic impacts of greater novelty.

In this chapter I begin this exploration by looking at the theme of catch-up, a preoccupation of China's reformers for over a hundred years. I use the idea of catch-up to underpin a key argument of this book – that culture and economic development are mutually dependent. At various times throughout history, China was at the leading edge of technological and artistic innovation. However, China's leaders failed to capitalise, largely as a result of excessive government intervention into society. Intervention included nurturing a talent base – scholar officials who would manage the relations between the mass population and the gentry, between commoners and elites. As I discuss in the following chapters, the Chinese state used imperial examination systems to produce obedient officials during the dynastical period. Governance through meritocracy made socialism an obvious choice for catch-up. Socialism was a rational model of progress and it needed educated cadres to administer it. By the end of the twentieth century, however, the limits of socialism had become apparent. In particular, socialism overplayed the role of productive forces and failed to develop the innovative potential of human capital, a key ingredient of China's cultural diversity during the first millennium.

The innovation ecology

How will China become more innovative, more creative? And why is this important for the rest of the world? I describe five layers of China's interaction within the global cultural economy. These co-exist and complement each other. Actors and investors move between the layers of this innovation ecology. I use the term 'ecology' in a provocative sense to show how change is taking place despite a high degree of state control of information. In the public imagination 'ecology' is associated with diverse phenomena: predators, pollution, destruction of habitats and acts of nature (Heise 2002). My application of ecology is less holistic and, as I discuss in the following chapters, more correlated with the concepts of 'field', 'environment' and 'cluster', in which multiple forces, connections (*guanxi*) and institutions moderate and direct change. In China, the dominant institution is socialism.

The CRD project mentioned on p. 11 typifies a state-directed approach to engagement with the creative economy. It is a socialist solution: to construct (*jianshe*) bases in designated areas that will hopefully produce higher outputs along with better quality outcomes. The CRD, and many projects like it now appearing, represent the fifth layer in China's innovation ecology. At the other end of the ecology there is less state direction, more self-organisation, and less concern for intellectual property. The first two layers are indicative of a nation moving unevenly and uncertainly from state-monitored cultural production. As Chinese policy makers experiment with a range of industry development models, and with forms of intellectual property licensing and distribution, many producers endeavour to evade compliance with best practice, whether defined by the Chinese government or by the international trading community. In other words, actors in China's innovation system are self-organising according to short-term rather than long-term considerations. This pragmatism reflects the uncertainty and risk

Table 1.1 The innovation ecology

Form	Strategic form
Low-cost production	Trade in tasks. Production work moves from higher cost centres and economies; mostly fee-for-service work denying local intellectual property development. The ubiquitous 'Made in China' brand
Imitation	Local actors and producers duplicate global and regional products without committing to intellectual property regimes
Co-production and formatting	Local actors seek international partners through joint ventures, co-productions, or through licensing content and formats
East Asian creative economy	Capacity building occurs as opportunity comes from exploiting cultural proximity and co-productions within East Asia
Industrial cluster	Specialisation, differentiation and quality deliver distinctive branded content, higher value added, and economies of scale
Peer communities	Post-collective models of user-led innovation in new media challenge the producer/supply model.

inherent in cultural production in China, a legacy of state interference in the cultural sphere.

I call the first layer *low-cost offshoring*. Rising production costs in developed industrial economies have seen the relocation of much standardized production to low-cost locations. This is a well-known story. The 'Made in China' phenomenon manifests in products that are designed elsewhere – often in developed economies – and fabricated in China. This offshoring translates into what economist now call called 'unbundling', or the latest phase of globalisation (Baldwin 2006); in other words, time-consuming processes and tasks are outsourced to China. This off-shoring of tasks occurs primarily in animation rendering and software fabrication, but is also evident in design, fashion, television and cinema. The intellectual property invariably belongs exclusively to a foreign entity. Despite the apparent exploitation of low-cost labour associated with the world factory model, innova-tion occurs on the edges as cultural expectations collide. As I discuss in Chapter 9, the offshoring party often serendipitously finds process and product innovation occurring on the factory floor.

The second layer is *imitation*, a key element in the rapid growth of media indus-tries in China over the past decade or more. It is also a strategic mode of production adopted by Japan during the post-War period. An effect of globalisation, imita-tion promotes flows of products in different continents simultaneously. While follow-the-leader activity does provide economic benefits for under-capitalised producers, it produces diminishing returns as more and more take the same route. This applies at the level of the firm as well as the level of the country. Pro-ducers engage in a game of denying imitation and claiming emulation so as to evade legal constraints. It is a feature of television, advertising, video games and software industries. Perhaps the best examples come from reality television, where international format ideas are cloned almost as fast as they appear (see Chapter 9).

Moving up the value chain to *co-production and formatting* delivers more 'legitimate' market opportunities and provides hope for actors seeking to interna-tionalise. This is the third layer of activity found in China today. The anticipated pay-off from joint ventures with international and regional production networks is the stimulation of local industries through training, employment, expertise, infrastructure investment and 'learning by doing'. The third layer, which I discuss in Chapters 9 and 10 offers the promise of success in truly interna-tional markets, working with global partners who offer improved value, often through association with best practice, new technology and better corporate governance.

East Asian animation and cinema are consolidating in their own 'backyard' and breaking into Western markets, where the returns on investment are exponentially higher. The *East Asian creative economy* is the fourth layer of the ecology. From learning to internationalise and share resources in the global pond, China's prox-imity to East Asian markets now provides a chance to exploit its cultural heritage. China sells less of its culture to East Asia than it imports but the increasing num-ber of regional film and TV co-productions demonstrates that the Asian creative economy needs China's cultural vitality, and not just the advantages of low-cost production.

The four previous categories demonstrate that success can be achieved in highly competitive markets. The fifth category, the *industrial cluster* or milieu, has now become almost mandatory in debates about regional economic development. It allows a more defined role for government. As economies push towards increased specialisation in trade and seek out high-value markets, policy makers target clustering as a competitive growth strategy. China is establishing cultural bases and media production centres, mostly in large cities, that may in the future challenge the dominant players.

This is the order of development that has occurred during the past decade in the Chinese cultural economy. Starting with non-creative outsourcing and finishing at value-added clustering, however, is not a direct trajectory, nor is it an ideal model. Most activity occurs in the more imitative and exploitative layers of the ecology. As I will explain in Part II of this book, this imbalance has occurred largely due to the overwhelming focus on productivity and the need to service the low-value fragmented domestic market. While these five layers of the innovation ecology describe production capacity, there is another important element, reflected in a shift from state-orchestrated scarcity to consumer-driven abundance. As diversity increases, and as more Japanese, South Korean and Western culture influences consumer choice, a new model of collectivism has evolved which has little to do with either Confucianism or Communism. The directed culture of the past is losing its influence. Consumers of information and culture are selecting from an ever widening buffet. But importantly, the innovation ecology is fostered as *peer communities* rather than cultural officials adjudicate on taste and value. Reality TV and blogs together combine to undermine the authority of experts.

These processes are taking place against a background of generalised social apprehension about globalisation and the relevance of Chinese culture in its region and in the world economy. Anxiety prevails within government about the trade deficit of China's cultural economy, in direct contrast with the apparent endless boom in manufacturing and exports. However, there is also growing apprehension about the long-term future of manufacturing. A consensus of opinion has formed around the idea that 'culture is a driver, rather than a passenger in the knowledge-based economy' (Cunningham 2006: 14). As I will show, this idea has gained purchase in many parts of China; the transformation of science parks into creative incubators and the gentrification of disused industrial space is only part of the response. The most significant shift, however, is a *change in the culture* of the cultural industries in China. As one Chinese evaluation of the international creative economy puts it, debates have long been dominated by protectionism and underpinned by propaganda: 'In the debates about culture, and in important policy decisions impacting on the cultural industry it is hard to hear expert voices – that of economists, managers, and those who own or invest in cultural enterprises – especially those who don't have a background in the liberal arts' (Miao and Chen 2003: 85).

Catching up to the West

In 2006, a writer by the name of Bai Haijun published *Believe China 2049 (xiangxin Zhongguo 2049)*, a book purporting to reflect China's status in the mid twenty-first century. The scenario – China 100 years after the founding of the People's Republic – was a clever marketing strategy, even if most of the predictions were not supported by credible data. In a section entitled 'the world in 2049', the author asserted: 'Based on general conjectures in the year 2050 Europe will account for 15 per cent of the world's economy (down from 21 per cent currently), the US will take 20 per cent and China, including Taiwan and Hong Kong, will account for 25 per cent. Japan will reduce its share while Russia will probably rise' (Bai 2006: 15).

National obsessions about China's developmental path and its place in the world have been a consistent feature of Chinese society over the past century. This kind of publication is nothing new. Books about China's emergence appear regularly and often disappear just as quickly. Prominently displayed in the front shelves of Beijing's Xidan Book market, they offer a variety of colourful and often nationalistic development scenarios to nourish local prejudices. Despite people's standard of living remaining low by international comparison, the idea of catch-up to the West is celebrated in important national events, such as the return to earth in October 2003 of Colonel Yang Liwei, China's first man in space.

For many people living in the most developed Western economy, however, the year 2005 signalled an awakening to a China threat. It was not the ideological threat of Communism but the menace of Chinese-style capitalism. Best-selling books bore alarmist titles, warning that China's emergence would impact on jobs and standards of living in developed countries.[4] Andrew Ross has written about the mood in middle America, arguing that the coverage of China's growth is fuelling 'the same kind of virulent reactions that greeted the rise of Japan as an industrial superpower a quarter of a century earlier' (Ross 2006: 10).

The cold-war rhetoric has faded; the war talk has turned to trade. 'Made in China', the symbolic juggernaut of Chinese manufacturing and exports, became a frightener for people in a nation where low-skilled jobs were disappearing to China. In Silicon Valley venture capitalists now ask start-ups to provide 'offshore outsourcing' plans (Ernst 2006). Much of this offshoring is conducted in China. The Chinese marketplace of 1.3 billion consumers, more than one-third of whom work in private employment in manufacturing industries, often in township and village enterprises, has significantly reshaped indicators of international trade (see Donald and Benewick 2005). In recent years, cheap Chinese goods, often designed in the West and manufactured in China, have displaced local brands in Wal-Marts and K-Marts at an ever-increasing rate. While China's gross domestic product (GDP) was ranked the seventh economy in the world in 2003, the relative buying power of a dollar, the 'purchasing power parity', means that China is realistically ranked in the top five, and according to some analysts as high as second (Shenkar 2005).

Does this economic growth mean that China will eventually become the business centre of the global economy? The 'China dream' – the title of a book by Joe Studwell (2002) – paints a sobering picture of international investments that produce little or no profits. Other business 'guide books' have appeared with titles bordering on hyperbole. The fantasy of one 'billion consumers' is irresistible copy, calculated to make any self-respecting marketeers' pulse race.[5] Despite business anticipation about China's consumer revolution, however, international companies have failed to capitalise on the Chinese market with the notable exception of fast foods (McDonalds, Pizza Hut, and KFC), slow drinks (Starbucks), and automobile manufacturers (Volkswagen) (Studwell 2004). By 2005, the ardent glow of international business expectation for earning massive profits in the Chinese market had begun to cool. As one commentator suggested, 'the world's late great China love affair' has gone sour (Anderson 2005: 23).

Anxiety about China's emergence is further tempered by the reality of social relations – the lack of openness to personal freedoms. The Chinese nation might be a manufacturing behemoth and a superpower in the making but democratic reforms, Nobel Prizes, and exports of Chinese contemporary culture are conspicuously lacking from the China miracle. In the euphoric Chinese twenty-first-century discourse, economic growth is associated with ascendancy. Economic prosperity will lead to greatness, a new version of Empire. But something important is missing from this success formula. Great civilisations in world history – including China in the Tang dynasty and Rome in the first half of the Christian millennium – have embraced pluralism and complexity. The Tang Dynasty (618–970 ACE) was the apex of artistic and creative diversity.

As I discuss in detail in Chapter 2, such periods of high innovation benefited from openness to trade. In the new era of 'independent innovation', creativity is endorsed as a public good. China is more open to ideas about reform of its education system, its enterprise management, and its media. Behind the Chinese Communist Party's rhetoric of 'harmonious society and peaceful emergence', which proclaims that Chinese culture and civilisation is a new template for global progress, there is an emerging sense of anxiety as Japanese and Korean popular culture targets youth cultures. Why is China not competing forcefully in the creative economy? Why is it not sending its culture as it did in the past? Can China be a great nation once again without an identifiable global cultural centre? Will the momentum for China's creative future come from a commercial class with global financial connections or will it emerge from within an East Asian creative commons?

The blind spot of Western scrutiny

As I will discuss in Chapter 6, the slogan 'Created in China' surfaced in 2003. Why then has China's creative emergence not grabbed international headlines? Is there a blind spot in our understanding of China? The answer has much to do with hardening of the categories. Optimistic scenarios of catch-up and 'the Chinese century' inevitably run up against negative traditions of framing culture through rear-vision mirrors. In approaching questions of China's emergence we need to be aware that academic approaches are constrained by, and embedded within disciplinary conventions. While this caveat may seem superfluous, a great deal of China analysis is captive to axiomatic conceptual structures grounded in static historical models of progress. Despite disciplinary segmentation of China Studies into anthropology, literary studies, sociology, economics, history, environmental studies, political science, law and international relations, most research into *change* within Chinese culture and society is framed by what the cognitive psychologist Howard Gardner (2004) calls socio-biological and historical-cultural approaches.

The socio-biological approach reiterates dominant structures, hierarchies and themes; for example, the Chinese Communist Party is monolithic, oriental despots preside over Asiatic modes of production, and things change slowly. Benjamin Schwartz has noted that in terms of projecting the future, theories of totalitarianism and oriental despotism 'assumed a watertight system immune to any fundamental change from within' (Schwartz 1996: 3). In this socio-biological approach a totalitarian state ruled by hardline ideologues remains chained to the past. While much of the world has been liberated from autocracy, China is without democracy – except perhaps for the brave new world of reality television where viewers can vote for their popular singing Idols (Keane *et al.* 2007). Similar themes of glacial change underpin much reporting of China in the international press. The mention of Beijing (and its frozen-in-time former designation of Peking) is shorthand, conjuring up associations of power and handpicked politicians who care little for democratisation and human rights. This is a view countered in 2004 by Joshua Cooper Ramo, former foreign editor for *Time* magazine. In *The Beijing Consensus* Ramo argues:

> To the degree China's development is changing China it is important; but what is far more important is that China's new ideas are having a gigantic effect outside of China. China is marking a path for other nations around the world who are trying to figure out not simply how to develop their countries, but also how to fit into the international order in a way that allows them to be truly independent, to protect their way of life and political choices in a world with a single massively powerful centre of gravity.
>
> (Ramo 2004: 3)

In short, changes in China are disrupting the geo-political order. As China transforms from within, the impacts are felt in its region, in developing countries, and in the developed industrialised world. While globalisation induces striking commonalities, the appearance of multinational franchises in China such as Pizza Hut and Starbucks does not portend the demise of socialism. The socio-biological approach, in addition, is used to explain rapid transformation, but this is a model of transformation shaped by ideological grand-narratives – accounts of dog-eat-dog capitalism, the diffusion of transnational business, the rise of consuming middle classes, and the rent-seeking activities of bureaucratic entrepreneurs within China.

The second approach is the historical cultural paradigm. In many respects this is complementary and emphasises what Appadurai terms 'trait geographies'. These are 'conceptions of geographical, civilisational, and cultural coherence that rely on some sort of trait list – of values, languages, material practices, ecological adaptations, marriage patterns and the like' (Appadurai 2001: 7). Discussions of China's trait geographies include institutions such as the Chinese family, philosophical tradition, the centrality of relationships (*guanxi*), ritual, dependency, and gift-giving. In other words, in order to understand China therefore we have to pay close attention to cultural contexts and in order to be successful business needs to understand the 'Chinese mind'. Taken to extremes, as it often is in business guide books, culturalism generates an excess of facile generalisation. Of course, if one is selling business guides to success, blanket statements such as 'Chinese are Confucians and Confucians are goal-driven' (Doctoroff 2005: 32) might just appear to be somehow profound.[6]

From the banality of business literature to the gravity of sinology, the emphasis on tradition remains a common theme. Geremie Barmé writes that 'those who are unlettered in the basic histories, languages and ideas of the last few centuries will ever only be semi-literate in the culture of China today' (Barmé 2005). In contrast, Teng and Fairbank have suggested that while knowledge of China's growth as a traditional society is a prerequisite, 'new forces are at work, induced by the modern experiences of the Chinese people' (Teng and Fairbank 1979: 2). Writing in 1954 in the introduction to *China's Response to the West*, they pointed out that the contemporary scene 'cannot be understood merely by reference to classical worthies like the Duke of Chou (ca. eleventh century BC) or by the philosophical maxims of Confucius (551–479 BC?) and Mencius (390–305 BC) or the thought of a medieval scholar like Chu Hsi (AD 1130–1200)'.

While cultural knowledge is important, there is a less clear line on what constitutes China literacy: one might have deep cultural and linguistic insights but misunderstand or misread the winds of change. Further, emphasis on deep cultural insight runs the danger of perpetuating stereotypes. Cultural explanations of contemporary behaviour are sometimes 'educated guesses' applied in hindsight. Can we be sure that temporally remote events are really having a significant or dominant impact on the present? Academics, politicians and journalists use the term 'with Chinese characteristics' as shorthand explanation to describe all manner of Chinese exceptionalism and variations of international behaviour. But such clichés invariably obscure rather than illuminate. With people in China now more Western in their outlook – or at least their knowledge of the Western world than at any time in the past – there is an inherent danger in reducing rationales for behaviour to either trait geographies or local responses to globalisation. We live in an era of unprecedented cultural and economic exchange. An over-emphasis on tradition and settled categories of thought can be counter-productive when it comes to creating new knowledge. Hagel and Brown (2006: 11) argue that as change accelerates, 'stocks of knowledge' diminish in value: 'the life-time value of knowledge rapidly shrinks as the rate of obsolescence in knowledge increases'. In times of stability, such knowledge stocks remain valuable and need to be protected. Hardening of the academic categories is particularly prevalent in media and cultural studies, the core foundational disciplines informing this study. The focus of most Chinese media scholarship over the past five decades has been 'structures of dominance': the Chinese Communist Party ideological machine, the control and manipulation of information, censorship and propaganda. The mainstream research agenda is influenced by a positivist communications studies tradition that attempts to ascribe behavioural effects to watching, reading and using media. In this regard, the Chinese Communist Party's ownership of the media – that is, the idea that the media are the mouthpiece – would appear to justify 'media effects', although very little 'empirical evidence' has been mounted to test the proposition that the Chinese ideological apparatus is totalitarian or even hegemonic. Control is systematic, but the effects of control are mainly inferred from events such as content crackdowns, strict censorship, and policy regimes. In fact, it is evident that Chinese people, like people in the free nations, actively negotiate meanings from their media. Users of new media become makers of meanings, like youth in the USA, Europe and Australia. This renders the effects tradition problematic. Sophisticated audience analysis is particularly problematic in China for international researchers unless there is some institutional assistance in reaching the audience. Textual analysis or content analysis of news media has served as the de facto evidence base.

Alternatively, when Chinese media are celebrated in the cultural studies and post-colonial studies traditions it is typically the works of film-makers who offer a version of Chinese culture that conforms to Western stereotypes, or dissident writers who perpetuate a pessimistic image of Chinese society and the state's unremitting political control. Political economy of the media offers a slightly different negative version of China's positioning, subscribing to a cultural domination model in which the control of world communications emanates from a centre – the US capitalist dream factory. Communication impregnates the periphery (China), aided by the inevitability of powerful interests, eventually undermining local cultural identity. The conventional view from such communication scholars is that new structures of dominance are forming as China builds new media conglomerates. In contrast to the economic policy narrative that celebrates the exploitation of intellectual property, Marxist political economy seeks out evidence of the exploitation of labour together with the dumbing-down of the public sphere.

These are not narratives of progress. While the political economy of the media does acknowledge that China is changing, many working in this critical tradition worry that it is becoming too globalised, in turn reducing diversity and ushering in too much 'inappropriate' global culture – Starbucks, Hollywood blockbusters and Hullo Kitty. In China fears of Westernisation also persist, frequently fanned by political expediency; for instance, anti-Japanese sentiment about war-time atrocity periodically whips up hysterical nationalism. But prescriptions of cultural invasion are perhaps premature. Cultural imperialism is confounded by the resilience of tradition, local specificity, and the lessons of recent history. Under Maoist socialism there was limited diversity; choice is now built into the development script.

The re-emergence of Chinese diversity, that is diversity *within* Chinese society, is an effect of communication technologies and greater social mobility. China is more confident on the world political stage and less xenophobic, if we accept the evidence of Korean and Japanese fashions, popular among the younger generation. Despite criticisms of too much Westernisation from conservatives, Chinese culture is extremely resilient and characteristically Eastern. Fears of the demise of a Chinese identity or self-image are not supportable by evidence. Unfortunately, much academic analysis in communication studies is captive to analytical categories handed down from Western Marxism and cold-war politics.[7]

Institutions and innovation

Change disrupts settled academic and journalistic categories. New kinds of enterprise formation problematise control theories inherited from the cold-war period. The transformation that we are now witnessing, from Made in China to Created in China, illustrates the state's focus on 'independent innovation' diffused within regional policy, allowing and encouraging new networks and alliances between government, individuals, small and medium enterprises and international finance. A more flexible approach to understanding processes of change is required, in contrast to the rigid models inherited from Western communication theory, which were developed in response to a clash of ideologies – namely free enterprise versus socialism. While the 'mental maps' that organise research are inherited from the past, the topography has altered.

Development in China is more than ever provincial and networked. Local governments have considerable capacity to effect change – to allocate valuable land to emerging enterprises and to attract small and large investors – albeit within the framework of five-year planning cycles. Much of the development is therefore driven by local entrepreneurs, not 'big' business. While the legacies of recent history remain important, we need to scrutinise China's uptake of international models more critically. The cultural and media industry development processes that are occurring in China, both micro-level (small and medium enterprises) and macro-level (government policy intervention) challenge the inherited discipline-specific and sector-specific models of analysis that have dominated Western research of China. To illustrate this I draw on analytical tools from disciplines such as economic and cultural geography, history, cultural policy, and development studies.

In order to understand the nature of change at a deeper level I show how culture interacts with institutions, both formal and informal. In *Economics and Utopia* Hodgson writes that 'Socio-economic systems are essentially and unavoidably built up of historically layered and densely entangled institutions and routines' (Hodgson 1999: 60). Veblen (1919) described institutions as 'settled habits of thought', while North (1981: 201) has referred to 'a set of rules, compliance procedures and ethical behaviours designed to constrain the behaviour of individual in the interests of maximizing the wealth and utility of principals'. North notes also that political-economic systems are made up of a complex of institutions bearing specific relationships to one another. Formal institutions are changeable by government fiat while informal institutions change slowly by a variety of processes, in particular transfer of ideas and technologies. Of course, the key institutions that have moderated change and innovation in the modern era (since the industrial revolution) have been the free market and socialism. Other important institutions include the family and the education system. When writers use the term institutional impediments to refer to China's stalled innovation processes relative to the West, they are usually referring to structural processes put in place to regulate national development, manage populations and normalise habits of thought.

Much of the literature on 'national systems of innovation' thus reflects 'national idiosyncrasies' inherited from the past. In China, patterns of conflict avoidance (low risk taking) and relationship building (favouring people within close networks) are often associated with limits to socialist innovation. Hodgson, for example, writes that 'it (socialism) has to learn to inhabit open systems and open spaces' (1999: 61). But this is not to presume that these institutions are deterministic or inflexible. As I have noted, decisions may be influenced by the past but international knowledge transfer increasingly plays a role.

Institutions include norms and practices endemic to the system, such as a propensity to cooperate rather than compete, to imitate rather than innovate, and to favour personal preservation over risk. As I will show in the following chapter, the root causes of institutional routines, norms and 'mental models' reach deep into Chinese history. Such institutions, moreover, are changing as integration into the global economy leads to the 'creative destruction' of inefficient practices.

2 Territory, technology and taste

> Such cultural triumphalism combined with petty downward tyranny made China a
> singularly bad learner. What was there to learn? The rejection of the strange and
> foreign was the more anxious for the very force of the arrogance that justified it.
> For that is the paradox of the superiority complex; it is an expression of insecurity
>
> (Landes 2006: 11)

The success and failure of nations to compete is a contentious theme in the field of
economic history. In *The Gifts of Athena* Joel Mokyr (2002) makes an argument
for the relationship between institutions and useful knowledge. By the former, he
refers to 'the trustworthiness of government, the functionality of the family as the
basic unit, security and the rule of law, a reliable system of contract enforcement,
and the attitudes of the elite in power toward individual initiative and innovation'
(2002: 285). Mokyr claims that 'propositional knowledge' has been a driving
engine of technological innovation in the modern 'Western' era. Propositional
knowledge, he argues, is different from 'prescriptive' knowledge, which is cod-
ified as techniques (*techne*). Propositional knowledge is *epistemic*: it observes,
classifies, measures and catalogues, as well as establishing regularities, principles and natural laws. Propositional knowledge therefore seeks knowledge about
'what' and 'how'. It is concerned with both process and progress, and in this
respect it is transformational. To this we might add culture. The economist Eric
Jones (2005) argues that Europe institutionalised a form of creativity that depended
for its energy on social competition, the foundation of which was its underlying
pluralism.

Why did China, considered to be the centre of civilisation during the Tang
dynasty, miss out on 'useful' propositional knowledge? Why did China not
establish the kind of efficient modern institutions that made the West competitive? Mokyr contends that in the modern West technological change was rarely
imposed from above, whereas in dynastical China technological change was gov-
ernmentalised. In other words, it was initiated by governments and regulated by
bureaucracies. He argues further that this occurred even during the high periods of Chinese innovation, the Tang and Song dynasties. The China historian
Samuel Adshead argues that the Tang was a time of 'complex pluralism' and that

knowledge lock-in came much later during the Ming and Qing (Adshead 2004). In defining complex pluralism he says: 'Intellectual fruition supplied the semantic field for conceptualisation, the semiotic medium for communication and action, and the syncretic field for legitimation' (2004: 130). This 'openness' to ideas was gradually lost in later dynasties as China asserted itself as the centre looking out. Polycentrism is therefore an important element in development. Adshead, along with other economic historians (Mokyr 2002; Landes 2006; Vries 2003), agree that complex pluralism, together with a range of market, social and technological advances, was a feature of European development. In Europe by the eighteenth century, competition in and among a system of smaller nation states had reduced the scope for bureaucratic rigidity. Landes asserts that Western imagination was the driving force from as far back as 1000 CE. He points to the rapid diffusion of ideas, in particular news of novelty: 'an intoxicating sense of freedom touched (infected) all domains' (Landes 2006: 9).

The Chinese translation of innovation – *chuangxin* – is literally to 'create or make something new'. Innovation therefore holds the key to framing both the Rise of the East (in the Sui and Tang), and the Rise of the West in the eighteenth century. Landes argues that by the Ming dynasty China had become a 'bad learner'. China was not imitating and borrowing, a charge that would be levelled against it several hundred years later. It was arrogant. Landes cites Joseph Spence's translation of the thoughts of the Kangxi emperor during the Qing Dynasty (1644–1911). '[E]ven though some of the Western methods are different from our own, and may even be an improvement, there is little about them that is new. The principles of mathematics all derive from the *Book of Changes*, and the Western methods are Chinese in origin' (Spence 1974: 74, cited in Landes 2006: 12).

While many historians dispute the Eurocentrism of Landes,[1] there is less argument to counter the view that China was slower to adopt to change from 1500 onwards, and was less open to ideas, partly as a result of rigid bureaucratic knowledge management and partly because of the need on the part of its rulers to maintain a safe distance from 'outsiders' from the West lest their influence became too great. Change was contained within the strictures of conformity to institutional rules – the Confucian processes that regulated relationships at all levels of society. By the Qing Dynasty (1644–1911) candidates for imperial exams were asked to write in a so-called 'eight-legged essay style', a rigid model of presentation that discouraged innovation. China was looking inwards more and more, a tendency that increased throughout the Qing. What was missing? The cultural economist Tyler Cowan (2002) has pointed out that both consumers and producers of culture need 'otherness' and they need the kind of exchange mechanisms that cultural markets provide. China opened itself in the early twentieth century, only to close down under Communism. In order to rediscover its lost preeminence China needs more than openness to ideas; it needs diversity.

These questions relate to changing the culture in broader sense. Culture is ultimately a social process; it is not static – although it is conventionally used to illustrate of periods of development (civilisation) in history books, text books and museum catalogues. However, elites in China have over the course of history sought to restrain cultural innovation against tides of heterodox propositions about society, political reform and nature. Orthodoxy was inculcated by the imperial examination system that privileged the landed classes – those who could afford to send their sons to study. Increasingly throughout history the sons of many of the landed classes received the privilege of inherited official status. This rigidly eventually imploded. Inevitably change occurred as institutional processes failed to adapt to globalisation. Such is the complexity of the field of world history.

Adshead argues that over the past two millenniums the drivers of economic growth in China have been territory, technology and taste (Adshead 2004).[2] Territory reflects development and expansion, the need to cultivate fields as well as attendant demands for capital investment to raise productivity. Territory is reflected in the growth of cities, absorbing labour from the countryside and producing innovation through industrial technologies and new waves of economic growth (cf. Hall 1999: 291). In the imperial past much territory was seized by colonisers and armies, allowing many to lay claim to power, wealth and prestige. The European colonisers also brought ideas to what were often, in their view, uninhabited lands. *Terra nullius* implied the non-existence of an existing culture: oftentimes the culture of the inhabitants of territories was over-written or absorbed into the new dominant culture. Territory also drives the need to developed sophisticated technologies of military control. This is an important theme in Chinese history: the influx of outside forces and the development of weapons, steel and strategy.

Territory reflects the importance of national sovereignty through the ascendancy of identity and civilisation discourses; in China the idea of territory has embodied dynastic struggles for power – the Mandate of Heaven, the Warring States period, and the 'three kingdoms' (*sanguo*).[3] The Warring States period (see Chapter 3), which culminated in the ascent to power of China's first emperor in BCE 221, was a period of territorial expansion. The kingdom of Qin, led by Shang Yang (c. 390–228) triumphed over its main rival, the kingdom of Wei. Shang Yang then established a unified legal code, enforced conscription, and rewarded military success with landowner rights, titles and pensions (Armstrong 2006). Territory also includes the Mongolian conquests, the voyages of the Ming Dynasty navigator Zheng He (who reminded far-flung empires that China was indeed the centre although not colonising these nations), and it ultimately reflects the incursion of the West upon Chinese sovereignty in the mid nineteenth century. Exchanges of culture regularly occurred across borders and along territorial trade routes – the Silk Road being the most well-known example in Chinese history.

With the rise of national independence movements in the twentieth century imperialism gave way to civil wars, leading to greater flows of people. For example, the Treaty of Nanjing in 1842 ceded Hong Kong to the British. The Chinese revolution of 1949 did not seek to reclaim Hong Kong, which had been occupied by the Japanese army. Hong Kong's re-occupation by the allied forces made it a safe haven for those fleeing from communism. Refugees brought new ideas, skills and money, and a hybrid Hong Kong identity evolved, facing away from China towards Japan and the West. In the cultural sphere of these 'new' territories governments provided patronage, regulation and subsidy. The Taiwanese government led by Chiang Kai-shek (Jiang Jieshi) and his successors promoted the Guomindang (nationalist) capital of Taipei as the home of Chinese culture.

Technological development is central to the transfer of useful knowledge and the rise of institutions. Technologies are both physical and social. Indeed, Chinese reformers in the late Qing dynasty spoke of the material superiority of Western technology. However, the West had long been aware of Chinese innovations. Physical inventions included writing, paper, and printing, the magnetic compass and gunpowder. The technology of hydraulic water-driven machinery for the spinning of wool and silk, used in the fourteenth century, was borrowed from China, ultimately accelerating the Rise of the West when combined with coal during the industrial revolution. Social and cultural technology transfer also includes the notions of meritocracy and transparency, exemplified by scholar-officials who maintained the system of governance and tax collection from the time of the Tang dynasty (Woodside 2006). These ideas about administration made their way to the West and were adopted in the eighteenth and nineteenth centuries. By the mid nineteenth century they formed the basis of new supranational institutions, the management of information and the flow of financial transactions. Modern world institutions underpinned the capitalist ascendancy. Western technology and knowledge assumed the status of 'advanced', while China sought to catch up in several domains of knowledge. Woodside (2006) argues the Chinese demand for Western management techniques over the past two decades surpasses intellectual interest in that other great institution, democracy.

The role of taste as a driver of economic progress is central to the modern post-enlightenment period and the rise of consumerism. In previous periods of history, taste was largely determined by elites who had the privilege of greater choice. Adshead writes, 'privilege could impart a further dynamic of its own as the creative periphery of the economy' (2004: 86). The link with territory and technology becomes clearer in relation to cultural exchange. The social technology of Buddhism provided new objects for consumption in buildings; celebration of festivals led to the construction of statues, incense use and banquets. In addition, the technology used to produce porcelain 'had implications for manners, aesthetics and more generally, civility' (Adshead 2004: 80). Tea drinking became an art form, proving a new medium for design, colour and decoration. In addition, the fashion for Chinoiserie in Europe generated international flows of decorative commodities in the late eighteenth and early nineteenth century. The explosion of consumer culture is usually attributed to the emergence of advertising and communication industries in the free-market West during the 1950s and 1960s. A current explanation of the effect of taste is the purchase of contemporary art by international advertising companies. Explaining a penchant for continual renewal of public art in their business space, Joseph Wang, Ogilvy's vice-chairman in China argues that the circulation of new aesthetic forms generates creativity within the organisation: 'We lease art pieces ... we are a creative business and require constant stimulation to generate "out of the box" thinking' (*China Business Weekly* 18–24 July 2006: 8).

Technology, talent and tolerance

The three Ts: territory, technology and taste, encounter a new dynamic as globalisation demands that regions and cities embrace innovation. A report from Hong Kong in 2004 noted:

> World cities now face formidable economic challenges in the global economy. They need to sharpen their own edges by offering distinctive products and creative services to the world market and to position and re-position themselves in the world economic chain of production. Meanwhile, they are eager to attract talents and foreign capital for sustainable economic development. The crux of these challenges is to maintain their own competitiveness in a more integrated and competitive world.
>
> (HKCI 2004)

Richard Florida (2002) has argued that the three Ts of today's competitive globalised landscape are *technology, talent* and *tolerance*. In Florida's 'simple formula' of innovation-driven growth, technology represents the leading indicator and this includes infrastructure as well as the location of high-technology enterprises. Tolerance reflects the openness to heterodox cultural values, expressed somewhat provocatively for Chinese policy makers as the presence of bohemians. Innovation appears to occur more frequently in places where there is less restriction on personal freedom. Talent, however, is an essential ingredient.

Florida substitutes his idea of the 'creative class' for a standard education-based measure of human capital. This creative class consists of a super-creative core (computer software programmers, media workers, creative industry professionals) and a broader umbrella of white collar knowledge workers. Much of Florida's work revolves around competition for talent. For instance, headhunting is part of the worldwide competition for skills, not just in the hard sciences but in the realm of administration and marketing. Florida's work has been gladly received by national and regional governments looking for the competitive edge. Indeed, Florida's insistence on human capital and labour mobility, a phenomenon that applies more to the USA than other places, has been described as 'fast policy' (Peck 2005). The 3T model says more about consumption and consuming classes than production: in this model it is the discriminating affluent, mobile 'creative class' who become the arbiters of place competitiveness, more so than tourists.

This ability to easily move occupations and residence, however, does not apply to many parts of Asia. While the focus on occupations is important and has the advantage of empirical clarity over sometimes haphazard attempts to calculate the value (and value added) of sectors, a key determinant of innovation remains change in the global economy. For instance, the economic transformations that have shaken Hong Kong in the past decade have to a large extent been caused by Hong Kong's positioning relative to China and the international economy. Offshoring and outsourcing of manufacturing to the Pearl River Delta in south China has assisted in redefining Hong Kong's role in the producer service economy. Hong Kong is increasingly providing services to Mainland China rather than innovating upwards as might be expected by an increase of creative class occupations relative to population (Mok 2006). Allan Scott (2006) is also critical of Florida's approach. He argues that simply focusing on mechanisms to attract as many creative individuals by providing high quality urban environments rich in cultural amenities and conducive to diversity is not enough. As I discuss in Chapter 7, the policy framework needs to be underscored by a more meaningful 'creative field'. By creative field Scott alludes to a 'locationally-differentiated web of production activities and associated social relationships that shape patterns of entrepreneurship and innovation in the new economy' (2006: 1).

Michael Curtin (2003, 2007) has written of such networks and associations in the development of 'media capitals'. He argues that creative migration has been central to the media industry success of Hollywood, Mumbai and Hong Kong. To take the example of Hong Kong, this entrepôt benefited from waves of creative talent, initially migrating from Mainland China in the 1940s and 1950s, from south-east Asia in the 1960s, and in the 1970s and 1980s from the international business centres that recognised Hong Kong as the gateway to East Asia. However, Curtin goes a step further and argues that success is more than just migration and attraction of talent. He says that successful media capitals – he uses the term in the sense of financial capacity as well as centre – have come into being through the 'logic of agglomeration' and 'forces of socio-cultural variation'. In relation to Hollywood, he says that through a refiguring of the spatial relations of production 'managers concentrated the creative labour force in a single location where it could be deployed among a diverse menu of projects under the guidance of each studio's central production office' (Curtin 2007).

Commentators have pointed to the technological ability of China's workforce (Ramo 2004; Fishman 2005) and the role played in industrial development by returning graduates from Stanford or Chinese business entrepreneurs from Silicon Valley (Saxenian 2006). Many of these returnees were lured back to the mother country through incentive schemes, or were simply tempted by the attraction of the world's biggest market. Many brought capital and a risk-taking consciousness forged in the crucible of innovation. This includes an awareness of failure as a learning process. In the cultural sphere the flow has been of a different order. Migration of creative personnel to China in the past few decades has occurred less than creative talent leaving China. The reasons are fairly self-evident. China does not resonate with Florida's third T – tolerance. This value is under-represented in China's emergence.

However, China's capacity to build on transferred technology and knowledge can not be underestimated and this is the foundation of catch-up. During the early years of the reforms in China it was widely believed that obsolescent technology was a prime reason why China lagged behind the West (Wall and

Yin 1997). In order to solve the problem of technology deficiency, China initiated the 'Torch Program' in the mid 1980s. The program was aimed at commercialising high-tech research and development achievements and providing industrial bases for high-tech industries and experimental sites for structural reform of China's innovation system. The technology science park model responded to a national innovation agenda. This has now metamorphosed into creative clusters, precincts, and creative industry bases. Expert 'foreign' knowledge has been added to validate the theoretical underpinnings of the shift from productivity to value added. Hu Anguang writes that as a significant 'latecomer' China has advantages of 'selectiveness, diversification, and creativeness' in terms of the design of its industrial model (Hu 2002). Incubators, combined with preferential government policies for domestic industry, are a potent symbol of catch-up. In spite of the new found popularity of creative technology clusters, diffusion of technology occurs at pace in the market. Ideas and technologies are often copycatted, producing what business writers refer to as 'a Red Queen' effect: the idea that change is occurring so fast due to industry 'churn' that it is hard to predict the shape of technology markets. China now has more mobile handsets than wired phones and according to one leading business writer 'seeks to compress 200 years of post-Industrial Revolution into a couple of decades' (Ohame 2005: 37).

De-territorialisation and the new economic trade routes

China's catch-up is also heavily embedded in global shifts, which have intensified since China's re-emergence from Maoist-inspired isolation in 1978. John Dunning (2000) has written about four significant changes in the world economy from the mid 1970s to the late 1990s. The first of these transformations was the increased role of 'intellectual capital', illustrated by the rising contribution of services in GDP. Many of these 'services' are point-of-purchase delivery and are local. Foreign companies wishing to gain a presence in developing markets need to draw on local expertise. Where internationalization occurs it is often through foreign direct investment or franchising using localized global brand names. As service-led growth impacts upon production, one kind of knowledge is combined with several other kinds to produce a good or service. For firms to increase, or deploy their intellectual capital effectively, it has become necessary to complement knowledge with that of other firms, often by way of some collaborative agreement. The globalisation of advertising industries is a case in point.

The second change in the global economy has been an increase in cooperative ventures and levels of integration among the main wealth-creating nations with alliances most pronounced in knowledge-intensive sectors such as IT, media and communications and Internet services. Probably the most high profile case of communications M&A was the alliance between AOL and Time Warner in 2000. The third change over the past four decades concerns market liberalisation. Within the global economy market liberalisation has increased with protected economies trading sovereignty for free trade concessions. US trade negotiators have played an important role in brokering such liberalisations, working through international forums such as the General Agreement on Trade and Tariffs (GATT), its successor the WTO, and international development agencies the World Bank and the International Monetary Fund. Such was the leading role of the USA in pursuing global market liberalisation that a list of 10 policy recommendations became known as the Washington Consensus. Authored by US economist John Williamson in 1989, this prescription for developing countries to reform their economies is regarded by many international policy makers as shorthand for the market-centred policies of privatisation and liberalisation (Naim 1999).

The Washington Consensus aimed to break down state protection of industries. Open flows of trade and investment have in turn increased interdependence between nation and enhanced globalisation. Artificially imposed barriers to trade began to fall during the 1980s as neo-liberalism displaced Keynesian economics in many advanced Western economies, culminating in the setting up of the World Trade Organization on 1 January 1995. By the late 1990s, 47 per cent of service sectors in industrialised countries and 16 per cent in developing countries had been liberalised (Winseck 2002).

Fourth, and most importantly, new major economic players have emerged within the global economy. The rise of the New Industrialising Economies of East Asia has created a shift in the locus of development in high-technology and communications industries. Three of these – Hong Kong, Singapore and Korea – are among the wealthiest countries in world. Several of the new players, moreover, are developing countries, although mostly in Asia and Latin America. Recently emerging countries have achieved growth through providing cheap labour for companies located in the First World.

This re-organisation of global capital occurs through *de-territorialisation*: 'the spectacular cases of off-shoring that are so prominent in the media' (Storper 2000: 49). De-territorialised production (goods, services, animation etc.) and outsourcing of call centres gives low-cost locations an opportunity to be included in global trade networks. But this window of opportunity may be limited. For example, Mexico's 'maquiladora' strategy of providing factories for processing US industries now faces intense competition from China where costs are even cheaper, quality control is better, and physical infrastructure is improving. As Daniel Rosen points out, while Mexico was changing to accommodate global business chains, China was changing faster (Rosen 2003). The solution for Mexico is to leapfrog or at least climb into a higher value-added spectrum of production, not an easy task considering the low human resource base. As many writers have pointed out, knowledge-intensive asset-augmenting activities tend to remain heavily concentrated in advanced industrialised countries (Dunning 2000). The reshaping of the global economy, and associated foreign direct investment flows, is therefore heavily influenced by low-cost location production. This applies equally to textiles as it does to making cinema (Christopherson 2005; Elmer and Gasher 2005; Miller *et al.* 2001).

The World Trade Organization, the wrecking ball and China's catch-up

In December 2001, China formally signed into the World Trade Organization, the premier global trading club led by its former capitalist foes. Repercussions were widespread across many industry sectors, so much so that the then Vice-Minister of Finance used the metaphor of a 'wrecking ball' to suggest a force that smashes old institutional practices and allows the marketplace to rebuild with greater capacity

> For many developing countries, the accession is a destructive force that smashes whatever is left in the old edifice of the more or less closed economy. More importantly, however, is the constructive force for building and strengthening institutional capability and taking an overhaul of the existing system of economic management. We should capitalize on the destructive construction by active participation in this organisation.
>
> (Jin 2002: 3)

China's late entry in 2001 allowed it to take the next step to invigorate economic reforms, which had begun to stall. The WTO wrecking ball facilitated the kind of Schumpeterian 'creative destruction' that resonated with discourses of catch-up (Schumpeter 1961). Schumpeter was born the year that Karl Marx died. Contrary to popular belief he did not believe in the future of capitalism. In *Capitalism, Socialism and Democracy* he wrote 'Can capitalism survive. No, I do think it can' (in Heilbroner 1996: 298). Nevertheless, he believed that the capitalist system was dynamic because of 'its ceaseless and self-generated changefulness'.

For the USA and other potential 'investors' in the Chinese market, China's entry to the WTO was an event whose significance was compared to the fall of the Berlin Wall. As US Trade Representative Charlene Barshefsky pointed out in 2000 during the lead-up negotiations, former cold-war suspicions were being laid to rest in the cause of global cooperation as the USA – the leader of the free world – helps 'communist central planning regimes' integrate into rules-based world trade. In Barshefsky's assessment China's accession would aid world prosperity and stability (Barshefsky 2000: 5).

Following WTO entry, there was a sense of expectation from many within the international business community that China would play by the rules and its emergence would create unprecedented opportunities for earning wealth with the Chinese middle classes, a social demographic varying between 48 million and 90 – 100 million (depending on comparative global incomes) (Nolan 2004: 16). As Donald and Benewick point out, 'In 1998 China was the fifteenth largest trading nation in the world. By 2003, it was the fourth and snapping at the heels of Japan' (Donald and Benewick 2005: 14). Today, along with India, China is regarded as the next titan, providing 'the biggest boost to the world economy since the industrial revolution' (*The Economist* 14 September 2006). Despite these predictions of a new superpower bloc, glossed as 'Chindia', business in China is resolutely path-dependent, non-transparent and tethered to the state. Nevertheless, investment in technology is drawn to China's growth miracle like a moth to a flame. 'This competitive jungle keeps prices low and forces survivors to continually invest in new technology' (Engardio 2007: 9).

In the same year that China joined the WTO, the new economy was the key theme of the Asia Pacific Economic Cooperation (APEC) Summit in Shanghai. Leaders from countries as geographically disparate as Peru, the USA and China agreed that the new economy was about transformation. The 2001 APEC Summit focused explicitly on how structural policy reforms could exploit networked technologies to generate greater productivity. It noted 'Productivity rises because unproductive activities are more easily identified and harder to justify and perpetuate in the presence of greater awareness'. Acknowledging the APEC leader's endorsement of the knowledge-based economy in report the previous year, the 2001 Summit document focused on the 'right policy environment' to yield the 'higher productivity' of the 'new style of economy' where policies 'transcend the traditional boundaries' (APEC 2001).

Whereas China's modernisation during the post-Mao Zedong reform period was built on harnessing productive forces and consolidating the industrial base, the developed free-market economies were proceeding through structural transformations that would in turn impact upon East Asia. The terms 'stages of development' and 'catch-up' are synonymous in much of the development and modernisation literature. The stages-of-growth model of Walt Rostow (1960) contrasts with Marxism's four-stage model of development – feudalism, bourgeois capitalism, socialism and communism – which is based upon the core belief that history moves forward through a series of conflicts, productive forces, divisions of labour (and property) and economic organisation.

An ardent believer in capitalism, and a national security advisor for the US government during the 1960s, Rostow emphasised free trade. His growth model spanned traditional society and high mass consumption via three intermediate stages: the preconditions stage, take-off and maturity. He believed that developing countries needed to be supported with foreign aid during the preconditions stage and furthermore that economic growth is not smooth but subject to successive forward leaps of an economy's leading sectors. Rostow's model states that some countries may depend on raw material exports to finance the development of manufacturing sectors. Similarly, the Marxist model favoured by Chinese intellectuals argues that a period of accumulation and technology transfer precedes take off. As I will argue below, this is a position supported by recent studies of East Asian take-off.

In contrast to Marx's view that profit maximization was the core motivation for capitalist development, drawn from his study of Britain's take-off, Rostow argued that 'man' was complex, driven not only by economic advantage but also by other factors including 'power, leisure, continuity of experience and security'. In *The Stages of Economic Growth* Rostow writes of (man's) patterns of choice: '(he) is concerned with his family, the familiar values of his regional and national culture, and a bit of fun down at the local' (Rostow 1990: 149). Such discretionary consumption choices, it should be noted, however, are not available at all levels of development and in all parts of a nation. Working from a different discipline, that of sociology, Maslow (1943) wrote about a hierarchy of needs, with basic physiological needs at the base of his pyramid and self-actualisation needs (including creativity and spontaneity) at the apex. A similar perspective is often applied to creative class arguments: affluence and mobility, particularly in the advanced economies, is driving the demand for material goods and self-actualisation. From a model of social equalisation under Maoist nation building, China is moving to what Communist Party theorists, following Engels, term a well-off (*xiaokang*) society. Indeed, Jiang Zemin's proclamation in 2002 that entrepreneurs are worthy of becoming party members, inadvertently legitimates market individualism.

In this era of 'independent innovation' in which the new professional classes invigorate institutions like the Chinese Communist Party (CCP), it is possible to detect traces of Richard Florida's 3T thesis of toleration, technology and talent, suitably sanitised to fit Chinese conditions. These ingredients are evident in China's near neighbours, which have moved through their own stages of development.

The East Asian flying geese

With the advanced Western nations moving swiftly towards becoming service-led economies following the Second World War, the only real option for the new industrialising economies of East Asia was to follow. The flying geese model (FG model) describes how developing economies are drawn into competitive forms of production and industry regulation. Developed by Kaname Akamatsu in the 1930s (see Ozawa 2003) it entails a sequential process of tandem growth among closely interacting nations through leader–emulator relationships. In contrast to the kind of economic integration typified by free trade agreements, this de facto integration model has no official requirements for entry. In other words, follower economies can 'free-ride' on the growth stimulated by the first goose.

The emergence of East Asia is built on the flying geese model and exchanges of skill, the transfer of production capabilities, investment and management. These intangibles, sometimes classified under the label of the new economy, have long been associated with global cities like New York, London and Zurich, internationalising via Japan and Hong Kong to Taiwan, South Korea and now China. The so-called 'East Asian miracle', a term used to describe the rapid catch-up of Japan, Taiwan, Korea and Singapore, was characterised by government protection of infant industries and a focus on differentiated manufacturing (World Bank 1993). New institutional practices developed in response to market liberalisations and trade agreements. Technological advances – including convergence and digitisation – provided opportunities for growth in the region while the corrective effects of the 1997 Asian financial crisis led to more transparency and less interventionist markets. As Ozawa *et al.* note, the Asian financial crisis of 1997 signified that 'governing the market' could not remain as the recipe for future growth (cf. Wade 1990; Ozawa *et al.* 2001).

However, this openness does not imply the retreat of the nation-state from policy making, nor does it imply a level playing field for international investment.

East Asia's 'catch-up' was achieved through a state-directed brand of capitalism. Aside from protectionism, characteristics included shared growth (subsidies and job security for employees), extended credit from central banks, and large industrial conglomerates. Ellis and Gadiesh (2006) have proposed three stages of development to describe the rise of Japanese and Korean companies. The first stage saw the building of local manufacturing capacity in order to provide low-cost production (outsourcing) to multinationals; second, Japanese and Korean companies borrowed capabilities through technology licensing and joint ventures; and third, they bought assets and brands abroad. This so-called 'turnaround' requires a top-down effort, often through central planning to eradicate the unproductive patterns of the past.

It is this combination of top-down support for catch-up combined with grassroots entrepreneurship that now frames China's catch-up. The rise of East Asian 'soft power' has captured much of the world's attention in the past decade, as these countries have moved into high-value service industries including the exportable content industries of film, television, animation, and video games. China's turnaround in these industries is a work-in-progress. The infrastructure is laid, the plans are made, but can the vision be realised? In the following chapters, I will show how China's past provides the resources for the Created in China project.

3 The culture-knowledge economy of traditional China

Marco Polo, the great Venetian traveller of the fourteenth century, must have gazed upon the sights of Lin'an (Hangzhou), then capital of the Southern Song dynasty, and wondered how man could construct such a place of infinite splendour. Polo described Lin'an as the most beautiful and magnificent city in the world. All under heaven was spectacular. In his *Travels* Polo wrote about the communication system by which important messages were rapidly dispatched and about the merchants who transported goods up and down the Yangzi river. Today the area that Marco Polo saw is spectacular in a different way. The great canals that carried traders have been replaced by four-lane highways and electronic networks delivering instant messaging. Hangzhou is a vibrant industrial centre, the capital of Zhejiang province, the engine of China's economic miracle, producing household commodities proudly bearing the Made in China label.

Whether Polo actually travelled to China is unresolved. Nevertheless, his *Travels* are synonymous with ideas of cultural exchange and knowledge transfer. In the previous chapter I argued that China underwent great periods of rapid change, followed by periods of resistance to change. A central theme in this history of cultural exchange is the role of tradition. Many writers have used the term 'traditional culture' in a static sense to frame China's response to the West in the nineteenth century, particularly to support the idea that European development advanced because it was more resilient, more scientific and less constrained by traditional values. China specialists, Teng and Fairbank (1979) point out that 'tradition' is a mechanism that expresses both continuity and change: they argue that 'China's ancient ways have undergone continuous modification as century followed century' (1979: 4). Indeed, it is worth re-emphasising that culture is not fixed. This holds true whether we speak of cultural artefacts housed in museums of galleries or popular cultural traditions repurposed in cheap accessible formats. Cultural tradition extends over time, evolving and absorbing influences.

This chapter charts a course through the history of cultural commerce in China. My account is an abridged one and I omit many important developments due to constraints of space. The purpose is to draw out antecedents, innovations and disruptions in the flow of cultural trade – and in the process to develop an argument about the benefits of cultural exchange to innovation. I begin with some foundational definitions of culture in China. I then introduce an origin myth, before moving to the pre-history of cultural exchange in imperial China.

Beginnings of the knowledge–human capital nexus

The origin of the modern Chinese word 'culture' (*wenhua*) dates to about 800 BC in the *Book of Changes* (the *yijing*).[1] In its classical form the morpheme *wen* referred to 'lines or markings'. As a measure of learning and refinement, *wen* provided a standard to emulate. The knowledge of rites and rituals became essential to social management and the literati class acted as the conduit for regulating and maintaining traditional values. The *hua* morpheme has the associated meanings of transformation, change and nature. From the etymology of *wenhua* comes the tension between continuity and change.

In classical Chinese *wenhua* has another meaning; it implies ruling by non-violence and refinement. Learning was imperative to the art of government. At points of dynastic succession, military families would ascend to power where-upon they were impelled to become competent in the arts of civilian governance. Challenges to the traditional social order were held in check by Confucian norms; for instance, the emperor was bound by the same ethical principles as members of a household. Ethical refinement defined by the canon of Confucian knowledge contributed to the consolidation of the Chinese high culture tradition. Traditional Chinese society exemplified a link between self-cultivation, refinement and governance. Although persons of the lowest rank were able to sit for the official examination system that once successfully negotiated conferred scholar-gentry status, this station was generally out of the reach of the common people. Confucius wrote that, 'The common people can be made to follow a path but not to understand it'.

Ritual (*li*) and benevolence (*ren*) consolidated tradition. According to the Confucian sages, the decorum and conduct of the common people would be positively influenced by exposure to the refined virtue of the superior man who observed ritual. Edward Shils wrote that, 'the charisma of the centre, discerned by study, cultivated by ritual and the reverence for ancestors, brings the peripheral common people closer to the moral order occupied at the centre by the emperor and his counsellors and officials' (Shils 1996: 65). Ritual and benevolence offered material and social benefits. The scholar-gentry class constituted a unique form of human capital. The economist William Baumol (2002: 63) notes, that 'having been appointed to powerful positions [they] were expected to recoup in the form of bribes the heavy expenses they incurred in preparing for the difficult imperial examinations that were required for such positions'. The scholar-gentry class had civil authority over lower ranks, including the merchant classes. They were exempted from corvee labour and were entitled to a state pension. The stereotype of the Confucian scholars, and to a lesser extent the intellectual in more modern times, is a person well versed in the arts but often far removed from the mundane routines of daily existence. Successful scholars administered the provincial and central organs of government, they had authority to interpret the *Five Classics*, and they could use their authority for personal aggrandisement.[2] In effect, the longevity of the classical Chinese tradition was due to the scholarly class's reluctance to tamper with a symbolic order that preserved their social ranking.

The bracketing of cultural refinement with social distinction endured throughout the imperial period. At the same time, a rich tradition of popular arts developed, informed by Confucianism but also absorbing elements of Daoism and Buddhism, as well as local myths and historical legends. The economist William G. Skinner (1964) identified the important role of market systems in China. Farquhar and Hevia (1993: 496) have argued that such market systems were 'both foundations of "little" cultural traditions and the means by which the "great" tradition was communicated throughout China'; that is, the great tradition of the literati – the great wheel of Chinese culture, slow moving and resilient to change – and the small wheel, the tradition of the market-based rural communities.

The pre-history of cultural exchange

In the previous chapter I showed how territory, technology and taste provided the foundations for Chinese economic development. My discussion now turns to specific forms of cultural exchange. The origins of cultural commerce in China extend back into the Neolithic age. According to an origin myth from the *Book of Changes* the beginning of human culture is associated with trade in commodities.

> After Fu Xi died Shen Nong arose. He carved a piece of wood into a ploughshare and bent another piece to make a handle, and taught the world the advantages of ploughing and weeding. This idea he probably took from the hexagram *yi*. He set up markets at midday and caused the people of the world to bring all their goods and exchange them and then return home so that everything found its proper place.
>
> (in Wm T. de Bary 1960: 197)

It is difficult to verify the extent of commerce and forms of cultural production that took place prior to the Shang dynasty (1600–1027 BCE). The *Book of Changes* itself was written much later, probably in the Western Zhou dynasty (1115–781 BCE). Much discussion of the Xia period from 5000 BCE to approximately 2000 BCE is speculation based on scattered remains of ancient tombs and records of the Han dynasty historian Sima Qian. Aside from myths of semi-divine culture heroes – the legendary Yellow Emperor and the sage-kings Yao, Shun and Yu – little evidence of daily life exists. Nevertheless, archaeologists surmise that the Yangshao culture of the central plains along the Yellow River region (now Henan, Shaanxi and Shanxi) dated from the fifth millennium BCE. This central plains culture was based on millet, pig, goat and dog. Cultural artefacts retrieved from burial sites are mostly composed of metal or clay; examples of fine-grained pottery artefacts and clay rattles have survived. Another stream of culture, the Daxi culture (5000–3000 BCE) was located in the Hubei and Sichuan regions, now inundated by the Three Georges Dam project. This region produced a distinctive red pottery.

People of the Longshan culture (3000–2000 BCE) of today's coastal Shandong created black polished pottery. Musical instruments from this period include bone and clay whistles and clay flutes (Guo and Sheng 1993). There is however no evidence to suggest that these items were used for trade.

The Shang period records provide the best indications of daily life in China following the Neolithic period. There is abundant evidence from the Shang and Zhou periods (1027–771 BCE). Handcraft industries flourished on the Chinese plains areas. According to Sima Qian, the written script emerged in current day Henan and Shanxi provinces during the Shang period, together with schools for education of the nobles and princes. Even during the pre-Confucian Shang dynasty, a belief prevailed that the government had a responsibility to provide education so that talented people could enter government and perpetuate the moral and ethical foundation of society. Burial grounds found at Anyang in Henan Province have revealed objects and artefacts from afar – seashells and turtle shells, salt, turquoise, jade, tin and bones. Records show rudimentary carvings on jade, bone, stone and on wooden flutes, pottery, bronze, gold and silver vessels and embroidery. Oracle bones, a means of divination dating back as far as 4000 BCE, were plentiful at the Anyang site. In ancient China the practice of drying cattle and buffalo bones and turtle shells, and then heating them till they cracked, provided a role for diviners and a source of wise counsel for the rulers. By the Shang dynasty interpretations were carved on to bones using a script that would form the basis of the Chinese written language. During the same period musical instruments such as whistles, big and small bells, gongs, drums, and flutes were introduced. Singers, dancers, musicians and acrobats provided services, mostly unpaid, for the ruling elites (Zhao 2003).

The Shang period was followed by the Zhou, usually divided into the Western Zhou (1027–771 BCE), the Spring and Autumn Period (770–475 BCE), and the Warring States period (475–221 BCE). The Zhou witnessed new developments in calligraphy as well as inscriptions on bronze and silver vessels, and jade carvings. Records from a book called the *Tongdian* (*The Comprehensive Manual*) indicate that Zhou historians kept a record of ceremonial music known as *yayue*. This royal court music was performed at sacrificial offerings, imperial court meetings and grand banquets. The term *yayue* literally translates as 'elegant refined music'. The *Book of Rites* notes that, 'The gentlemen of the ancient times did not indicate his social position in words but in the manners and the music entitled to him' (Guo and Sheng 1993: 41). Social rank determined the size and type of performance, the quality of instruments and the number of dancers. The distinction between 'elegant and refined music' and 'folk music' had emerged in the Shang but was formally acknowledged during the Zhou Dynasty. The sounds were derived from metal (bell), stone (stone chime), string (*qin* and *se*), bamboo (*di*, *chi*, *xiao* and panpipes), clay (*xun*), wood (*zhu* and *yu*), gourd (*sheng*) and leather drum. Music was considered essential to maintaining order; the function of elegant and refined music was therefore educational, it served a regulatory role and strengthened the hierarchical formation of the state.

During the Spring and Autumn period, the Zhou kingdom centred at Luoyang (in today's Henan province) came under increased strain from its principalities. This was the era of the great philosophers. Poetry and prose prospered. During this time of the so-called 'hundred schools of philosophy', bamboo, bark and silk scrolls were carried by officials and advisors to the king. Education developed. Two kinds of schools emerged: the Schools of the State were located in Luoyang as well as the various capitals of the many states that existed; Schools of the District formed in villages and in townships, supported by public funds (Guo and Sheng 1993). During the Zhou period memorisation and rote learning were widely condemned as artificial education. The system of myriad city-states consolidated into larger bounded territories that eventually became the seven powers known as the Warring States. Alliances, intrigue and open warfare ensued, and the Warring States became independent kingdoms ruled over by large families headed by a king (*wang*). Agriculture prospered, new territories were seized through conquests, and technologies such as hoes, knives and sickles developed. Trade increased due to the expansion of forms of currency as well as territory (Morton and Lewis 2004). Records from the historians reveal that Chinese silk was known in India as far back as the fourth century BCE (Curtin 1984).

By the end of the turbulent Warring States period, the followers and students of Confucius were generating cultural and intellectual commodities for use in the private schools. It is said that Confucius was the first to establish a private school; this had more than 3,000 students (Guo and Sheng 1993: 225). The philosophers Mencius, Xunzi, Mozi and Zhuangzi established their own traditions. The teachings of the Hundred Schools period, together with the historical records of the contending states provided materials for the production of the classic books. But the legacy of Confucius was the greatest. The Confucian system, although undergoing numerous iterations throughout history, was essentially founded on the idea that learning is acquired by the diligent study of messages passed on by learned teachers. These teachers were sought after. Guo and Sheng write that 'Another form of educational activity in this period was the practice of the contending feudal states of luring into their domain a large number of scholars, partly to serve as a source of ideas for enhancing the prosperity of the state and partly to gain an aura of intellectual respectability in a land where respect for scholars had already become an established tradition' (Guo and Sheng 1993: 225). The Jixia Academy in the State of Qi (now Shandong) was an important centre.

The Qin dynasty (221–206 BC) is directly associated with the imperial dynastical system and China's first emperor, whose name Qin (pronounced *chin*) gives us the modern English word China. Unification of speech and writing took place under the theory of state known as Legalism. Cultural development accelerated with dissemination of books concerning agriculture, medicine, astronomy and mathematics. Other books were deemed to be redundant. Qin officials carried bamboo book scrolls, not of the Confucian classics, but of the regulations of the Legalist code. The earliest recorded medical book, *The Yellow Emperor's Inner Classic (Huangdi neijing)*, is said to be written in the Qin. This book comprised

81 chapters or treatises in a question and answer format between the mythical Yellow Emperor and his ministers. By the end of this dynasty the self-designated august emperor Shi Huangdi had turned on the Confucian scholars, burning their books and, according to historical legends, burying many of them alive.

The despotism of China's first emperor was followed by the Han dynasty (206 BC–221 CE) along with further systematisation of relationships between elites and commoners. In the Han the state instituted the imperial academy along with the first examination system based on the Confucian classics. This 'empire school' (*taixue*) facilitated the emergence of a knowledge economy. In 140 CE the leading scholar Dong Zhongshu advised the Emperor Wu Di to formalise orthodox knowledge, effectively marginalising the contending voices of the Hundred Schools period. The educational curriculum from this time was underpinned by rote memorisation of selected Confucian classics and the sayings of ancient sages. In the reign of Emperor Wu Di a Music Bureau was founded to train musicians, and perform rites. This bureau eventually extended its remit to include songs and folk ballads of common people (Guo and Sheng 1993).

Speciality book markets and schools appeared in Luoyang and Chang'an (now Xian), the capitals of the Han dynasty. Books were laboriously hand-produced using brush and pen and were exchanged in a special market (*huaishi*) that assembled twice each month (Zhao 2003). The most famous text was *The Historical Records* by Sima Qian, while Xu Shen's *Solution of Text and Words* (*shuowen jiezi*) also appeared. The Han was a period of territorial expansion, which gave impetus to the importance of recording history. The invention of paper occurred later in the Han and is generally attributed to a person called Cai Lun, further stimulating the circulation of books on topics as diverse as sexual advice, law and fortune-telling. Markets prospered in which goods were both bartered and exchanged for money (Hansen 2000). Bronze craft, lacquer, jade, painting and sculpture were evidence of a revival of cultural commerce.

The Han period also witnessed the opening of China to 'foreign' influences. By the beginning of the Han Dynasty in the second century BCE, China had established itself as a universal empire based on idea of the mandate of heaven. This was the notion that succession was delivered by good governance, an idea initially conceived in the Zhou Dynasty. The Silk Road, through what is now Xinjiang, had opened up a path to the Roman Empire by the first century CE, and this trade route brought woollen and linen textiles into China as well as coral and pearls, amber, glass and other precious stones (Curtin 1984). Continual border conflict meant that the Han emperors were caught up in territorial skirmishes with the Xiongnu, a barbarian tribe who maintained a fast-riding cavalry.

These ongoing altercations had important effects. First, they initiated diplomacy based on trade. The Xiongnu were appeased with fineries of the Han civilisation – gold and silk in return for animal skins, rugs and rare stones (Hansen 2000). Second, the battles against the Xiongnu led the Chinese general Zhang Qian into the new 'Western regions', later to be known as Central Asia (Whitfield 1999). Third, the Chinese mainstream absorbed new cultural influences; for instance, the tall 'celestial' horses that have come to be associated with Tang and Song oil painting were introduced during the western exploits (Watson 1973). The skirmishes with the Xiongnu also led to innovations in Chinese music. The percussive style of music of the nomadic tribes was absorbed into the mainstream of the Han Imperial Army; this new music utilised drums, gongs, bell type percussive instruments, panpipes, a cylindrical double reed instrument called the *jia*, and the transverse flute (Guo and Sheng 1993: 422). It subsequently served as ceremonial music in the royal courts. The nomadic Xiongnu themselves moved westward and were replaced by another barbarian tribe, the Xianbi. Other instruments introduced into the Chinese mainstream during this period included the *hongkou*, a kind of Persian harp, and the pipa lute, which was derived from the plucked string instruments of the caravan trade along the Silk Road. In the so-called Northern Dynasties period (the 420s), imported music flourished. The entry points were Xiyu in present day Xinjiang and Xiliang in present day Gansu. The former incorporated music styles from Central Asia while the Indian influence was absorbed into Gansu. These styles were later incorporated into Tang court music.

The Chinese empire imploded due to ongoing conflicts and would not be reunified until the Sui dynasty in 589 CE. During this time the Silk Road was travelled by traders from Iran, India and Tibet – and in the eighth century by armies from the eastward moving Arab empire, which was first centred in Damascus, later Kufa, and then Bagdad. Buddhism, Islam, Zorastrianism, Manicheanism and Christianity moved along this trade route during various periods. Susan Whitfield's account of life along the Silk Road provides us with valuable impressions. She writes of the gains of trade: the Roman desire for silk, the role of Parthian traders as middlemen, Central Asia's positioning as a source of jade and other gems, the trade in Astrakan fur, salt from Tibet, and gold from the Altai mountains that was used by artisans in Chach (present day Taschent) and Samarkland to fashion beaten gold ornaments. Spices, cotton and ivory from India travelled along this route to the large cities of Chang'an and Luoyang (Whitfield 1999).

By the tenth century, the Silk Road had lost its appeal to long distance traders due to the likelihood of conflict; the focus of trade turned to the maritime route. The ocean had served to direct trade as early as the second century; Indian and Indian-Malayan merchant ships had plied the spice trade along India's east coast to Guangzhou. The Arabs and the Persians later used this Spice Route. Bagdad, Rome, Guangdong and Guangxi were accessible to Madagascar, providing a means to establish contact with India, Sri Lanka (Ceylon), the Mediterranean, and the Persian Gulf. Chinese embroidery, pottery and porcelain handicrafts reached distant destinations, eventually arriving in Europe in the sixth century. Chinese textile designs were popular in Rome and Iran, while Iranian designs were introduced into the Chinese repertoire (Watson 1973).

Music, carving and paintings from foreign areas reached the Chinese plains. This was the high tide of the import and export of cultural goods, which culminated in the Sui, Tang and Song dynasties. Porcelain production, books, opera venues, colleges, and private schools provided evidence of the increasing scale of cultural commerce. The historian Samuel Adshead (2004) says that before the Sui and Tang dynasties the intellectual world of China was 'provincial, static and monochrome'. During the Sui and Tang dynasties, Buddhist cultural influences were reflected in carvings and paintings. The Mogao caves at Dunhuang in the western Gansu province and the Longmen Grottos, not far from Luoyang in central Henan Province provide extensive evidence of Buddhist art, despite being plundered at various times throughout history.

The Tang Dynasty marked the beginning of fiction writing, further precipitating the expansion of book markets. While stories had circulated in the preceding dynasties, these were mostly confined to tales of the supernatural, brought about by the introduction of Hinayana Buddhism, and tales of famous persons exhibiting wit and erudition. During the Tang, however, imaginative romance tales began to appear, some written by candidates for the Imperial Examinations, who would present these stories to examiners to show their versatility. The expansion of prosperous commercial centres during this period, notably Chang'an and Luoyang, provided material for fiction. The professionalisation of storytelling in the Tang led to the emergence of street and palace performers. As Benn (2004) notes, the vast majority were independent entertainers who were tolerated but generally distrusted by high officials. They had a reputation for being itinerants, moving from place to place and exhausting the population's surplus income. They were also stigmatised by the orthodox classicists and moralists. The various titillations provided by the independent performers of the day were embodied in the so-called hundred acts – 'snake charmers, sword swallowers, fire eaters, and weight lifters, as well as more dignified music, singing, dancing, and acting' (Benn 2004: 159).

Stories often concerned courtesans and singsong girls. Booksellers thrived and sold large numbers of books; private art collections and collectors began to appear. Businessmen interested in cultural commerce made their living by specialising in painting and calligraphy sales. The calligrapher Wang Xizhi was a notable example of an early cultural entrepreneur; a five character painting by Wang once sold for 102 liang of silver (100 liang = 50 grams). At that time an official Zhong Shaojing invested all his assets in buying works by Wang Xizhi (Gong 2005). The Tang was the golden age of poetry. Poets such as Li Bai, Du Fu, Gao Shi, Cen Shen, Wang Changling and Li Qi were innovative in style and popularised poetry. The era saw the emergence of *ci* poetry, texts set to existing musical tunes. In the capital of Chang'an music flourished; indentured officials regularly outlaid amounts of money to patronise musical troupes, in particular female singers from central Asia. Foreign styles in music became fashionable and international performing troupes supplemented the thousands of musicians and dancers employed to perform daily in Changan's Academy of the Performing Arts and the Pear Garden, the latter an elite academy established by Emperor Ming Huang (Guo and Sheng 1993). Valerie Hansen recounts records of women riding horses, wearing tight dresses in the Central Asian style. The Qin music score, *The Orchid*, appeared in the Tang, composed by Qui Ming (Zhang 2005).

The Song dynasty comprises northern and southern periods, the former (960–1126 CE) a period of unification following the fall of the Tang, the latter (1128–1279) a time in which northern China was overrun by Jurchen tribes, forcing the capital to relocate from northern Bianjing (Kaifeng) to southern

Lin'an (Hangzhou). In the Song Dynasty, China experienced further economic prosperity, despite the encroaching Turkish and Mongolian tribes. Agriculture, handcrafts and commerce advanced in tandem with painting, calligraphy and ceramics. Cultural trade flourished and agents surfaced as cultural intermediaries. Emperors were not merely patrons but purchasers. The imperial system of official selection provided a catalyst for scholarship.

This was a period of high creativity in the visual arts; influences from Daoism and Buddhism led to a style of landscape painting that relied upon acquisition of technique over time and the artists' absorption in nature. The moment of creation, however, was spontaneous, putting down on paper the image that exists in the mind. For many, the Song represents the pinnacle of Chinese painting. The painters of the day were classified in three categories: palace artists, scholar officials and popular artists. While the palace artists were supported by patronage and scholar officials' work was non-commercial, the popular artist aimed at economic benefits, generating a market for cultural artefacts. There were said to be over 800 artists plying their skills for commercial gain in the Song. The painting and calligraphy market in Lin'an was prosperous and well attended.

The Qingming Shanghe tapestry, usually attributed to Zhang Zeduan, was an example of the commercial focus that emerged in the Song. Zhang became a palace artist in the Imperial Painting Academy of the Northern Song, an academy set up by the emperor Song Huizong to establish and propagate aesthetic standards. Perhaps more than any other work of art, museum artefact, opera or story from the time, the Qingming scroll illustrates the dynamics of cultural exchange and street life in China at a time when Europe was experiencing cultural repression under Christianity, its so-called Dark Age. The original of the Qingming scroll is 528 centimetres long and 24.8 centimetres wide. It presents images of some 550 people, 60 animals, 20 wooden boats, as well as 30 rooms and pavilions and about 20 transport vehicles. The reputation of the painting led to numerous reproductions and reinterpretations, often commissioned by emperors. Its value and its importance as a historical document lie is its realistic representation of commercial activity and social intercourse. But more than just a record of life in imperial China and a means to capture valuable tourist revenue for the Kaifeng city government, the Qingming scroll symbolises the legacy of cultural commerce in China. The painting passed through many owners, including acquisition on at least four occasions for imperial collections and numerous exchanges among private collectors, prior to its rediscovery as a cultural heritage artefact in 1950.

The title of the scroll reflects the Qingming festival, an important time in Chinese traditional culture when people tend to their ancestors' graves – although some critics have queried if this in fact is the theme, if Zhang Zeduan really was the artist, and if Bianjing really is the location depicted in the scroll. Nevertheless, at the time the scroll was painted, street fairs were popular in the northern Song cities and this exchange function provides much of the vibrancy, in contrast to the more static mountain landscapes characteristic of the Chinese oil painting tradition. Markets and fairs in the northern Song capital of Kaifeng promoted the curio trade.

Important curio markets appeared, such as the Kaiyuan temple in Yuezhou, which was a focal point for overseas businessmen. The publishing industry flourished. By the first half of the thirteenth century almost all the Tang and Song poems and novels had been published. The publishing industry was stimulated by the development of movable type for printing during the eleventh century and the demand for Buddhist sutras. The centre of publishing at the time was Lin'an.

The emergence of large urban centres in the Song stimulated a need for entertainment and this led to the practice of professional storytelling. In the Southern Song storytellers organised guilds to promote their activities and to propagate new scripts. The tales of this era were a further innovation; they embraced a full picture of real society rather than pandering to the tastes of elites. The performing arts by now had become commodities and singers and dancers who performed for the imperial court and the nobility were released, further stimulating the cultural economy. There were large entertainment markets called *washe* in the larger urban centres. The *washe* was a place for performances, usually located in business districts, together with night markets. Storytellers plied their wares, although their use of the vernacular language (*baihua*) was often considered inferior to the classic style. Each *washe* had several theatres (*goulan*). In Bianjing (Kaifeng) there were more than 50 theatres and in Lin'an there were more than 20 *washe* and *goulan*; the performances in each were different (Wang 2002; Hu and Zhang 1991; Guo and Sheng 1993).

China turns inwards (Yuan, Ming and Qing)

The Yuan dynasty (1280–1368 CE) is best known for the conquest of China by the Mongols and the great Kublai Khan, the grandson of Genghis Khan. A short-lived dynasty lasting just 88 years, the Yuan had its capital in Beijing. It was a period of trade expansion. Traffic along the Silk Road increased, bringing not only Persian and Central Asian traders but Europeans. Rosemary Scott writes of how the Mongol emperors expanded transportation infrastructure as well as facilitating commerce and cultural exchange. Under the reign of Kublai Khan, 'for the first time merchants were recognised as creators of wealth, and artisans were considered important enough to be excused corveé labour' (Scott 2006: 49). Visitors to China came from Italy and France. Franciscan monks travelled to China between 1253 and 1255 under the instruction of the French regent Louis IX. The most famous, however, were Venetian merchants; some like Marco Polo came and stayed.

Despite the Mongol occupation, the Yuan was a time of artistic growth. The popular novel developed in everyday language, allowing a greater use of satire, a necessary device under the Yuan regime (Morton and Lewis 2004: 123). Za opera (*zaju*), which had first appeared in the Tang, developed in north China. *Zaju* was a special term for a kind of performance that included singing, dancing, music, comedy routines and acrobatics. New important operas were created, such as Guan Hanqing's *The Injustice of Dou'e* and Wang Shifu's *The Western Chamber* (Hu and Zhang 1991). Under the Mongol regime Yuan *zaju* followed moved south, temporarily eclipsing Southern Opera. The northern music was robust and vigorous, while the southern music was soft and gentle. In fact, some of the most striking characteristics of Chinese music stem from this north–south dichotomy. At the end of the Yuan Dynasty Kunshan opera emerged, an art form requiring high levels of skill and the ability to sing for long periods at a time. This was a highly choreographed style which laid the foundations for the emergence of Beijing opera at the end of the eighteenth century.

During the Ming (1368–1644) the cultural economy developed further, particularly in the prosperous and populous Jiangnan area south of the Yangzi River. Taste was a driver of the cultural economy. Wealthy classes had time to enjoy the arts and shops proliferated in the large cities trading in calligraphy, painting and picture mounting. The famous artist Zheng Banqiao had a fixed price for his paintings: 6 liang of silver for large size, 4 for medium and 2 for small size paintings. The popular novel came of age during the Ming. *The Romance of the Three Kingdoms* (*sanguo yanyi*) and *The Water Margin* (*shuihu zhuan*) were published and widely circulated.

Another significant cultural incursion during the Ming was the influence of Jesuits on Chinese court life – and the corresponding transmission of knowledge about Chinese culture and technology back to Europe. The Jesuits, initially led by Matteo Ricci (1552–1610), had come to China to convert but soon found out that the Chinese were interested more in clock making than Christianity. There were some notable conversions though: a well-known convert to Christianity Xu Guangqi introduced Western knowledge of mathematics, astronomy and cartography (Morton and Lewis 2005: 132).

On the cultural front more than 300 recorded operas existed; of these, more than 200 were composed during the Ming (Zhao 2003). These included folk as well as professional operas. The audiences came from all social classes and different stages were built for the rich classes and the commoners. Folk music developed while palace music waned in influence. During the late Ming Dynasty the first daily newspaper was produced. The *Jing* had 10 pages and a print run of 10,000. The Ming dynasty is well-known also for its ostentatious displays of court life revolving around the palace known as the Forbidden City. A painting academy was established in the reign of the Yongle Emperor (1360–1424) while trade in porcelain grew along with an increased scale of production. Imperial factories produced exquisite porcelain, not just for their royal patrons but for wealthy connoisseurs.

During the Qing dynasty reign of Emperor Qianlong (1736–1795) the arts flourished in Beijing. The Emperor was an avid collector, a poet and a patron. During his reign the Jesuits exerted more influence on styles of art. The most notable was Giuseppe Castiglione, a favourite of Qianlong who introduced a European aesthetic into the Chinese oil painting canon. Chinese literature also travelled to Japan during this period. The most well-known stories of the Qing were *The Journey to the West* (*xiyouji*) and *The Dream of the Red Chamber* (*honglou meng*). In particular the *Journey to the West* symbolised cross-cultural exchange, the story of how Buddhist sutras came to China from India in the seventh century. These stories made their way to Japan. From 1600 a steady stream of letters from Jesuits living in China helped to create an image of China that resonated with the tales of Marco Polo. China was exotic and oriental. The trade in porcelain was accompanied by a European interest in Chinoiserie; the techniques of porcelain production were first adopted in Meissen Germany in 1710 (Morton and Lewis 2004: 130). Joe Studwell writes that 'late eighteenth and early nineteenth century Europe based its pagodas, wallpaper and decorative Rococo style on Chinese design' (Studwell 2002: 12).

The end of empire

While the Qing was a period of economic expansion, from the perspective of creativity, it was a time of decline. Achievements of the past were treasured, but 'imitation, elaboration and decoration ran riot' (Morton and Lewis 2004: 145). Europe had its Renaissance, its Enlightenment, and was in the midst of an Industrial Revolution. From the periods of complex pluralism – the Sui and the Tang – China had moved towards a more bureaucratic model of high culture, evident in the ostentatious displays of the Dowager Empress Cixi (1835–1908). The Imperial examination system was failing to produce the talent base necessary to allow China to adapt. The West was closing in. The problem China would face over the next 150 years was how to catch up. Over the next several decades the Chinese nation countenanced contrasting approaches to catch-up: learning from Western technology, turning to Communism as a development model, and eventually in the mid 1980s initiating a massive push to develop a Chinese innovation system.

4 Revolution, reform and culture in modern China

I am just sixty years old, but I can still work
And I find it as easy as when I as young
It's not that I am boasting of my strength
But here in my heart I have Mao Tse-Tung

(from Songs of the Red Flag 1961)[1]

During the late nineteenth and early twentieth centuries, cultural producers, writers and artists in China absorbed an increasing variety of foreign influences and ideas. A turning point was China's opening to the West after the Treaty of Nanjing in 1942. The designated treaty ports of Canton (now Guangzhou) and Shanghai became centres of intellectual fervour, political protest and commercial culture. By the 1920s, the political imperative of nation building led to new understandings of the role of culture. Foreign ideas, notably ideas inherited from Soviet Marxism, were seeded into the field of Chinese traditional culture. The resulting hybrids were productive – in the sense of their rapid dispersal – but for many they were aesthetically less pleasing than the elegant culture of Chinese tradition. However, the utilitarian role of culture superseded aesthetics.

Debates ensued about appropriate forms of culture, in particular, whether the role of culture was to enlighten (*hua dazhong*) or to popularise (*dazhong hua*). At different times these dual functions stood in uneasy opposition. In the initial period of cultural nationalism during the first decades of the twentieth century, culture was linked to the urgent task of moral development but this political fervour co-existed with a dynamic commercial cultural market. The revolutionary period under Maoism saw the introduction of a distinctly Soviet approach to cultural governance. After China's opening to the international community in 1978, heterodox ideas were mixed into a so-called 'cultural fever'. This period of reflection about China's cultural repositioning was then superseded by a nascent cultural market, a period in which the state retreated from its leading role in subsiding cultural activities.

Modern China: new culture

The history of modern China is conventionally charted from the mid nineteenth century when Western foreign incursions brought the outside world to China's ports. The foreigners were seeking tea, spices and silk in exchange for opium. The technological superiority of the West was demonstrated in the Opium Wars of 1839–1842 and 1857–1858, leading to a succession of reforms movements and internal rebellions that weakened the hegemony of the Manchu state. Beginning with the 'self-strengthening' movement from the 1860s under the slogan 'Chinese learning as the essence, Western learning for utility' (*zhongxue weiti, xixue weiyong*), calls for reform were not only directed at specific social institutions considered to be too traditional, corrupt or ineffective, but were directed at changing the 'mentality' or 'spirit' (*jingshen*) of the Chinese people, or at least those segments of the population capable of responding to the challenges of modernity.

Benedict Anderson (1983) has argued that the development of print technologies and capitalist forms of social organisation were instrumental in the disintegration of traditional conceptions of community. It was the convergence of capitalism, the technology of print and the diversity of languages in sixteenth-century Europe that led to what he called 'imagined communities'. The adoption of vernaculars by printers and publishers allowed people who might never meet to establish a sense of common understandings; the expansion of print capitalism served as the basis for the transmission of political ideas and visions of nationhood. The emergence of print capitalism in China in the late nineteenth century validates Anderson's thesis to the extent that the mass media rapidly precipitated the transmission of political ideas. The potential of the print media had been demonstrated in the 'modern'-style periodicals published by Protestant missionaries. The influence of publishers such as James Legge in the 1860s hastened the belief that the media could be used to disseminate radical political ideas (Lee and Nathan 1985). Of course, the emergence of print capitalism in China needs to be contextualised against the historical influences of the end of the Qing Dynasty. Great social dislocations occurred throughout the country. Civil unrest and warlordism were rife together with European colonialism, an imperial court incapable of reforming itself, the influences of the Meiji Restoration, Japanese imperialism, and a disenfranchised intellectual stratum.

The reform movements that followed the collapse of the Manchu dynasty were led by scholars and political activists who had benefited from the modern insights of Western scholarship, either by study and travel overseas or through reading translations of new foreign works. These scholars included Kang Youwei (1858–1927) who conceived of the idea of *datong*, a treatise on 'the cosmopolitan society'; Yan Fu (1853–1921), who translated numerous foreign works including Thomas Huxley's *Evolution and Ethics*, J. S. Mill's *On Liberty* and Adam Smith's *The Wealth of Nations*; and Liang Qichao (1873–1929), who was probably the most strident advocate of reform.

The writings of these scholars and activists pronounced the challenge of modernity and heralded a new understanding of culture as 'a fundamental bearer of difference between countries and peoples' (Liu 1995: 239). This anthropological conception came to prominence in China at the turn of the century, a time when the evolutionary theories of Darwin, Huxley and Spencer were challenging the status quo of Confucian cosmology. The idea of evolutionary stages, according to which European civilisation led the way, was promulgated via Japanese translations of Western sociologists and anthropologists, in particular in the discussions that ensued from the work of E. B. Tylor (*Primitive Cultures*), E. Westermarck (*The History of Human Marriage*) and F. H. Giddings' *Principles of Sociology* (Wang 1991: 121–131).

The debates about evolution and stages of civilisation introduced the problematic relationship between race and culture. Probably the most influential writer in this regard was the Japanese scholar and educationalist Fukazawu Yukichi (1835–1901) who was influenced by Guizot's *Histoire de la civilisation en Europe*, and Buckle's *History of Civilisation in England.*[2] The Western evolutionist sense of 'civilisation' was subsequently rendered in Japanese as *bunmei* (equivalent to *wenming* in Chinese), whereas the anthropological sense of 'culture' became *bunka* (*wenhua* in Chinese). The impact of the new understandings of culture was devastating for reform-minded intellectuals. In the minds of many intellectuals China's racial stock was superior but its civilisation, far from being at the apex of the hierarchy was backward, its progress stymied by a pre-modern cultural tradition. The problem from this perspective was how to bring about a fundamental change in culture and at the same time awaken the population to the national predicament – the fact that China was no longer the 'great civilisation' or the 'middle kingdom'.

Liang Qichao and the new citizen

The reformer Liang Qichao met the missionary publisher Timothy Richard in Peking in 1895, and it was through this meeting that Liang first recognised the power of media publicity in the quest for national consciousness-raising (Lee and Nathan 1985). The political journal became an instrument of popular mobilisation. Following the unsuccessful 'Hundred Days Reform' in 1898, the leaders of this movement were exiled to Japan. From his experience in Japan Liang Qichao became more convinced that the press was essential to a nation. First, because it contributed to the progress of civilisation by exercising intellectual freedom and guiding public opinion, and second, the newspaper spoke to the entire nation and hence helped create a national community (Tang 1996). In Liang's opinion, the political press was the messenger of modernity. The task then remained to refashion new forms of culture from the old civilisation, forms that would serve the cause of progress.

From the period of the Hundred Days Reform (1898) to the end of the second decade, reformers such as Liang Qichao saw the role of culture as a means of 'awakening' the population to the task of national reconstruction. Liang wrote,

'In order to develop nationalism in China, there is no other way than to renew the people' (cited in Tang 1996: 26). Inherent in this renewal was a new ideal of moral development, 'a morality to be followed by citizens for the good of their nation', best represented in the 'new ethics of the West' rather than the 'unfit' ethics of traditional China (Pusey 1983: 238). One of the most influential books of the 1890s was Yan Fu's translation of Thomas *Huxley's Evolution and Ethics* (*tianyan lun*). The link between Charles Darwin's 'survival of the fittest' and T. H. Huxley's 'self-restraint and social cooperation' is encapsulated in Liang Qichao's notion of 'fit virtues'. The kind of moral development prescribed by Liang was a 'public morality' (*gongde*), which in incorporating self-restraint would allow people to 'group' and integrate. Accordingly, people needed to be educated to understand that progress was tied to values of cooperation rather than self-interest. However, Yan Fu was critical of the argument that Western knowledge was the utilitarian foundation upon which China could prosper, 'Chinese knowledge has its foundation and function; Western knowledge also has its foundation and function' (Yan, cited in Teng and Fairbank 1979: 151).

The periodical press allowed political reformers to promote their views to an educated reading public. The development of print capitalism soon displaced the role of the scholar-official. As Lee and Nathan point out, 'the intellectuals who became involved in the periodical press as writers and editors found themselves adopting a somewhat different role – no longer that of the state-orientated scholar-official, but that of a 'popular' spokesman for society' (Lee and Nathan 1985: 379). Significantly, the content of the periodical press incorporated a new approach towards cultural government. Writing in 1898, Liang Qichao advocated the pedagogic function of the popular novel, to promote in the common people new ethical understandings so that they might awaken from their slumber:

> There is indeed a great deal of truth in Mr. Kang Youwei's observation that people with low levels of literacy will often stay away from the classics but cannot do without fiction. Fiction should therefore seek to teach where the Six Classics have failed to teach, to convey lessons where the official histories have failed to convey, to illuminate where the recorded sayings are unable to illuminate, and to govern where laws have failed. In the world, experienced men are few, and the ignorant are innumerable; those well-versed in literature are few, and those who can barely read are legion. The Six Classics are indeed elegant, but if they are not read and understood, they are just pearls cast before swine.
>
> (Liang, cited in Denton 1996: 72)

According to Liang, simplification was necessary if fiction was to perform the function of political education and moral development. Realising that commercial success depended upon establishing a broad audience base, many of the periodical presses dispensed with the elegant and abstruse literary language (*wenyan*) of the classics in favour of vernacular forms. Liang stopped short, however, of completely dispensing with classical prose, preferring to fashion his work with a mixture of the elegant traditional style, the vernacular of the day, and a stream of foreign references.

The expansion of the modern commercial press during the dying embers of the Qing Dynasty provided a vehicle for the exchange of information and ideas. The political periodicals produced by reformers and revolutionaries, both from within the treaty ports and from exile in Japan, gained ground during periods of political unrest and foreign aggression, culminating in the May Fourth demonstrations of 1919.[3] However, despite the efforts to promote ideas of reform through fiction that was morally uplifting, commercial considerations continued to intrude upon the enlightened concerns of those who saw culture's role as part of the government of the people. While the periodical press flourished, so did the cultural forms that elite intellectuals had railed against. As Lee and Nathan (1985) have pointed out, the problem confronting reform intellectuals was that the great majority of the burgeoning audience for the periodical press came not from people educated in the new modern schools but from a traditional background. The intended 'elevating' effect of the 'new literature', as it came to be known, had to contend with the 'popularising' impact of publications appealing to a broad less-educated readership.

The political journals sought to distance themselves from popular escapist forms. Modern forms of popular fiction were advanced as a vehicle of reform and mass education in contradistinction to 'decadent forms' of popular fiction and frivolous tales. Titles such as *Playful News*, *News for Laughter* and *News for Leisurely Entertainment* were available alongside collections of translations of Western fiction and scientific articles (Lee and Nathan 1985: 386). The pernicious influence of decadent fiction, according to elite intellectuals such as Liang, was manifest in social ills including superstition, dishonesty, avarice, the formation of secret societies and attachment to sensual pleasures (Denton 1996: 80). An elite-minded social reformer, Liang had condemned the 'moral degeneration' of decadent forms while exalting the uplifting and civilising potential of 'new fiction'.

Whereas the more literary publications carried translations of Western scholarship and literature, the downmarket end featured mostly murder and detective stories. The commercial nature of publishing brought a competition for readers that featured tabloid style journalism and a diversity of formats intended to cater to the tastes of an urban population more interested in salacious gossip and revealing exposes of the lifestyles of 'government officials, "foreign affairs" experts, compradors in the treaty ports, merchants, status hungry nouveaux-riches, and decadent scions of rural landlords who migrated to the city for fun and pleasure' (Lee and Nathan 1985: 383).

For the authors of popular fiction, however, the function of literature was to entertain. In the words of one editor, 'When you are exhausted from a night out and return home, you can turn on the light and open the magazine, or enjoy a spirited conversation on the stories among friends, or peruse the stories with one's beloved wife sitting by one's side' (Denton 1996: 244).

Commercial popular culture continued to flourish throughout the 1920s and 1930s. The popularity of these genres and their exploitation of traditional themes had the effect of sustaining an intellectual backlash from elite intellectuals who saw the escapism of popular culture as antithetical to the cause of educating the common people. Many of these cosmopolitan intellectuals, attracted to European romanticism and realist fiction, viewed art and literature as a pantheistic celebration of the creative impulse and a vehicle for the ideal of universal humanism. Two such literary societies formed in the 1920s were the Literary Research Association and the Creation Society. The slogans associated with these societies were 'literature for life's sake' (realism) and 'literature for art's sake' (romanticism and expressionism) (McDougall and Louie 1997).

Reform and revolution

The early reform movements of the first two decades of the twentieth century were not dramatic society-wide transformations but they established the seeds of what would later become a mass movement. Located in the large coastal cities where the influence of Western imperialism was most evident, they attracted ardent nationalists to the cause. In the more rarefied domains of Peking University an anti-traditionalist movement was generating new followers. The vulgar pursuits of commercialism were counterbalanced to some extent in Chen Duxiu's *New Youth* (*xin qingnian*), a journal established in 1915, which promoted Chen's catch-cry of 'science' and 'democracy'. Launching a sustained attack on the historical legacy of Confucianism, Chen – along with fellow reformer Hu Shi – became pioneers of the New Culture Movement. Chen Duxiu was a liberal thinker who sought to apply science to the domains of society, politics, ethics and morals. Wang Hui writes:

> For Chen Duxiu and his colleagues of *New Youth*, however, the main purpose of applying the concept of science was to remould subjective mentation, or to re-cognise the mental state of the self through science. In other words, they applied science to mean self-reflection and assumed the progression of human society would be a natural result of self-reflection.
>
> (Wang 1995: 38)

Taking up the clarion cry of 'awakening the population' that Liang Qichao and others had identified as the role of the modern novel, Chen advocated social reform based on a scientific process of self-reflection and renewal. Awakening included two 'basic levels': political awakening and ethical awakening (Wang 1995a: 40). Chen Duxiu later converted to Marxism, accepted the theory of historical materialism as the new science of progress, and was rewarded for his conversion by becoming the first secretary-general of the Chinese Communist Party in 1921. Chen came to believe that historical materialism was a scientific account of all social phenomena and furthermore that it provided an explanatory basis for the determinative role of economics.

Invariably, discussion of culture under socialism proceeds from its use as propaganda. From a Western perspective the term 'propaganda' conjures up a negative sense of manipulation, misinformation and brainwashing. The Chinese word for propaganda (*xuanchuan*), however, carries a much loftier sense, meaning 'to propagate, to disseminate, or to give publicity to'. The modern use of propaganda was consummated during periods of armed struggle. The Soviet influence infiltrated both Communist and Nationalist cultural circles during the civil war period and during the anti-Japanese struggle as propaganda offensives spread across the countryside. The Chinese revolutionary movement initially used agit-prop forms to win the support of a largely uneducated peasant audience. After 1949, propaganda techniques were further developed and used in nation building campaigns.

In the succeeding struggle for power, the revolutionary leadership under Mao Zedong viewed the May Fourth 'petit-bourgeois intellectual' literature as too closely aligned with the imperialist system that the revolution opposed. In addition to his distaste for refinement, Mao contended that the urban literati who aspired to participate in the revolution were as much in need of reform as the culture they espoused. Mao's idea of a 'revolutionary peasant culture' collapsed the opposition between the literate high tradition and the unsophisticated common tradition and forged a 'proletarian culture' – a 'national, scientific and mass culture' (Denton 1995: 430). The kind of cultural reform proposed here rejected culture that did not belong to the people of China (foreign culture), as well as opposing feudal and superstitious (unscientific) forms, and calling for the elimination of bourgeois forms (non-mass). By creating the oppositions, and prescribing policy to ensure cultural renovation was carried through, the Chinese subject would be effectively remade. In other words, culture would act directly on society.

In his insightful study of ideology in Communist China David Holm (1991) writes about the arguments over 'national form' that took place in the communist base camps in Yan'an in north-west China in the 1940s. Two camps emerged: cultural populists and literary intellectuals. The former maintained that because of peoples' familiarity ready-made forms such as local operas, folk songs and tales were most appropriate for the task of mobilisation (Holm 1991: 54–55). The process of utilising old forms, termed 'pouring old wine into new bottles', had already been advocated by Mao Zedong's political secretary Chen Boda, who in 1939 wrote:

This ... requires that one selects the forms [the common people] have grown accustomed to over a long period, pack [new content] and give it appropriate refashioning; only then can they take delight in receiving it (*le yu jieshou*) and digest it thoroughly.

(Chen, in Holm 1991: 53)

Unsurprisingly, those who had been influenced by the heady fever of the May Fourth Period in the 1920s opposed these views. During this renaissance period the cry was 'destruction of old forms' and their replacement with modern Western genres and styles of literature. Proponents of this line maintained that use of old forms resulted in the problems of 'ready-made concepts, metaphors and moral values' which despite ease of transmission were counter-productive to revolution and the reformation of consciousness (Holm 1991: 52). In the end the populist camp prevailed, if only for the utilitarian value of ready-made forms.

In due course the elevating mechanism of culture espoused during the Yan'an talks gave way to the more necessary and utilitarian goal of popularisation. This is when the mass media came to prominence as propaganda technologies. In determining what cultural forms were necessary for the task of revolutionary class struggle, the Chinese leadership confronted a dilemma: how to make cultural forms pleasing to the masses at the same time as educating and arousing them. By now the national form was socialist realism, directly imported from Stalinist Russia. Socialist realism had the advantage that it could be readily inscribed into existing popular art forms.

Subjects in need of political training: the mass audience

Identifying the targets of cultural propaganda was an additional task. The revolutionary credo of 'understanding the needs and interests of the masses' had its roots in the Chinese revolution. Propagandists were aware of different audiences with different cultural backgrounds, occupations and levels of education. A resolution passed in 1929 at the Gutian Conference had made this clear. It was noted that a survey conducted by Mao Zedong in Xingguo county in Jiangxi province had come up with a profile of vagrants, considered the outsiders in Chinese rural society. Vagrants were 'gamblers, Taoist priests, porters for religious processions, Buddhist priests, fortune-tellers, and wandering players (*xi kezi*) who performed with puppets' (Holm 1991: 19). It is interesting to note here the correspondence with official evaluations of 'travelling entertainers' during the imperial period – despite the overthrow of the imperial system most entertainers were still regarded as itinerant.

On 2 May, 1942, during an address to party cadres Mao Zedong defined 'the problem of the audience' in terms of the revolutionary task of literature and art. The audience of the day was not the audience targeted by propaganda during the guerrilla struggles of the 1930s, even less 'the students, office workers and shop assistants' targeted prior to the War of Resistance, but rather an audience of workers, peasants and soldiers' (Denton 1996: 458–467). Those who came from the ranks of the intelligentsia were asked to remould themselves and their thinking, to assimilate the opinions of this mass audience, and then to sift and refine these opinions into cultural forms through which the masses would then recognise themselves. The induction of urban intellectuals into the ranks of the socialist cultural elite meant immersion in the daily life of the masses in order to build awareness of the psychological interiority of the audience of revolutionary culture. This process, in theory at least, resolved the 'contradiction' between intellectuals and peasants – a 'contradiction' which Mao himself had experienced firsthand. In his address to cultural workers at the Yan'an Forum, he cited his early experience as a young student, his reluctance to countenance manual labour, and his disdain for workers and peasants. He said, 'But after I became a revolutionary and lived with the workers and peasants and with the soldiers of the revolutionary army,

I gradually came to know them well, and they gradually came to know me well' (in Denton 1996: 462). Some years later during the anti-rightist campaign of 1957, the implementation of the theory of contradictions resulted in intellectuals compelled to work with their hands while peasants and workers enrolled in universities. In the Cultural Revolution, this was taken to a new extreme as intellectuals were thrown out of universities and schools and forced to confess to bourgeois aspirations.

While 'knowing the masses' was officially regarded as establishing a correct relationship between the leadership and the masses, it ultimately meant revitalising and reinventing the culture of the common people. China's cultural workers were directed to produce literature and art that, according to Mao Zedong, met the 'urgent needs' of the masses, now defined by the leadership. These urgent needs were not for 'more flowers on the brocade' but rather 'fuel in snowy weather'; in other words the masses needed clear and simple instruction in how to undertake revolution. Claiming to know the cultural needs and expectations of the masses therefore was a form of audience research in contemporary China, one that allowed the Communist leaders to claim an understanding of public opinion. Despite the neat theoretical resolution of contradictions between the leadership and the masses, however, the latter were ultimately the object of propaganda, a constructed entity, an imagined community who would respond to stimuli: in Mao's own words, they were 'blank sheets of paper' on which 'the most beautiful characters could be written' (Mao 1971: 500). According to the workings of dialectics, the contradiction between intellectuals and peasants would be dissolved, the masses would be the subject of history and the revolution would be a glorious triumph of the proletariat, led by enlightened cadres. In this unity of contradictions between intellectuals and peasants, culture was the mechanism of adjustment.

From the 1950s until the end of the Great Proletarian Cultural Revolution in 1976, culture disciplined and educated the population. This moulding function was made possible by massive social restructuring. With culture and propaganda converging, the Chinese state recruited its cultural workers as the messengers of progress. Cultural activities fell under the jurisdiction of central authorities. Inevitably, the ideological component came to determine the productivity of culture. Diversity and novelty were put aside in favour of standardisation and quotas. In addition to Maoism, cultural policy followed the prescriptions of the Soviet theorist Zhdanov who argued that literature must become 'a small cog' in the social-democratic mechanism (Wang 1992: 716). Zhdanovism emphasised the creation of a body of exemplary myths, the rejection of complexity, as well as the censorship of 'unhealthy and decadent' subject matter. The central propositions underpinning Zhdanov's aesthetics were the utilitarian role of culture and its direct reflection of society.

Taking its foundation from Leninist reflection theory, Maoist revisionism then produced an important conceptual breakthrough. Human cognition was essentially a linear process in which sensations were directly linked to perceptual knowledge. This 'theory' located the audience of cultural messages as mere processors of information rather than agents who actively select meanings. By extension of this linear model, certain representations will have determining effects on consciousness. The audience of cultural messages were passive.

As for the mass media, its function was to 'reflect' reality, namely the reality of class struggle in the Maoist era. Accordingly, positive propaganda portrayed exemplary characters who produced an effect on the 'inner self' (*jingshen*). Negative or unhealthy representations – various forms of what came to be known as 'spiritual pollution' (*jingshen wuran*) – on the other hand, would result in psychological disease. This fundamental belief in the theory of reflection remained influential among China's cultural commissars who felt it was their duty to protect the audience from viral infections. The treatment was direct – censorship of the offending representation, re-education for those responsible, and a course of remedial education for the masses to remedy any damage done. Positive education was even referred to as inoculation or sterilisation. The top-down model of communication denied the audience any real part to play other than to recognise the truth of official communication. The audience was situated at the reception end of the communication process.

Cultural production was therefore directed towards making the population internalise the truth of class struggle as the key to a great society. With the revolution accomplished, the bourgeoisie banished, and the dictatorship of the proletariat achieved, cultural standardisation aimed to maintain the hegemony of the Communist state. This levelling process was in turn tied to the education system. It began with a linguistic revolution, the erasure of classical Chinese and the *baihua* vernacular that had largely replaced it in fiction. The new standard was a common language *putonghua* (literally common tongue) – the language as spoken on the streets by the urban masses. This common tongue had previously been advocated by Qu Qiubai in the Yan'an period of the late 1930s. Qu had argued that a common tongue would facilitate the dissemination of the new culture and 'end the domination of the mass reading public by reactionary and escapist forms of commercial popular fiction' (Holm 1991: 33). However, the cliché-ridden, heavy-handed official discourse that replaced the expressive *baihua* and the multi-vocal classical language imposed its own hegemony over meaning. Dictionaries were rewritten with entries that explained social relations in terms of class struggle, revolution and nationalism.

For China's writers and artists the task was clearly prescribed. Yet, it would be untrue to say that production was formularised so as to completely erase the individual. In *Literary Dissent in Communist China* Merle Goldman wrote, 'Even when a regime dictates the writer's subject matter and literary style, the actual creation must still be by the writer himself' (Goldman 1967: 6). Indeed, many writers held to the ideal of speaking out with courage against injustice. The majority, however, bought the party line that literature should depict life as it is, not as it might be. When socialist realism did conjecture outside of lived reality, it described a glorious future where peasants and workers were heroes (Goldman 1967).

The function of popularisation eventually superseded elevation and enlightenment. During the 1950s the expansion of radio monitoring networks complemented by wired loudspeakers throughout the country led to modifications of the propaganda model in order to suit the new medium (Chang 1997: 87–88). However, this was about efficiency rather than a dilution of intensity. By the late 1950s and early 1960s, the politicisation of culture defined a unified cultural field in which meanings and relationships were determined and non-negotiable. This led some commentators to refer to the kind of control over meaning as 'cultural despotism' (Su 1993: 137).

The high tide of cultural despotism arrived during the Great Proletarian Cultural Revolution (1966–1976). Cultural activities were sanctioned by Mao Zedong and senior CCP leaders, including Mao's wife Jiang Qing, resulting in a further diminution of diversity. Aside from the model soldier Lei Feng and the heroes and villains of Madame Mao's model operas, the most well-known example of cultural propaganda during the Cultural Revolution was one of Mao Zedong's favourite fables, 'The foolish old man who moved the mountains' (*Yu Gong yi shan*). This was the story of an old man, Yu Gong, who was determined to move two mountains which were causing inconvenience to his family. With perseverance, and in spite of the ridicule of neighbours, the old man and his family worked with primitive tools to move the soil and rock. Eventually his diligence was rewarded when God sent down angels to help the old man move the mountains.[4] The point of this parable was to draw attention to the determination of people to transform reality, the belief that anything could be achieved through effort. Through such selected homilies and lessons, Maoist ethics – selflessness, altruism, self-denial, hard work, frugality, self-discipline, diligence, and honesty – were popularised.

Reform not revolution

Cultural forms were used as mechanisms of social reform in modern China. In this reforming project the mass media assumed a central role. The kind of subject sanctioned by cultural propaganda in the Maoist era was a self-sacrificing, altruistic collective subject. People were called to undergo conversion to the cause of revolution following which they were trained to be socialist citizens. By a combination of disciplining and moulding – and denying people options to develop their psychological capacities – a more docile national subject was formed. The subject was then further moulded through cultural propaganda disseminated in the educational system, in study sessions, and through the mass media.

Dramatic changes were to take place in Chinese society during the next two decades. Many of these changes were directly attributed to the CCP's economic reforms presided over by Deng Xiaoping. These reforms were wide-ranging, not only in the sense of re-aligning material interests, but also in seeking to reform people's conduct, the latter component currently formulated as 'spiritual civilisation' or 'cultural and ethical progress'. Upon becoming paramount leader in 1978, Deng not only attempted to distance his government from the disaster of the Cultural Revolution but also sought to redefine people's roles as Chinese subjects. The Chinese government's endorsement of wealth creation therefore stands out as the most definitive break with the policies of Maoism. Deng Xiaoping's much-quoted dictum 'to get rich is glorious' effectively broke with Mao's regard for egalitarianism. In effect, the values of collectivism and altruism that had served to stabilise society were displaced by the more individual concerns of self-interest, success and prosperity.

The role that cultural representations played in the remaking of the Chinese social consciousness during the revolution cannot be underestimated. However, times had changed. As Richard Kraus writes, 'State-sponsored culture, when no longer a monopoly, must contend for audiences, rather than take them for granted, and runs the risk of becoming irrelevant' (Kraus 2004: 64). Cultural production expanded and diversified due to political liberalisation and the impact of philosophies of the market. China's cultural producers were forced to survive with reduced state funding, in many cases without any subsidy. A consequence of the commercialisation of production was that cultural workers became less willing to view their roles simply as spokespersons for CCP ideology. This re-positioning marks the beginning of China's cultural industries.

5 Cultural fever, critical theory and cultural industries

The trade in international ideas about progress, success and prosperity increased in the 1980s as translations of foreign works, often unauthorised appeared on book shop shelves. The exchange of ideas impacts upon the transition from Made in China to Created in China. It is necessary therefore to understand how some important ideas about culture, the sovereign individual, and economics infiltrated the Chinese intellectual community. In this chapter I look at some of the key developments that have influenced the cultural economy and I tell of how some Chinese intellectuals have learned to love the market, while others, faithful to a socialist vision of collective progress, have positioned themselves as strident opponents of all things associated with consumer culture.

Almost 50 years ago a vision of nationalist glory was promoted in the smoke-filled halls of the People's National Congress in Beijing – a vision that would consolidate the hegemony of the Chinese Communist Party following the revolutionary power struggles that culminated in the Chinese people's 'liberation' in 1949. China would be a superpower. Production would skyrocket, fuelled by the energy of a massive population striving for the next stage of the Communist revolution. In the process China would overtake the Western powers.

The potency of this image inspired the aptly titled Great Leap Forward (1958–1961), galvanising the population to increase production to bring about a communist utopia. The Chinese nation's ascendancy would be propelled by the superiority of a political ideology and its ultimate expression in collective labour. The Communist Party leader Mao Zedong spoke passionately, drawing on scientific metaphors to describe how the productive energy of the people would be released:

> Now our enthusiasm has been aroused. Ours is an ardent nation now swept by a burning tide ... our nation is like an atom. When this atom's nucleus is smashed, the thermal energy released will have really tremendous power...
>
> (Mao, quoted in Selden 1979: 382)

China's Great Leap Forward was a monumental disaster. Politics prevailed, bureaucracy stifled innovation and the mentality of striving for unobtainable goals led to inefficient work practices which were masked by exaggerated reporting of outputs. Enforced collectivisation further weakened incentives to produce. National output declined 35 per cent during the period 1958–1962 (Nolan 2004).

Even though the catch-up optimism of the Great Leap Forward unravelled by 1962, and was thrown into further disarray by the Great Proletarian Cultural Revolution (1966–1976), productivity remained a central platform of national development. It was the guiding theme when Deng Xiaoping took over the controls of the Chinese Communist Party after the short and unsuccessful stewardship of Mao's anointed successor Hua Guofeng. In 1962, long before his succession as Communist Party supremo Deng had claimed: 'As long as we increase production, we can even revert to individual enterprise; it hardly matters whether a good cat is black or white – as long as it catches mice, it is a good cat' (Deng, cited in Chesneaux 1979: 115).

Deng Xiaoping made surplus and industrialisation primary development strategies. The 'four modernisations' – of agriculture, industry, science and technology, and the military – reflected the national obsession with productivity. The focus on industry was intended to compensate for the low productivity of agriculture, which employed 70 per cent of the nation's population at the time the reforms began (Chesneaux 1979). Supported by pragmatic reformers – Zhao Ziyang in the 1980s and Zhu Rongji in the 1990s – Deng took the prognosis of inefficiency and non-competitiveness seriously and implemented strategies to transform the welfare state model, the so-called 'iron rice bowl mentality' – although without engaging in the kind of economic shock therapy policies that characterised the Soviet economy post-1989 (Mar and Richter 2003). The Chinese reforms adopted a gradualist programme to transform the command economy into a commodity economy. Meanwhile, the advanced Western powers moved further ahead under capitalism. By the 1990s, the East Asian tiger economies of Taiwan, Korea, Singapore and Hong Kong had managed their own catch-up, transforming from manufacturing to service economies.

The 1990s saw a new release of productive capacity in China. Financial assets locked in state-owned enterprises were redistributed, and in many cases siphoned into private enterprise, often by bureaucrat-managers deliberately stripping state assets for private gain. Capitalism became the de-facto logic of reform, and brought with it the tendency to generate a multitude of small-scale, family-focused businesses flanking large unproductive state-owned enterprises. With the expansion of private enterprise, much of it financed by international investment, China moved inexorably towards integration into the global economy. As international business waited in anticipation for more protectionist barriers to fall, the problem of stimulating productive forces continued to confront Chinese reformers. Inefficient and over-staffed state-owned enterprises were the target of policy in the Fifteenth National Congress of 1997, leading to greater freeing up of public resources in order to establish a 'modern enterprise system', and echoing the principle of 'holding on to large (state-owned enterprises) while letting the small go to market' (*zhuada fangxiao*).

China's Tenth Five-Year Plan (2001–2005) signalled the prominence of the information society (represented as a pillar industry) with an emphasis on raising productivity through the use of information technology. It was at this historical juncture, coterminous with China's accession to the World Trade Organization, that culture emerged as a major development issue. During the ratification of the Tenth Five-Year Plan the term 'cultural industries' (*wenhua chanye*) was formalised. This formalisation of the cultural industries had a long gestation. The subsequent cultural industry and innovation model advocated by reformers led to a frenzy of policy making, often made on the run, by provincial and local governments anxious to find an appropriate 'cultural industry strategy'. The Chinese Academy of Social Sciences played a leading role. Since 2002, it has produced an annual report known as the *Blue Book of China's Cultural Industries*.

These developments were also embedded in a larger development discourse, championed by the Chinese Academy of Sciences. This was the Chinese national innovation strategy (NIS), a response to a rising tide of international reports about knowledge-based economies, innovation as competitive advantage, and a shift in the world economy from goods to services that has seen much of the routine production of commodities outsourced to the newly industrialised world (see Chapter 2). However, Chinese responses to such global shifts ultimately focused more on process innovation than product innovation. New supply chains emerged to exploit the Made in China economic development model. Offshore production was outsourced to subcontractors and independent suppliers. With China taking advantage of non-unionised labour to procure overseas contracts, factories proliferated, particularly in medium-sized Chinese cities. This massive focus on the low-cost advantage has led to an imbroglio, an undermining of the assumed long-term relationship between social and economic development and material productivity. China has already absorbed so much manufacturing from Taiwan, Japan, Hong Kong, the USA and the European Union (EU), that limits to growth are beginning to appear. The desire to attract manufacturing to China, whether final products or 'trade in tasks', has resulted in blatant disregard for environmental protection and workplace safety. Many overseas businesses, constrained by corporate governance and strict union conditions in their home countries, are willing to exploit these advantages. Moreover, costs are rising in China's cities and low-end production is moving to less-expensive locations. China's large municipalities of Shanghai, Beijing and Chongqing, with an excess of unproductive factory space, are seeking cleaner, greener solutions to development.

In the lead up to the drafting of the Eleventh Five-Year Plan in 2006 a discernable shift occurred, away from obsession with productivity towards sustainability and high value-adding (*gao fujiazhi*). Multiple and overlapping economies (and schools of thought) contended, with new versions of cultural development coming onto the reformist radar. The terms new economy, service economy, knowledge-based economy, cultural economy, experience economy – and ultimately creative economy – appeared almost simultaneously. In particular, the often interchangeable 'cultural' and 'creative' economies, offer new development solutions but in turn require a rescaling of the expectations of stakeholders who had previously received generous subvention. International scholar-consultants offering advice about creative cities and creative industries made high-profile visits to Shanghai and Beijing. The net effect was to bring together new coalitions from industry, academic and policy in order to create a groundswell of support for China's great new leap forward.

The evolution of expectations about success, together with the rise of gold and white collar classes – the former according to Jing Wang (2008), predominantly business elites working in joint ventures – has provided an opening in China for a neo-liberal ethic of self-cultivation. Under Maoist-style socialism a top-heavy bureaucracy, coupled with a welfare state, served to negate the self-governing subject. The recent emphasis on economy, whether singular or multiple forms – such as new, knowledge-based, information, experience, and creative economy etc. – has facilitated the diffusion of liberal notions of self-government.[1] Stories about the changing face of China have frequently appeared in the international media during the past two decades: urban youth emulate international fashion trends, rags to riches entrepreneurs proclaim the value of hard work and enterprise, and peasants tell how their lives are more meaningful with greater choice. And so it continues. Is this the end of ideology? Are Chinese people expressing their repressed entrepreneurial nature? Are they realising the truth of markets and the errors of socialism?

The shift from Marxist egalitarianism to capitalist enterprise, however, is not so seamless. For many people in China, social equalisation and redistribution of resources vindicated the Communist revolution. Faced with the choice of how far to reform, 'wholesale Westernisation' (*quanmian xihua*) was never taken seriously by reformers. The idea saw the light of day briefly during the Reform Movement of 1898 when Tan Sitong, a student of the reformer Kang Youwei, promoted the idea of a world without boundaries and advocated opening China to foreign trade (Teng and Fairbank 1979). During the May Fourth Period many debates ensued about the relative benefits of Westernisation compared with the maintenance of tradition. In the main, Western knowledge came to symbolise better science, technology and management. Ideas about modernity and progress were wrapped in the cloth of modern theory.

The seeds of post-industrial society

The re-emergence of commercial culture in China in the mid 1980s was reminiscent of the commercial activity that followed the expansion of print capitalism in the first decades of the century. During both periods mass commercial culture eventually rose to challenge elite forms. The rise of literary culture during the 1980s, in particular the avant-garde modernist schools, recaptured the fervour of the aesthetic renaissance of the first few decades of the twentieth century. However, the 1980s literary cultural revival was short-lived. The principle of 'art for art's sake' found expression during the so-called 'culture fever' movement (*wenhua re*) (1985–1986). Echoing the intellectual fervour of the pre-revolutionary period, this 'reconstruction of culture' played out on issues of modernity and Chinese identity. Despite the similarities with the 1920s, and the fact that the ideals of science and democracy were re-articulated in the modern era, there are a number of important differences. As I discussed in Chapter 3, the call for a new modern culture at the beginning of the twentieth century was predicated on discourses of evolution and civilisation, and had as its catchcry the transformation of the Chinese subject. According to this vision 'new culture' would lead to a new morality, one that was modern and progressive and 'fit' for the new nation-state to be. Notwithstanding differing stances towards tradition the advocates of cultural renovation saw higher forms of art as having civilising influences, elements that were lacking in vulgar commercial culture.

The culture fever and its associated 'schools of thought' came to prominence together in wide-ranging debates about society and technology within the Chinese Academy of Social Sciences. New journals were published and unorthodox ideas were circulated. For instance, in the decade from 1977 to 1987, the number of periodicals published increased from 628 to 5,687 (Ding 1994: 118). This was also a period of great intellectual enquiry. The call to 'develop' Marxism was taken up with a sense of optimism by many younger critics. New theoretical models of science and knowledge deriving from Western figures like Popper, Kuhn and Lakatos challenged the notion that reality could be known and grasped directly (Kelly and He 1992: 35). For many Chinese intellectuals this represented a discrediting of Marxist-Leninism. If there was no such thing as a reality that exists prior to, and independent of thought, how then could there be a fixed locus of truth?

In trying to resurrect what was useful in orthodox Marxism, many scholars turned even more to theories from the West. Intellectual debates in the early 1980s centred on the so-called 'three theories' – systems theory, cybernetics and the theory of communication. The works of Norbert Weiner, Daniel Bell, John Naisbitt and Alvin Toffler were highly influential. Weiner's cybernetics model extended the argument mapped out by Frederick Taylor's management theory, namely that individuals could be made more productive and overcome biological limitations. This was good news for Chinese scholars, keen to find administrative solutions to falling national competitiveness. The ideas of Daniel Bell, a non-Marxist, were particularly influential in debates about the shape of culture in China and ultimately formed a bridge for the reception of Frankfurt School 'critical theory'. Bell's 'post-industrial society' with its notion of stages of development and its condemnation of mass culture sat easily with many critics in China looking for an alternative to mainstream Marxist-Leninism. In spite of Bell's dismissal of Marxism, Chinese critics managed to link his theory with Marx's analysis of the determining role of the productive forces (Brugger and Kelly 1990: 37). The post-industrial thesis accorded with the technological determinism emerging from the Chinese Academy of Social Sciences. Bell's theory of the transition from a goods producing economy to a service economy had an echo of the utopianism of communism. The population would be delivered from their backwardness and the intellectual class would assume a leading role in the professional and technical class.

Alvin Toffler's initial influence in China was largely due to his visit to the Chinese Academy of Social Science in 1983 to publicise *The Third Wave*

(Toffler 1981), which was subsequently published in China. Toffler's ideas about the role of knowledge in assisting development are hardly revolutionary, but in the context of China's steady economic growth and focus on information technology it is not surprising that in 2006 he was named one of the 50 most influential thinkers in China. Toffler also made friends in high places in China during the 1980s and 1990s by promoting the idea that China would be a superpower by harnessing the advantages of its domestic market. Naisbitt's book *Megatrends*, published in 1982 identified him as a kind of seer, a fellow traveller, one who recognised the role of information and technology in future societies long before the internet and Manuel Castells' influence.

Also prominent in this period was a self-conscious imagining of the cultural intellectual's role as saviour of the nation. The 'high culture' espoused by sections of the literary establishment was counterposed to the high 'official culture' of the Chinese state. Despite different stances towards questions of artistic autonomy, both high cultures saw their role as imparting moral elevation and raising the cultural level of society. According to Chen Gang (1996: 32), 'The premise of the new enlightenment was first to establish an idealised form of culture, and then to define that the culture of the common people was low level culture. The only way for the common people to raise their cultural level would be to enter the channel of idealised culture'. It is not difficult from this to detect parallels with the Confucian intellectual tradition in which knowledge of higher codes of refinement indicated social distinction and authority.

The culture debates were very much a process of self-reflection and an act of self-preservation by a social stratum who several years earlier had been officially designated as 'stinking number nines' and subject to ridicule and persecution. The rehabilitation of the status of intellectuals during the 1980s contributed to the impression among many participants in the debates that literature and art had been released from the tyranny of partisanship, its role no longer exclusively to disseminate CCP ideology but also to act as a bearer of universal and some-times anti-hegemonic values. According to Jing Wang, the anti-establishment and utopian aspect of these debates was exaggerated. The intellectual van-guard of a 'new civilian culture' (*minjian wenhua*) oriented towards 'human rights, democracy, pluralism, and open-mindedness' in opposition to the 'old official culture oriented towards authoritarianism, close-mindedness, conser-vatism and inhumanness' was misplaced (Wang 1996: 71; see also Su 1991: 21–35).

Revisionist accounts of culture drew their inspiration from a number of sources. The influence of anthropology in the Chinese Academy of Social Science during the early 1980s was significant, possibly due to the perceived apolitical nature of cultural relativism. Levi-Strauss' structural-anthropology, for instance, allowed a compartmentalising of culture while the 'inclusive' anthropological definition of culture as a 'complex whole' offered by E. B. Tylor (1874) a century earlier was able to co-exist beside the official definition of culture as 'the sum total of all the material and spiritual wealth created in the historical development of society'.[2] The revisions of culture's value, inspired by Western scholarship, led to a pluralisation of the concept of culture, a move which was amenable to arguments about the relative merits of Western and Eastern civilisations.

Culture moves towards the market: the birth of the cultural industries

Whereas conduct was regulated largely by social ethics that were embedded in cultural forms in traditional society, the state took a more direct role in the modern era. Many of the embedded forms were redundant to socialism, which favoured a materialist and scientific view of development. Engineering culture was more than just a slogan. As I have shown in Chapter 3, culture became a field of oppositions. In Maoist China cultural activity was systematically organised. State-funded public cultural institutions (*shiye*) were directly monitored according to a hierarchical management structure that mirrored the structure of the Chinese Communist Party. Apart from the somewhat *ad hoc* cultural policies of the Cultural Revolution, this highly structured model prevailed until the beginning of the 1980s, a decade during which the agenda of economic reform rendered such direct control untenable. Following substantial increases in agricultural and industrial productivity resulting from decentralisation policies, a more 'arm's length' approach to management was deemed by China's leaders to be conducive to the efficient and profitable running of enterprises. In due course this would flow into the cultural sphere.

The decentralisation of China's cultural sphere began in 1978 following the Third Plenum of the Eleventh Central Committee of the CCP. Also in train was the rehabilitation of advertising. During the previous three decades of socialism, the creative potential of China's cultural workers had been utilised in promoting the truth of Party doctrine. Under a system in which cultural goods were produced according to quotas and distributed according to plan, advertising was redundant and even 'wasteful'. Within only a few years of the Third Plenum, however, advertising had become commonplace on Chinese television screens. On 14 January 1979, however, an editorial appeared in Shanghai's *Wenhuibao* calling for the restoration of the good name of advertising. Among the social benefits now accorded advertising was that 'outstanding advertisements can be used to beautify the people's cities, pleasing both the eye and the mind.' On 28 January 1979, China's first television advertisement appeared promoting a herbal wine on Shanghai television. A month later viewers witnessed the first foreign advertisement, a promotion for the Westinghouse Corporation. In November 1979, the CCP Central Committee had formally ratified advertising in the mass media. Within a few years China Central Television (CCTV) was exchanging television programmes with America's CBS in exchange for commercial airtime. The product differentiation that was the spirit of advertising soon found embodiment in the notion of the consumer (*xiaofeizhe*). According to official explanations, advertising was the means to link producers and consumers. The needs and psychology of the Chinese consumer attracted scholarly attention evoking theories of needs from Maslow to Engels, while on a public policy level, consumer associations appeared in cities. China marked the annual 'International Consumers' Rights Day' in 1987.

The momentum for the rehabilitation of commercial culture increased during the mid 1980s, following the opening up of Chinese society to the outside world. The political relaxations bestowed by the Deng regime were indirectly responsible for allowing new leisure pursuits to flourish, among which included 'popular readings',[3] dancing, karaoke, hiring videos and watching TV serials. The expansion of mass-media infrastructure during the 1980s, in particular television and publishing, greatly contributed to a recreational boom, which was endorsed by the reform regime as enriching people's lives. Leisure time had become 'private time' in contrast to the 'public' concept of leisure in the Maoist era which saw free time as something to be regulated and gainfully used in shaping a disciplined and healthy population, and which entailed a suppression of activities considered immoral and irrational (Wang 1995b). Books, magazines and newspapers devoted to new cultural activities mushroomed on bookstands as academic discussions about culture – the 'culture fever' (*wenhua re*) – trickled down to the general public. Between January 1985 and June 1986 some 200 books and articles on culture were published, and by 1987 there were at least seven new magazines incorporating the term 'culture' in their titles.[4] With restrictions lifted on censorship a range of subjects became available for publication. Pulp magazines, many illegal, flourished catering to popular tastes which included detective stories, traditional knight-errant fiction, triangular love stories and pornographic stories. Such was the expansion of the print media that by the late 1980s, many serious literary journals, despite receiving state-funding, felt compelled to go 'downmarket' to attract readerships. During this period many writers took the opportunity to turn their attention to writing television screenplays as a means of lining their pockets. Cultural entrepreneurs, sensing the beginnings of a decline in literary publishing also began to make the move into television.

Consumer interest in 'foreign' popular forms stimulated the growth of commercial culture in China during the 1980s. Television dramas from Brazil, Japan, and even the USA turned up on Chinese TV screens. Proximity to Taiwan and Hong Kong allowed pop music influences to penetrate the Chinese market. The radio market of the Pearl River Delta in Guangdong Province played a key role in changing the propaganda model of broadcasting. Located close to Hong Kong and in direct competition with the signals from Hong Kong broadcasters, the Guangdong People's Radio chose to respond to the challenge of diminishing audiences by copying the commercial techniques of its cousins across the strait and by instituting a new radio channel. The Pearl River Economic Radio had its first broadcast in 1986, introducing a mix 'of entertainment, information about daily life, and societal news instead of preaching' (Chan 1994: 76). The new format was a resounding success. Joseph Chan writes that from 1986 to 1987, the audience share of Guangdong People's Radio jumped from 46.7 per cent to 78 per cent with the Pearl River Economic Radio accounting for 54.9 per cent alone. News of the station's success soon reached further. Within a few years, the model of personality programmes, talk back radio, economic news and pop music became influential throughout China, resulting in an ethic of competitiveness among broadcasters and a willingness to apply market strategies in building audiences.

For many of China's cultural workers, the 'cultural market' had become a short-hand term to describe alternatives to the state-funded public cultural sphere. In the cultural market new rules of survival needed to be learnt. These new rules entailed mediations between the supply-side model of official culture and consumer-driven commercial culture. From a governmental perspective, however, 1985 represented an important landmark for the development of the cultural market. The State Council's Bureau of Statistics first included culture and arts in its statistical categories, confirming the 'industrial characteristics' of the tertiary sector (Zhang *et al.* 2002: 4). However, despite general public acceptance of the benefits of a commodity economy and the growing trade in cultural services, official statements on the productivity of culture chose to speak in terms of its use rather than exchange value. Official response to the success of the commercial cultural sphere continued to be muted – a combination of apprehension and celebration. In 1991, the Ministry of Culture formally proposed the term 'cultural economy' to the State Council (Report on opinion re economic policy about cultural undertakings)[5] (see Zhang *et al.* 2002: 4).

The success of the commercial cultural sphere was paraded as evidence of the government's policies of diversity and deregulation. In the *China Publishing Yearbook* summary of cultural achievements in 1991 – hitherto a listing of official public-funded cultural activities and achievements – it was announced that, '[A]s the reform and opening effort deepens and the socialist market economy grows, the country's cultural market is radiating from the south-eastern coastal region to the inland, from commercial cities to the surrounding rural areas, with repercussions even in remote border regions' (*China Publishing Yearbook* 1992: 375). Reports were quick to point out, however, that 'some difficulties still exist in the country's cultural market', in particular the question of legislation pertaining to its administration (1992: 376).

In July 1991, the Ministry of Culture convened a conference in Qingdao to address the regulation of the cultural economy. Seventeen items of cultural legislation were passed relating to the production and distribution of cultural artefacts (*China Publishing Yearbook* 1992: 374). Further reforms followed Deng Xiaoping's much publicised visit to the south of China in January 1992 and the official formulation of the 'socialist market economy' at the Fourteenth Party Congress in October that same year. Jiang Zemin's report to the Fourteenth Congress explicitly mentioned 'improving policies relating to the cultural economy'; later that same year the State Council general office published a major strategic policy document in which the term 'cultural industry' (*wenhua chanye*) was used.[6] Following the Fourteenth Congress, tight ideological controls over China's mass media that had existed since the 1989 Tiananmen demonstrations were relaxed, along with the ousting of hard-line leftists who controlled the media, literature and the arts.[7]

In the domain of cultural policy, 'enterprise' values of efficiency and competition were enlisted to make cultural institutions more accountable and self-reliant. Many print and television media were suddenly asked to forgo their annual subsidy, although Party organs were immune from this cost-cutting exercise. This was the beginning of the end of guaranteed security and immunity from market failure. A speech emanating from the Ministry of Culture was reported in the *China Cultural News* on 8 December 1993. With the unambiguous title 'In the reforms develop the cultural industries', this was the first comprehensive explanation of the term cultural industry (Zhang *et al.* 2003: 4).

The year 1993 was significant for a number of reasons. Following the Fourteenth Party Congress, the scale of reform deepened with economic solutions extended to resolve the problems of state-funded cultural institutions. The market emerged as the most contentious issue confronting cultural bureaucracies and the literary intellectual sphere. Prior to the removal of state subsidies the previous year, the official cultural sphere of state-funded publishing houses and distribution outlets, print media, and state-funded television units had been financially insulated from the frantic demand-driven trading of the informal cultural entrepreneurs, the 'book kings',[8] video and audio pirates for whom the commodity nature of cultural forms was already a fundamental article of faith.

The latter half of 1993 represented a turning point in attitudes towards the cultural market. Academics from the Chinese Academy of Social Sciences led the way in shifting attention to the inevitability of the cultural market as a determiner of value. 'Objective economic laws' were promoted as the reasons why cultural units – like other commodity producing enterprises – should 'stand on their own feet'. China's subsidised cultural workers were learning a lesson about market economies. The tide of commercial activity was already evident in a proliferation of underground and semi-legal cultural activities. This sphere of distribution was in turn primed by demand for cultural product from Hong Kong, Taiwan and the West.

In October 1993, three Beijing writers paid 12,000 yuan (US$1410 approximately) to take out an advertisement in the Beijing Evening News to promote a television drama script. The writers were Xing Zhu, Yuan Yiqiang and Gao Lilin and the script was called '*Hongshun dayuan 35 hao*' (Li 1995). They received more than 70 expressions of interest, finally selling for 160,000 yuan (US$18,820). Many serious writers also turned to writing television scripts, even selling their manuscripts at literary auctions–a new kind of market for cultural entrepreneurs (Schell 1995; Zha 1995; Kong 2005). These new markets for culture allowed writers and artists a choice: the freedom of offering their works to the highest bidder or taking their salary from the state. The term *xia hai*, literally 'to jump into the ocean' was already widely used to refer to those who left the security of academia for the challenge of commerce.[9]

Cultural production was not immune from the logic of economic incentive as a panacea for creative stagnancy. The realisation that market forces might act as the best arbiter of the relations between producer and consumer significantly undermined the authority of cultural intellectuals to determine value. The outstanding achiever in this respect was the 'hooligan' writer Wang Shuo who since the mid 1980s had written short stories, novellas, screenplays, and television scripts. Wang even managed to set up his own company, the Current Affairs Cultural

Consultancy Company (*shishi wenhua zixun gongsi*), which, as well as managing his own output, collaborated with many ventures by leading Chinese writers and producers. By 1995, his company had invested or acted in a consultancy role in 20 television series (Lu 1995).

Co-incidentally, 1993 was the 100th anniversary of Mao Zedong's birth and is remembered for the mass-media-driven sentimental outpouring for a lost icon. Alongside the official documentaries and publications a myriad of mass-produced souvenirs appeared: medallions, timepieces, T-shirts as well as unofficial titles detailing Mao Zedong's secret life and a 'reputed' affair with young movie queen Liu Xiaoqing (Schell 1995: 305). If there was any evidence needed for the supply–demand model of the cultural market, the Mao craze delivered it. The Chairman's favourite revolutionary songs were committed to a disco remixing under the title *The Red Sun: Odes to Mao Zedong Sung to a New Beat*. Bookstands were suddenly adorned with new titles such as *Mao Zedong's Skill of Language* (*Mao Zedong de yuyan jiqiao*), *Mao Zedong's Humour* (*Mao Zedong de youmo*), *Mao Zedong's Sons and Daughters* (*Mao Zedong de ernumen*).

Meanwhile Chinese television viewers witnessed the 21 episode serial drama *Beijingers in New York*, which was shown on CCTV in October of 1993. This was directed by Feng Xiaogang and Zheng Xiaolong and based on the book written by Cao Guilin, *Beijingren zai Niuyue*, and serialised in the Beijing Evening News in 1991. The narrative concerned the fortunes of Beijing couple who immigrate to New York in the 1980s. A kind of window on capitalism and its discontents, it was nevertheless described by some commentators as a 'textbook' for survival in a commodity-driven society – a society in which profit is the motor of social relations. The critic Can Bai (1994: 22) noted 'Some thought that it outlined and described the many bitter experiences of Chinese people in this highly commodity conscious society, and that it served as a good textbook for a market economy'. My own survey conducted when I was studying at Tianjin's Nankai University at the time of the series confirmed this perception. Of 76 respondents I surveyed almost half remarked that the series showed that Chinese people needed to change their way of thinking, or consider new ways of doing business in order to be successful.

More significantly, it was the entrepreneurialism of the producers that con-tributed to the hype. The fact that this 21-episode serial cost US$1.5 million to produce, far exceeding previous productions, signalled a new horizon for the television industry. The serial was largely financed by a loan from the Bank of China while production costs were recouped through advertising arrangements, product placement, sales of merchandise and distribution in overseas Chinese communities.

At the same time that the series was being broadcast a major development was occurring in the publishing world. A novel written by Jia Pingao, a respected liter-ary figure from Shanxi, had attracted funding from 'second channel' publishers.[10] The novel, *Abandoned Capital* (*feidu*), purported to be a tale of decadence in a feudal time-space. An allegorical swipe at contemporary society, sexual scenes supposedly imitative of the banned classic *The Golden Lotus* (*jingpingmei*), and comparisons with the Qing dynasty tales of elite decadence, *The Dream of the Red Chamber* (*honglou meng*), made the book a best-seller in a number of weeks (see Kong 2005). Despite being classified pornographic, the book was reprinted and available on street stalls in late 1993. The book had sold an estimated 1 million copies by the end of 1993 (Zha 1995: 137).

By the early 1990s, commercial popular culture had found a ready market in urban China. Standards of living were moving upwards and sociologists were confirming the rise of a Chinese middle class. Statistical information shows a six-fold increase in urban consumption of recreation, education and cultural services from 1985 to 1995 (*China Statistical Yearbook* 1996). The problem of how to protect the Chinese citizen from illegally produced cultural products such as pornographic videos and books escalated as cultural entrepreneurs took advantage of the thaw to flood the street markets with pirated material. One of the most popular authors in urban China in the early 1990s was Jin Yong (Louis Cha), the Hong Kong master of knight-errant fiction.[11] Volumes of illegally produced imitative fiction bearing Jin Yong's name appeared on private street stalls (*shutan*).

The two civilisations: a useful dialectic?

Moral development and the threats of 'spiritual pollution' had been ongoing concerns for the Chinese Communist Party since the early 1980s. The 'socialist spiritual civilisation' idea was coined by Ye Jianying in 1979 and taken up by Deng Xiaoping the following year. For a government obsessed with material progress the turn to the so-called 'spiritual' had to be managed lest it release too many heterodox views. Identifying the 'spiritual' became a focus of debate within the Chinese Academy of Social Sciences as well as within the Party Literature Research Centre. The result was a victory of socialist pragmatism over feudal revisionism: there was a 'socialist' realm of cultural achievement and moral development, as opposed the 'less developed' Western culture found fertile ground. If socialist moral development was to be the counterargument to the commercial and amoral tenor of foreign media, its cause could only be popularised by articulating a historical basis for its deployment. This foundation was the more superior, progressive and civilised nature of the Chinese people.

Ann Anagnost (1997) notes that 'spiritual civilisation' was first articulated in China by a writer called Gong Fazi in 1902. Writing from Japan, Gong had noted the distinction made between the material and the spiritual in the progressive European and American societies of the day. Gong argued that 'spiritual civilisation' was essential for the strength of a nation but it could not exist without the material. Echoing Gong Fazi writings of 1902, the definitive contemporary pronouncement on 'socialist spiritual civilisation' was made by Hu Yaobang in 1982:

> Material civilisation provides an indispensable foundation for socialist spiritual civilisation which, in its turn, gives a tremendous impetus to the former

and ensures its correct orientation. Each is the condition and the objective of the other.

(Hu 1982, *People's Daily* 8 September)

As a leitmotif of progress, the spiritual–material dialectic soon assumed a prominent role in the language of economic reform. Its reception by the general population, however, has been at times ambivalent. Soon after the 'socialist spiritual civilisation' morality campaigns began in the early 1980s, a popular saying emerged among urban Chinese: 'when the material is in short supply, the spiritual is used to make up for it' (*wuzhi bugou, jingshen lai cou*) (Ding 1994: 128). The 'socialist spiritual civilisation' drive was nevertheless successful, its penetration into the social psyche attributed to the popular belief that people's morality was being eroded by materialism. Black-market activities, official corruption, and trading in 'fake' commodities were pernicious manifestations of moral decline. The term worked on a number of levels. First, it captured the moral high ground for the Chinese Communist Party by appropriating the concept of 'the spiritual' from China's critical intellectuals; second, in doing this, it acted as a 'translation mechanism' between the general and the particular, the nation and the individual, the public and the private, the citizen and the consumer, and between official mainstream culture and popular cultures. For instance, the vocabulary of 'socialist spiritual civilisation', as well as embracing large 'themes' such as patriotism, idealism, education and discipline, also addresses the more mundane areas of economic, legal and personal relations: what is the right code of conduct within a socialist market economy? How should taxi-drivers, shop assistants and service staff act towards customers? What is the proper relationship between a boss and employees? What are the obligations of vendors and so on?

The River Elegy debate

By the mid 1980s, the culture debates had became embroiled in a re-examination of the past, an attempt to locate the roots of China's crisis in culture. The apogee of the debate about culture occurred in 1988 with the screening of a six-part television documentary called *River Elegy (Heshang)*. The series was an unprecedented criticism of Chinese civilisation and culture, challenging the legacy of state authoritarianism, the slave mentality of its people and the ossified social structure. Essentially this was the problem of 'catch-up' rephrased as rejection of Maoist authoritarianism and a celebration of many Western, in particularly the Western mindset. Returning to the kind of evolutionism championed by the turn of the century reformers, the programme's writers asserted that China should cast off the baggage of its cultural tradition and emulate the more modern outward-seeking culture of Western nations. Entailed in this prescription for radical modernisation was the liberation of the individual subject from the official doctrine of collectivism.

The series was produced under the supervision of Chen Hanyuan, vice-director of CCTV. Conceived originally as a paean to the Yellow River, the mythical source of Chinese civilisation, in the hands of writers, Su Xiaokang and Wang Luxiang, director Xia Jun and a line-up of invited talking-heads, the series became a full-scale assault on China's moribund culture (Barmé and Jaivin 1992; Wang 1996). Praised by then Secretary-general Zhao Ziyang, the series attracted an estimated viewing audience of 200 million. Following the screening CCTV was reportedly deluged with thousands of letters from viewers seeking scripts to hand out 'in order to help all Chinese understand themselves' (in Barmé and Jaivin 1992: 140). It seems that helping people to understand themselves was more than just making people reflect on the tyranny of history, the shackles of culture and the peasant mentality of the population. The series inadvertently suggested a prognosis for change that would devalue the role of the fragile intellectual public sphere.

The culture debates of the mid 1980s had identified a desire to establish an identity space for the intellectual 'as an autonomous, self-determining, self-regulating and free subject' (Liu 1992:121). The motif of culture as modern consciousness recycled the May Fourth ethic but it was a vision likewise doomed to failure. If there was a defining period that signified the demise of literary culture's pretensions of representing a space of resistance to politics, moreover, it was 1987. According to Jing Wang, the literary pursuits of the 1980s had until then been grounded in the utopian fantasy that art constituted 'an enclave of resistance' to the totalising politics of official culture (Wang 1996: 160). But China's literary intellectuals failed to recognise the role that economics was playing in the broader reform of society.

Within the Chinese Academy of Social Science, the relationship between economics and transformation soon became paramount. Pragmatism was on the agenda and, as always, there was a need for theory to justify the latest stage of development. A study published in 1991 by the Group for Research on Social Development established the basis for the socialist commodity economy, which would be officially 'launched' by Deng Xiaoping the following year on this southern tour of Shenzhen. The report laid the foundations in announcing six key areas of transformation. First, it argued that a planned commodity economy was a natural progression from the highly centralized and inefficient administrative economy. Second, with township and village enterprises playing a role in economic development, the nature of the surplus work force was changing. Third, the transformation from a rural to an urban society had implications for information transfer, communications and transport as populations moved to the new industrial centres. Fourth, China's opening society had stimulated investment, exports and tourism. Fifth, the market-entry momentum of the reforms was leading to a more complex mixed economic structure with state-owned, collective, individual and private enterprises. This mixed ownership was further complicated by combinations of collectively and state owned, state and privately owned, and collectively and privately owned ventures, Chinese–foreign joint ventures, businesses run by overseas Chinese or foreign investors, and those operated by investors from Hong Kong and Macao (Zhang 1996: 73) Finally, it argued, China had begun to move from a society based on ethical principles to one based on legal principles.

Industries in the making

China's media and cultural industries evolved slowly from 1978, the time of China's opening to the world. Within China's regulatory bureaus two dominant models continue to frame the extent of liberalisation. First, a hierarchical public service model prevails as a default position. In some respects this institutional model (*shiye*) can be compared to the public broadcasting systems that have long existed in Europe, UK, Japan, Canada and Australia. Public broadcasting was adopted in these countries for a number of reasons, ranging from a desire to maintain control of content in the name of nation building to the more pragmatic concern with narrow bandwidth; that is, if there were to be limited entrants, it was necessary to have a statist voice. In Western markets the core argument for public broadcasting is about the public interest maintaining a plurality of voices; in China the argument is also expressed as public interest, but as one of guiding and educating the masses, who are generally regarded as ethically incomplete.

The second model is an industry model (*chanye*). The evolution of media and cultural industries in the 1980s forced reconsideration of the separation between the sender and the receiver, between the media's role as ideological custodians of public morality – the traditional elevation function – and their self-reliance as enterprises. Fundamental distinctions began to emerge between official cultural institutions and new entrants, often financed by local capital. This increased by the end of the 1990s as the investment climate was liberalised. Industry consciousness extended to those formerly charges with monitoring messages. While the mouthpiece principle remained constant, the reality was that politicisation of content increasingly alienated audiences who were tuning to imported popular culture – television, music and novels.

Part II

From Made in China to Created in China

6   Innovation systems, creative economy and catch-up

Innovation is the soul of a nation's progress
> Neon sign, Nanjing Road shopping mall, Shanghai.

My exploration of China's creative economy so far has been largely based on historical accounts. I have shown how cultural markets were central to social life and economic development during the imperial period and how these commercial activities co-existed with official patronage of art and culture. Moreover, cultural innovation occurred throughout history despite the weight of tradition. In times of openness, notably the Sui, Tang and Song periods, Chinese culture absorbed influences from afar. The margins of the empire were important in the evolution of cultural forms and genres – in music, painting, sculpture, pottery, literature and the performing tradition. Independent entertainers and cultural intermediaries spurred the evolution of cultural forms by promoting trade of cultural products from the margins to the centre, throughout the empire, and across cultural continents. The dynamism of cultural markets, bazaars, opera theatres, street life, and tea houses contrasted with the selective display of culture in the royal courts of Beijing, Kaifeng, Chang'an, Hangzhou, Nanjing and Luoyang. Throughout Chinese history the centre tolerated the commercial sphere of cultural activity and facilitated its vitality through festivals, the most prominent being the lunar New Year and the mid-autumn festival. But emperors and high officials looked upon independent artists with suspicion, at lease those that were not co-opted into court academies.

As I discussed in Chapter 4, Chinese Communist Party cultural policy adopted an even more hardline stance against the independence of cultural producers. Commercial culture in particular was deemed too bourgeois, too reactionary and not appropriate for nation-building. Official management of culture during the period 1949–1978 was paralleled by a Marxist utilitarian definition of culture, one that described 'the sum total of all the material and spiritual wealth created by human beings in the course of the historical development of society' as well as 'in a narrow sense, ideology and related institutions and organisations' (*Cihai: Sea of Words* 1989: 1731. Chinese Encyclopaedia).[1]

The following chapters chart a different development course and draw upon my participation in what I call the 'Created in China' project. This was a series of events and forums commencing in 2004 that inspired an alternative cultural development course to that determined by the Tenth Five-Year Plan. 'Created in China' had its roots in Beijing and Shanghai. By 2006, it had moved inland as far as Chongqing in the south-west. In so far as this movement gained momentum among the intellectual and business communities before crossing into political discourse, it created an 'epistemic community' of actors, both Chinese and international. These advocates of creative sector reform interacted sporadically in forums and meetings, pushing the idea of 'Creative China'. The turn to creativity was, however, initially resisted by the national policy-making committees and regulatory ministries. The movement in turn responded by advocating the strategy of 'modelling'. In their study of global business regulation, Braithwaite and Drahos (2000: 30) note that within policy networks, decision makers will often 'dither in a confusion of complexity they cannot grasp', and open themselves to influence from 'entrepreneurs who encourage them onto a plausibly interest-enhancing path'. The strategy used within these emergent webs of influence was to offer case studies of international 'models'. Without wishing to gloss over the complexity of China's policy-making processes, the 'created in China' movement demonstrated how new ideas about development can rapidly gain impetus within epistemic communities. The advocacy achieved potency in the face of increasing imports of Korean popular culture. If a 'backward' country like Korea could become 'creative' and prosperous so fast, could China also follow? Could China export its creativity to Korea?

The sudden recognition that China needed to invest in creativity was a revelation to many old-style leaders brought up on the vision of extending national productivity through double-digit growth. They had seen China move from economic backwardness to national prosperity on the back of low-cost manufacturing. In the socialist view the cultural sector was non-productive; it was the superstructure, reflecting the economic reality and guiding people along the pathway of progress. This theory of the unproductive nature of culture, moreover, was not confined to socialism. It has dominated debates about cultural economics in most advanced economies.

From 2003 to the end of 2005 I was part of a research team investigating the internationalisation of creative industries. The research hypothesis was that China would embrace changes occurring in developed economies, in the process leapfrog from the industrial age into the post-industrial age. Could the new China, built on low-cost manufacturing and competitive outsourcing, transform into a creative nation? This was about more than just acknowledging how post-industrial society might play out in China (Bell 1974), or how global production networks and regionalisation (cf. Dicken 2003; Storper 1997, 2000) would impact upon entrenched state intervention into the economy. The creative industries would offer various internationalising ingredients and prescriptions: the new economy, post-Fordism, flexible production, outsourcing, and offshoring. It resonated with Organisation for Economic Co-operation and Development (OECD) knowledge-based economy prescriptions for development and the proposition that 'content' was once again 'a growth industry' (OECD 1996, 1998). Our research intended to show how culture, services and knowledge were converging in a variety of economies – the new, the knowledge-based, the information, services and the creative economies, to name but a few. From a policy-advocacy perspective it was about demonstrating how creative occupations provide a diverse range of intermediate inputs into the broader economy. The hypothesis was ambitious, at least in the sense that the weight of evidence from Made in China appeared to diminish the necessity of creativity in the Chinese marketplace.

The provenance of the changes that would eventually sweep China was the UK Creative Industries Task Force (DCMS 1998). Upon taking power in 1997, the senior minister at the Department of Culture, Media and Sport, Chris Smith, had sought to procure more money for the arts through the use of the term 'creative industries'. Critics saw this move as an opportunistic re-branding: conservative Britain became 'cool Britannia' (Garnham 2005; Oakley 2004). More than just a superficial image makeover, however, it entailed a degree of shifting culture into new categories, and in doing so upset the status quo whereby low-profit and 'no-profit' performing arts had traditionally made a case for public support based upon their inherent danger of market failure. Now resolutely non-commercial activities (visual and performing arts, theatre, dance etc.) were forced into a marriage of convenience with established commercial media (broadcasting, film, TV, radio, music), design and architecture sectors, and new media (software, games, e-commerce and mobile content) (Cunningham 2006).

This was the 'creative industries'. This expeditious rearrangement of the categories allowed culture and the arts to appear more profitable, although the value of the new creative industries was largely attributed to the high-earning commercial and IT sectors rather than the loss-making performing arts. The shift to enterprise rhetoric and the need for artists to prove their business bona fides coincided with a push by the UK to market its ideas internationally; in short, it contained within it an export drive for British creativity and design. Certainly, this rhetoric of development was influential beyond the UK. It gained quick traction in several countries where public investment in culture was assumed to service the public interest. As I will discuss below, the migration of these 'knowledges of the creative economy' (see Kong *et al.* 2006) moved swiftly through Pax Britannica networks, finding fertile soil in Hong Kong, Singapore, Australia and New Zealand.

However, the question we were seeking to answer was: could the idea of the creative industries take root in China? Some colleagues with extensive experiences in Chinese cultural studies were sceptical. In 2004, Jing Wang had doubted that the idea of creative industries could be accepted under a system so guided by central planning, particularly at a moment in time when the 'cultural industries' were freshly minted state policy. She writes, 'The thorniest question triggered by the paradigm of creative industries is that of "creativity" – the least problematic in the western context. How do we begin to envision a parallel discussion in a country where creative imagination is subjugated to active state surveillance?' (Wang 2004: 13). Wang was undoubtedly correct in her assessment of the ascendancy of cultural industries and its differentiation from the new foreign interloper. She points out that the Chinese cultural industries embodied 'three subtexts': a state-owned sector undergoing partial commercialisation, state monopolies, and the emerging varieties of mixed ownership that I referred to in the previous chapter. In 2002, the cultural industries, together with these 'contradictions', were formally charged with leading the expansion of the cultural market. What was not understood at the time, however, was the role that municipal governments would play in choosing their own development paths. As we find out, creativity was to become a powerful signifier of progress, and creative industries would offer far more scope for enterprise and autonomy.

The turn to creativity in China is an important element of the great new leap forward. In order to understand the impact of the idea, however, it is useful to explore the transplanting of the term creativity from its Western origins into what was by 2003 fertile Chinese soil. Lydia Liu provides a way of understanding this cross-cultural translation through the idea of a 'super-sign'. Liu writes about the translation of terms such as 'barbarian', 'sovereignty' and 'rights' into China during the period of China's engagement with Western powers in the mid nineteenth century. These terms were central to the treaties which ceded territory to the occupying powers. For instance, the British negotiators forbad the use of the character for barbarian (*yi*), a term that had a much more diffuse usage throughout Chinese history. Liu asks if we can recapture the true identity of language when such problematic terms are embedded in new territories. She says that a super-sign 'is not a word but a hetero-cultural signifying chain that criss-crosses the semantic fields of two or more languages simultaneously and makes an impact on the meaning of recognizable verbal units …' (Liu 2004: 13).

The term 'creativity' is also a super-sign: it operates across linguistic and cultural barriers, and across disciplinary boundaries. The most widespread translation for creativity in Chinese is *chuangzaoli* (literally the power of creation). Discussions of *chuangzaoli* inevitably derive from the fields of cognitive and behavioural psychology, reflecting emphasis on gifted individuals more so than embedded cultural capital.[2] The non-standard mandarin translations of creativity (*chuangyi*) and of creative industries (*chuangyi chanye*) were adopted in Hong Kong and subsequently exported to China.[3] The term brings together the morphemes *chuang* (to initiate or create) and *yi* (meaning, concept). The new word was initially unfamiliar to many Chinese policy makers; on the other hand, it was imbued with imported freshness, often a good indicator of acceptance in Mainland China. However, the etymology was ultimately Western: *chuangyi* did indeed criss-cross the semantic fields of two or more languages simultaneously.

Creative industries quickly became an article of faith among media businesses and among cultural and urban policy makers in China, echoing its popularity at the time in Singapore and Hong Kong. Widespread benefits would accrue from creativity – benefits that were individual, collective and organisational. Creativity was a green idea in a country where the 'Made in China' model had turned skies a brownish grey. It was also unlimited, if it could just be tapped. By 2004, it was clear that something new was occurring in Beijing and Shanghai. The creative economy was a 'new wave' ready to break. A short list of its benefits for China included wealth creation, renewal of traditional resources, enhanced productivity combined with cleaner greener production, education curricula revitalisation, and the ever-present theme of industrial catch-up.

Cultural industries and the national innovation agenda

The creative industries, however, had to convince a conservative community of cultural reformers. A decade before the Tenth Five-Year Plan, the cultural market had been growing at pace. In the early 1990s publicly funded cultural institutions (*shiye*) were asked to reposition themselves as industries (*chanye*). As I discussed in the previous chapter, the terms 'cultural industry' and 'cultural economy' were recognised in internal Party documents as early as 1992. This led to widespread discussions as to how to best stimulate the industrial development of culture: how to account for the value, employment, and enterprise dynamics of cultural industries. Formal acceptance of these terms took much longer. It was not until October 2000 and the Fifth Session of the Fifteenth Party Congress that the 'cultural industries' were formally proposed as part of the recommendations (*jianyi*) document for the national Tenth Five-Year Plan.[4] In March 2001, these recommendations were ratified in the Fourth session of the Ninth People's Congress (*renda*) (Zhang *et al.* 2004).

The cultural industries in China were directly linked to innovation. The translation, *chuangxin*, literally means 'to make new'. Innovation has carried great national freight since the revolutionary era of Mao Zedong. During the times of high socialism innovation was expressed as *gexin*: *ge* was 'to transform' while *xin* signified new. Manifestations of *gexin* ranged from reforming feudal practices and replacing these with scientific Marxist models, refashioning the thought processes of reactionary elements, and 'putting new wine in old bottles' – a euphemism for using old cultural forms to disseminate new ideas. The real champion of innovation, however, was Jiang Zemin, whose words on the subject were reported in the *Enlightenment Daily* on 5 March 1998:

> We must now put the stress on innovation. We need to establish national awareness; to set up a national innovation system and to strengthen entrepreneurial innovation capacity, to put science and innovation in a more important strategic position, and accordingly allow economic construction to revolve around scientific progress and the improvement of the quality of workers.
>
> (Cited in Yi 2000: 41.)

Further embedding innovation into the national psyche were the correlations between economic reform and national innovation systems policy (NIS), which was officially instituted in 1998 as the 'knowledge innovation program' (*zhishi chuangxin gongcheng*). Some commentators, drawing upon the literal Chinese meaning of innovation (to reform), have argued that China's innovation system was re-established in 1976 when the excesses of the Cultural Revolution were finally overturned (Li *et al.* 2002). The suggestion is that innovation was equivalent to reform, and in a more direct sense, revolution. Whether there was an innovation system under Maoism is a moot point. History seems to confirm that innovation was more *ad hoc* than systemic. The Cultural Revolution was a time that witnessed chaotic reversals of policy. Nevertheless, there is general agreement that the years 1992 to 1998 spurred the development of a more deliberate systems approach to economic reform. By the mid 1990s, the OECD's *Oslo Manual* (1990) was required reading for socialist planners. WTO accession in December 2001 signalled a need for deeper institutional reform, and in the eyes of radical reformers, a tide of 'creative destruction' was necessary. Observers – including senior government officials – used the metaphor of a 'wrecking ball' to suggest a force that smashes old institutional practices and allows the marketplace to rebuild with greater capacity (Jin 2002).

The concept of a national innovation system (NIS) stresses the importance of increasing returns to knowledge accumulation and the crucial role of new technologies and human capital. Precursors to the NIS were the information society discussions of the 1950s. In the USA in 1953, Paul Hatt and Nelson Foote had proposed sub-divisions of the service or tertiary industry sector into quaternary and quinary sectors based on information management (fourth sector) and knowledge generation (fifth sector). In the 1970s, Daniel Bell's writings on post-industrial society were influential in pushing the idea of a new social order. While Bell wrote primarily about technological change, he also concerned himself with culture. *The Cultural Contradictions of Capitalism* was the title of one of his books. Bell argued that culture had become detached and self-determining and in particular that the avant-garde was shaping and leading audiences rather than the market (Bell 1978). Culture was moving fast, changing fast, and audiences were diversifying. By the year 2000, the rate of turnover of cultural products was unprecedented. It was not so much the avant-garde or the market that were now shaping and leading; audiences and consumers were driving the innovation of services in interactive formats that included reality TV, mobile phone, and SMS applications. Innovation was occurring at a fast rate due to both technology (push) and consumption (pull).

National innovation systems drew upon evolutionary and industrial economics (Guinet 2002). The issue of evolution is central to the uptake of creative industries in China. Are the cultural (or creative) sectors industries *per se*, or might they be better understood as an element of the innovation system of the whole economy? If the latter, the determining characteristics would concern non-linear interactions between different stages of R&D and innovation, as opposed to traditional understandings of the culture as 'welfare enhancing', drawing resources from the rest of the economy (Potts 2006). In effect, this line of reasoning was destabilising to the conventional Chinese socialist view of culture as inherently pedagogic. The question therefore was: would the cultural/creative economy idea gain sufficient momentum within the propaganda system to influence key policy makers?

With national innovation systems hitting the radar of the Chinese government, the green light for cultural industries spawned a steady stream of articles and books focusing on development strategies to transform and regulate China's burgeoning but largely inefficient cultural economy. A National Base for Cultural Industries Innovation and Development Research had already been established at Shanghai's Jiaotong University in 1999, which in collaboration with the Chinese Academy of Social Sciences launched a series of industry reports reminiscent of the UK creative industries mapping projects (see Table 6.1). In 2002, the State Council gave the go-ahead for a second 'national research base', this time located at Peking University.[5]

The announcement of the cultural industries as a foundational element of the Chinese government's economic and social reform plans produced a plethora of cultural industries development strategies, mostly associated with exploiting traditional cultural resources. Culture was loosened even more from its ideological moorings, told to be more self-reliant, and sent to the market. This 'culturalisation of the economy' was a product of increasing apprehension about globalisation following China's accession to the World Trade Organization. To make the cultural economy stronger and self-reliant meant identifying resources, most of which at that time appeared to be located in traditional culture. China's 56 minorities were subsequently reinvested with economic potential.[6]

The core idea 'created in China' surfaced in 2003. Two scholarly articles appeared in June advocating strategies to reform the nation's over-reliance on manufacturing and an education system heavily reliant on rote learning.[7] By 2004, the idea was fermenting. Early indications of the creativity movement appeared at the Second International Forum on Cultural Industries in 2004. Taiyuan, the chosen site for this event, is in central north China's Shanxi Province. This was an important occasion, complete with celebrity, ceremony and exhibitions for trading of cultural assets. A previous event had taken place in 2002 in Chengdu in Sichuan province. In Taiyuan a group of US entertainment industry businesses led by the organisation American Television in China had come to broker entry into the restricted Chinese audio-visual and cultural market. Their presentations emphasised co-production models and tax incentives for local production willing to provide resources; in short, the kind of welcoming mats extended to the

Table 6.1 Number of cultural institutions, industries and employment (2001–2005)

Year	No. of cultural institutions (shiye)	No. of industry (chanye) units and (individual operators)	No. of persons employed in public cultural service (shiye)	No. of persons employed in cultural industry (chanye)
2001	59,000	209,000		
2002	56,900	253,000		
2003	56,500	293,000		12,740,000[a]
2004	55,600	301,000 (362,000)	471,354	9,960,000[b]
2005	55,800	329,500	493,659	

Sources:
a   http://www.gd.xinhuanet.com/newscenter/2006-05/20/content_7041309.htm
b   *The Statistics of China's cultural and related industries 2004 in brief (State Statistics Bureau: Beijing).*

US film industry in many global locations. Others spoke about the importance of legal mechanisms, the need for copyright regimes and more transparency. In the main the Americans were lavish in their praise of Chinese culture, creativity and enterprise.

I had attended the conference in Taiyuan purely by chance, following on from another event three months earlier at Beijing's Renmin University where I presented a paper on the creative elements of the Sydney Olympics. My invitation came about as a result of a relationship with the director of the Humanistic Olympics Research Centre, Jin Yuanpu. I had been introduced by Zhang Xiaoming, vice-director of the Humanities Research Centre of the Chinese Academy of Social Sciences. Zhang is the lead editor of the series of *Blue Books on China's Cultural Industries*. (The first of these reports was published in 2002.)

I met Zhang Xiaoming in October 2003 in Beijing. Zhang indicated that there was some interest in Beijing policy circles in the idea of the creative industries, mainly as a result of the newly published *Baseline Study of Hong Kong's Creative Industries* (CCPR 2003), a 227-page report identifying Hong Kong's competitive advantage in several creative industries sectors. The problem, he confided, was that the idea of creative industries was hardly understood in China at the time. In addition to the misunderstanding, the central government's cultural industry platform had become the default position for discussing the machinations of the cultural economy. In April 2004, Zhang alerted me to an article published on a new online forum. I was searching for evidence of the uptake of creativity in China. The article by Liu Shifa (2004b) advocated the proposition 'From Made in China to Created in China' (*cong Zhongguo chuangzuo dao Zhongguo chuangzao*). This phrase would become a slogan and eventually a branding strategy. Up to that time I had engaged in a number of futile discussions with Chinese journalists and media scholars who dismissed outright the value of creativity. Of course, these were people professionally trained to reflect reality rather than imagine alternative realities – 'to seek truth from facts'. The idea of creative industries was antithetical to their callings.

I made a point of emphasising the 'Created in China' concept during the Beijing Olympic culture conference. In the audience that day was Su Tong, the Executive Director of the Creative China Industrial Alliance (CCIA), a non-profit organisation, which at that time was less than a month old. The next day, I visited the organisation's 'think-tank' in Yayuncun, the area of Beijing where the Olympic Games were to be staged. In contrast to the academic environment of university researchers, the CCIA centre is designed to stimulate open thinking. Slogans celebrating the value of creativity and imagination confronted me. I met a number of members of the organisation including Liu Shifa, then a section head at the Internet Culture Division of the Ministry of Culture. We discussed the role of the Creative China Industrial Alliance in the unit's green room, supplemented by powerpoint presentations, Chinese tea and multimedia design concepts. I would make many more visits to the CCIA greenroom in the following years.

When I asked Su about 'From Made in China to Created in China', he introduced some of his organisation's ideas on cultural exchange and learning regions.

The slogan 'From Made in China to Created in China' was first presented to the public in May 2004 during the Seventh Beijing Science Expo, where the organisation had mounted a display with the intent of promoting the concept of creative industries. One key idea Su mentioned during our initial discussion was 'innovative productivity'. He said 'for a long time in China we liked to use the term material productivity. Our assumption was that productivity is directly equated with material production'. In other words, a focus on production and performance indicators in China had impacted negatively on creativity. This of course is borne out by China's key role as an assembler of imported components, and the ubiquitous 'Made in China' products proliferating in discount stores globally. Su was almost apologetic about China's past mistakes. There was a need to emphasise people's capacity to be more creative, he said. He was quick to point out that creativity is not just about big cities and the middle classes; it needs to be distributed to become people-centred. He told me how the Creative China Industrial Alliance had conducted a creative branding campaign in early 2004 around a wheaten food festival in Taiyuan, the capital of Shanxi province in north-west China, a place left behind by globalisation.

Locating the Second International Forum on China's Cultural Industries in Taiyuan was perhaps a statement of intent by the Ministry of Culture. Situated on the north-west plains of China between Shaanxi, Hebei and Henan provinces, the area is regarded as the cradle of Chinese civilisation, the ancestral home of the legendary Yellow Emperor of the Xia dynasty (5000 BCE–2000 BCE). Today Taiyuan is the centre of China's coal industry and as a consequence the environment has suffered severe degradation. One of the first things that I noticed after arriving was the poverty of the city, in stark comparison with Beijing from where I had just come. In contrast to the colourful bright neon signs advertising Armani and Microsoft, weak local brands jostled for attention in the greyish brown sky.

One-hundred-and-eight kilometres south of Taiyuan is the ancient walled city of Pingyao built in the Zhou dynasty (eleventh century BCE to 221 BCE) and fortunately preserved from the excesses of the Cultural Revolution Red guards who took their task of obliterating feudal culture very seriously. In 1997, Pingyao was listed as a World Heritage Site. However, Pingyao was important for more than just its ancient ruins. The city developed into a merchant centre in the late Qing dynasty, a time when enterprising locals established China's first modern banks. Now it functions as an emblem of a lost civilisation, and pins its hopes of a renaissance on tourism. Not surprisingly, cultural tourism was the subject of much of the discussion at the conference. Listening to the excitement about cultural industries, I recalled Ian Buruma's wry observation that 'Theme parks ... are to East Asian capitalism what folk dancing festivals were to communism' (Buruma 2003). Tradition suddenly appeared as the cash cow of the conference. Provincial leaders gave keynote presentations, eager to promote unique traditional cultural resources. These views on local enterprise were supported by humanities academics careful to integrate the idea of the cultural industry into the governmental rhetoric of advanced modern culture.

The invited 'image master' was the Hong Kong and Hollywood kung-fu star Jackie Chan, who introduced the conference and wished China well in its pursuit of cultural development, then promptly disappeared. The theme was economic sustainability and many of the presentations reflected on the government's commitment to the idea of increasing the vitality of cultural industries and reaching out to new markets. Significantly, a few papers at the conference signalled a new direction. He Chuanqi, the Director of the Centre for Modernization Research from the Chinese Academy of Social Science, began by reminding the audience that the cultural industries were not a new idea – they had been around since antiquity. In a wide-ranging survey of the development of the cultural economy he cited Maslow's five-level model of human needs, and how humans have progressed over time from basic needs such as food and shelter to social needs – and finally to emotional and intellectual satisfactions (He Chuangi 2004). He noted China's 4000-year history and its 23 world heritage sites (now more than 30), indicating China's backward position in development. China was fundamentally locked into the agricultural and industrial era in comparison to advanced economies that had moved into the knowledge and service industries.

Lui Shifa from the Creative China Industrial Alliance was another speaker. In the midst of the largely cultural development focused discussion, his presentation was an alternative model of catch-up. Liu was proposing a shift of emphasis from the cultural industries model that had three years earlier been ratified by China's State Council. This was the model endorsed by this 'international' gathering. Liu proposed three points of intersection: digital China, creative China and cultural China. Noting that one of the core problems facing China was the 'duck style feeding' (*tianya shi*) of students in educational institutions, Liu argued that China needed to make a transformation from an economy that over-emphasised learning from others – one that 'inherits tradition, follows others, copies, and brings in' other cultures – to a 'creative economy' where creativity is the priority strategy and originality is acknowledged and valued (Liu 2004a: 90). Creativity had to be instilled, not drilled. In China, he said, government was the primary consumer of services and hence its role ought to be lead the creative movement, by amongst other things reducing direct subsidy to producers and instead acting as a procurer of creative goods and services. Other initiatives, although not spelt out in detail, included taxation incentives to pump-prime the creative economy, a strategic reassessment of intellectual property protection, and a bringing together of government, enterprises and education in creative industry pilot projects.

Creating the environment: from culture to creativity

Two months after this major provincial level gathering, the Director of Cultural Affairs in the Chaoyang District Government in Beijing attended the 'City to City' Conference in Hong Kong. Hong Kong had made the running in the creative industries by producing the influential *Baseline Study of Hong Kong's Creative Industries*, which was published in 2003 by a team at the Hong Kong University

Cultural Policy Centre led by Desmond Hui. The report had adopted the UK methodological process of 'mapping' the value of designated sectors, including occupations. The Baseline Report was the evidence base that was needed to convince city leaders. International experts including Philip Dodd, the Director of London's Institute for Contemporary Art, had been instrumental in promoting the concept of creative cities networks while acting as a messenger for the UK's creative industries agenda. Dodd had visited mainland China and Hong Kong in 2002 before establishing a UK–China cultural exchange facilitation agency in 2004, in the context of the intended emphasis on exploiting creative value somewhat ironically called *Made in China*.

China's first symposium on the creative industries was held in Shanghai in December 2004, organised by the Propaganda Department of the Shanghai Municipal Committee of the Chinese Communist Party, the Shanghai Municipal Committee of Economic Development and the Shanghai Academy of the Social Sciences. It was attended by Chinese speakers and it was clear that a consensus was emerging about the role of creativity. In particular, the fast tracking of creative industries policy in Shanghai was championed by Li Wuwei (2006) from the Shanghai Academy of Social Science[8] and He Shouchang from the Shanghai Theatre Academy.

In 2005, creativity came on the agenda of government, think tanks and social science academics in China. During the ensuing year the value of cultural clusters, centres and precincts provoked animated discussion at several 'international' conferences and seminars. In January 2005, Desmond Hui from the Hong Kong University Cultural Policy Centre was hired to conduct a similar 'baseline study' of Beijing's Chaoyang district. It seemed as if the creative economy was set to follow the path of the high-tech sectors through national and local tax incentives and foreign investment. A stream of articles and books appeared. In July 2005, Beijing hosted China's first international conference *Creative Industries and Innovation*. The conference used the slogan 'from made in China to created in China' to great effect.[9] Nonetheless, despite the focus on creativity, the Chinese organisers were unwilling to directly translate the word creative industries, opting for the government's preferred term, cultural industries. Nevertheless, in a keynote speech, the vice-minister of education, Wu Qidi spoke of the importance of creative industries:

> In the era of the knowledge economy, the rate of growth of creative industries already constitutes a breakthrough industrial trend in many developed nations and regions. These nations and regions have made creative industries an important industrial strategy by actively fostering and promoting policies. Nations and cities have raised their core competitiveness.
>
> (Wu 2006: 263–264)

Wu Qidi spoke at the same time of the challenge for education and the Ministry of Education's emphasis on developing creative talents. She noted 'We have strengthened the foundations of creativity', referring to changes in the curriculum, and the encouragement of students 'in competitive activities that have a creative and innovative nature' (Wu 2006: 265).

Two events followed in relatively quick succession. The first was a special symposium on 'Cultural and Creative Industries' in Beijing in September 2005, which was organised to present the findings of China's first creative industries mapping. Desmond Hui notes the nervousness of officials. 'In the Chinese version of the program the word "creative" was omitted but allowed to remain in the English translation. However, when the final report was presented to the Chaoyang government, the authors were asked to revert to the term 'cultural and creative industries' (Hui 2006: 319). The idea of creative industries had won qualified support in Beijing. Within two months of this event a 'Shanghai International Creative Industries Week' was instituted, supported by the Propaganda Department of the CCP Shanghai Committee. The organiser was the Shanghai Creative Industry Centre (SCIC), an umbrella organisation formed in January 2005 to coordinate a range of activities and to attract international consultants to the cause. On 6 December 2005, the Shanghai Creative Window was formally launched under the administration of the SCIC, in an office space located in Luwan District. The Window has become the 'front office' of SCIC, dealing directly with international consultants and organising industry events such as the annual Shanghai Creative Industries Week. While the SCIC performs an economic facilitation role, the more governmental Shanghai Creative Industries Association operates in tandem under the Shanghai Propaganda Department. Like many Chinese organisational systems, there is a degree of overlap between the two entities.

By the end of 2006, draft Eleventh Five Year-Plans for Beijing, Shanghai, Chongqing, Nanjing, Shenzhen, Qingdao and Tianjin had embraced the creative industries. Beijing, with its cultural crown jewels such as The Great Wall, The Forbidden City and The Summer Palace, opted for the hybrid 'cultural creative industries' (*wenhua chuangyi chanye*). In December 2005, Beijing instituted its First International Cultural Creative Industries Expo (see Chapter 11). The adoption of the new translation of creativity *chuangyi*, instead of the conventional Chinese adjective *chuangzaoli*, underscores the resolve to internationalise the language of reform.

How had this change occurred so rapidly in China? Why had creativity – a concept previously confined to the rarefied academy of the arts and approached with clear suspicion for decades by Communist ideologues – been rehabilitated and set the task of reforming unproductive sectors, renovating education, and providing solutions for post-industrial urban planning? The answer to this lies in the genesis of the concept and its association with the restructuring of the economic activity in large Chinese cities. The international correspondence of the super-sign of creativity is therefore important in understanding its attraction.

Scholar-consultants and creative industries

One of the central issues in debates about the value of culture is its innate heterogeneity. Likewise, the notion of creativity conjures up various associations.

The term 'creativity' is applied loosely to a multitude of phenomena, particularly in the business sphere. As many scholars have discussed (Cunningham 2006: Ross 2006: Garnham 2005), the uptake of the term creative industries by regional and national governments globally has been based on a kind of faith in its ability to transform non-productive culture into value-added enterprise. Andrew Ross writes that, 'creativity was a renewable energy resource, mostly untapped; every citizen had some of it, the cost of extraction was minimal, and it would never run out' (Ross 2006: 5).

In contrast to the slow incubation of the 'cultural industries' the 'creative industries' was a fast burner. However, the imported concept needed national intermediaries who would act as translators. Kong *et al.* (2006), writing about the transfer of ideas of the creative economy across East Asia, have noted that 'Asian commentators were both "inside" and "outside" in relation to Euro-American knowledges'. Their insider status emerges from the fact that they are embedded in what sometimes appears to be a privileged international network of knowledge, one that brings new understandings of the inter-relationships among new industries and new sectors. But they remain outside, distant from the origins of the ideas, which were developed by foreign thinkers in foreign languages. The ability to make sense of these discourses and to circulate them rapidly into the purview of policy makers demonstrates just how powerful the super-sign of creativity had become.

As mentioned above, the creative industries model had come from the UK. Aside from Richard Florida's influential notion of the creative class, which found adherents among city planners, the concept of creative industries failed to garner national uptake in the USA, instead finding its level in regional 'cool city' development policies (Peck 2005). The British Council subsequently seized on the opportunity to claim ownership of the concept in China from 2005. While the USA focus on 'content industries' was largely concerned with how to further deals with the emerging media conglomerates such as the China Film Radio and TV Group and the Shanghai Media Entertainment Group, the British had recognised that the key to creating a position was through talking to city governments and placing an emphasis on expertise in design, branding, business services and industrial design. These were areas in which the UK creative industries had established a lead.

If Chinese participants had an insider–outsider relationship in the process of defining the contours of the Chinese creative economy, the same uncertainty applied to international visitors. From mid 2004, 'scholar-consultants' associated with the creative and cultural economies played a key role in facilitating its diffusion. The role of foreign knowledge is worth special scrutiny. Experts appeared thick and fast offering advice about creativity indexes, creative classes, milieus, clusters, and networks. However, what was often lacking in these international prescriptions for sustainability and creativity was the specificity of Asian culture and politics. Sometimes scholars were engaged to appear in conferences and forums. The content of the presentations was arguably less important than their presence. In short, the Chinese way of brokering new ideas is to invite as many as possible, and then to select out into models (*moshi*) those that are suitable. Much international advice was received, absorbed and filtered. Many of the consultants were duly acknowledged as contributors to China's new great leap forward.

In 2005, John Howkins, author of *The Creative Economy*, was engaged as consultant, initially by the Shanghai Intellectual Property Administration, under the jurisdiction of the Shanghai Municipal government, and later by the Shanghai Creative Industries Association. In August 2005, the British Council offices in London received a delegation from Shanghai and in November 2006, the Howkins Institute for the Creative Economy was established in Shanghai. In this process of seeding ideas with senior policy makers and city planners in Beijing, Shanghai and Chongqing, several leading consultants played important roles: Desmond Hui from the Hong Kong University Centre for Cultural Policy Research, Patrick Mok from the Cheung Kong Centre for Creative Industries, and experts from the Queensland University of Technology in Australia, which had created a prototype for a creative industries incubator in 2004.[10]

The diffusion of ideas into the Chinese mainstream proceeded rapidly. As mentioned above, the pure 'creative industries' model of the UK, with its emphasis on 'individual creativity', was influential, although the emphasis on the intellectual property of the individual creator in the original was downplayed. The Creative China Industrial Alliance, which was operating in Beijing where Ministry of Culture officials had initially rejected the term, advocated the compromise hybrid idea of *individual and collective creativity*. Likewise, the prescriptions for economic development offered by Richard Florida, namely his emphasis on toleration and bohemian indexes, were less enthusiastically received than the more pragmatic UK model of the creative industries with its prescription of sustainable rents from creativity.

Creativity and category confusion

By the time the cultural industries emerged in China, unanimity prevailed about the national importance of culture, even if strategies to exploit culture were undeveloped. After all, China's national culture was identifiable. The intrusion of creative industries in 2005 unsettled the established categories, with the new term demanding a greater degree of accountability to assert its bona fides. However, the benefits of the intangible creative economy in China are difficult to measure, not just because of the rubbery nature of Chinese statistics and the disappearance of much 'intellectual property' into the black market. For instance, how do you measure the value of the service sector components of cultural products? How do you account for multiplier effects associated with design and marketing? These kinds of problems do not disrupt the accounting of the manufacturing industries, on which China has based its development model. What is in? What is out? What is the core and what is non-core? Are they just another industry or do they deserve special attention? Moreover, while 'creative industries' appears to break down the foundations of rigid notions of culture, some regard the term as oxymoronic.

How can creativity, essentially something emanating from the individual, be an industry?

To understand the nature of these misunderstandings, it is useful to briefly explore the processes that are regarded as engendering creativity, both upstream (conception) and downstream (marketing). The notion of the creative value chain focuses on processes, the most basic breakdown of the process being inputs, production and outputs. Moreover, between production and outputs there are varying degrees of originality and imitation. The value chain of a piece of contemporary music begins with the musician noting down a series of notes such that the composition is copyrightable. In actual fact, the creative ideas may have devolved from his or her experiences immediately prior to composition or several years before. The composition may be a new combination of sounds, something accidental or planned. John Howkins writes about Igor Stravinsky's *Rite of Spring* thus: 'When Igor Stravinsky was writing *The Rite of Spring* in 1911, he was living in a small room in Clarens Switzerland. Robert Craft has recounted how the landlady received complaints from the other tenants that he was playing the "wrong notes". Stravinsky, unamused, later retorted, "They were the wrong notes for them but they were the right notes for me"' (in Howkins 2001: 125). Various processes and intermediaries combine to make the combination of sounds and lyrics more commercial: other musicians, producers, publishers, commercial agents, record labels, radio play lists, personal appearances, distribution outlets etc.

Despite the romantic view of creativity, process is central. To take an idealist position, creativity is *ex nihilo*: it comes out of nowhere, at least it seems. If we take this view originality simply cannot occur. We need the past to create; for instance new words, slang and hip expressions are generally combinations of existing meaning systems. In the Buddhist tradition, the idea of beginners' or empty mind predisposes the sage towards illumination uncluttered by the past. Many of the great Chinese lyrical poets during the Tang Dynasty drew upon this 'method' or alternatively shifted their reality with liberal amounts of wine. In *The Creative Mind* Margaret Boden notes that creativity is fundamentally value laden. She argues that 'creativity is the ability to come up with ideas that are new, surprising, and valuable' (Boden 2004: 1). However, a work or product may be creative for the person generating it, but this does not necessarily make it surprising or valuable. The work or idea may be private and personal, or it may be a product. Howkins pushes the argument further in this direction: a creative product is an economic good or service that results from creativity and has some economic value (Howkins 2001: x). He defines the creative economy thus: $CE = CP$ (creative product) $\times T$ (transaction).

Most economists agree that the capitalist economies, and particularly the USA, have placed a higher value on novelty than socialist nations (see Hodgson 1999). In turn, Western liberal democracies have instituted intellectual property laws (copyrights and patents) that have rewarded creativity, whether artistic or scientific. Not surprisingly, the emphasis on intellectual property confirms that creativity is time bound: it can be registered. The past, on the other hand, both constrains and extends creativity. In the media industries, the past – and especially the recent past – is the key to success. Many television programmes thrive by being repetitive or derivative. One can ask: just how creative or original are formatted game and reality shows that reproduce formulas? Just how original, for instance is Harry Potter?

Bilton (2007: 53) points out notions of value 'are dependent upon the subjective, individual interpretation of "symbolic" goods in the mind's eye of the consumer'. As opposed to conventional commodities (for instance, foodstuffs) creative goods and services 'have to work much harder to engage with and manipulate customer perceptions of value, through critical reappraisal, customized marketing and innovative modes of packaging and delivery'. Taking an evolutionary economics approach to the creative industries, we can observe that creativity is embedded within a more complex system of economic coordination than is conventionally understood in the arts (Potts 2006). Design, for instance, adds value to the packaged foodstuffs on the supermarket shelves.

Conclusion: great expectations

Are there corresponding differences in China between personal creativity, economic creativity, and aesthetic creativity? The important question we need to ask is: what does China expect of creativity? What can the creative industries do for China that cultural industries or innovation policy cannot? Many writers, speakers and officials in China conflate the terms cultural and creative industries, sometimes intentionally. This slippage adds to the tension between preservation and novelty generation, between public cultural institutions, cultural industries and enterprises. Does not China's national policy already emphasise innovation? When I attended the Beijing Forum at Peking University in October 2006, one of the interpreters translated *chuangyi chanye* as 'innovation industries'. While a basic translation error, this nevertheless demonstrates the proximity of concepts. Innovation has had several years of governmental support; and innovation centres have mushroomed. But in some critics' view they have engaged in precious little breakthrough innovation. Indeed, there has been more emphasis on incremental innovation and exploitation of existing ideas and formats than the production of intellectual property. Why is this so? Are there historical legacies to account for Chinese applications of the creative process? Will the shift to creativity as a command metaphor unlock some hidden potential, turn on the originality tap, and release new productive forces?

Kong *et al.* (2006) have suggested that the creative economy is embedded within a relational geography of diffusion and adaptation in Asia. They point out that discourses of creative economies in Asia are often adapted in superficial ways. Certainly, much of the current hype over creative industries in China calls for a stronger evidence base. A few people I spoke to fear the concept may become too general to maintain its momentum. Further to the emphasis on industries, infrastructure and markets, however, there is another creative story that may ultimately erode the policy high ground. This is user-led innovation. It is the most radical model of the creative process, bringing with it a high degree of disruption to existing institutions, products and processes, and leading to what Joseph Schumpeter (1961) famously called 'creative destruction'. The kinds of destruction that occur include changes to traditionally defined industry boundaries and entry barriers, changes to regulatory approaches, as well as greater competition to keep pace with technological developments demanded by users. On a transformative level, the role of users as innovators breaks down linear models of diffusion and challenges conventional investment in R&D. The role of communities of practice within the creative commons leads to a more rapid collision of ideas, which produces the effects of innovation but without the same proprietary lock-in. In China's creative industries strategies this model is seldom discussed.

7   Cities and the creative field

Throughout history cities have been crucibles of creativity. In antiquity large cities on inland trade routes experienced golden ages; in modern times, port cities and cities close to transport, finance and communication systems have lured investment and talent: some, like London, New York and Tokyo became finance and entrepreneurial hubs as well as cultural centres (Sassen 1991). These cities sit atop a hierarchy of approximately 30 'world cities'. Financial cities with lesser international cache (Miami, Frankfurt, Singapore) occupy a second tier. In addition, the world cities 'list' includes those that dominate large national economies (Sao Paulo, Paris, Sydney, Seoul), and subnational or regional centres (Osaka-Kobe, Hong Kong, Vancouver, the Rhine-Rhur conurbation, Chicago) (Friedmann 2002: 7).

While urban planners and sociologists attended to the rankings of world and global cities, scholars in the disciples of economic and cultural geography meanwhile saw the central role of the city within transnational media networks of production and distribution. Michael Curtin (2003, 2007) has coined the term 'media capitals' to describe the effects of agglomerations of finance, cultural diversity and creative talent. Typical examples of media capitals include Los Angeles (Hollywood), Hong Kong and Mumbai (Bollywood). Such discussion of cities as attractors of capital and talent has been further fleshed out in contrasting ways (Florida 2002; Landry 2000, 2006; Landry and Bianchini 1995; Zukin 1995). For these writers, cities have many resources that can be utilised to advantage. Of course, all cities are not equal in terms of assets, liveability and location. Some cities and towns have attempted to generate instant creativity in order to lure investment and tourists; for this reason there have been criticisms of expedient 'cookie cutter' creative industries districts and cultural quarters (Oakley 2004).

Scholars have pointed to the post-industrial city as a model to address a range of urban problems, including economic sustainability, tolerance, dynamics of innovation and civic engagement. The city stands as the locus of social diversity in an era of mediated abundance. Peter Hall (1999) maintains that cities have always played important roles as sites of innovation. Hall says that the common ingredients of all major cities over time are openness to trade, new forms of social organisation, tensions between freedom and hierarchy, and mixing of people and cultures. Moreover, transformations, discoveries, and social reforms have occurred mostly in large cities, and often in capital cities.

In this chapter I turn the analysis towards understanding the recent proliferation of 'creative' clusters, centres and precincts. Over the past few years disused factories and districts in China's large cities have transformed into creative clusters (*chuangyi jiju*) and creative precincts (*chuangyi yuanqu*). This transformation echoes the gentrification described by Sharon Zukin (1981) in *Loft Living: Culture and Capital in Urban Change* which saw districts like SoHo and Tribeca gain a reputation as avant-garde centres. As the proportion of New York's work force engaged in manufacturing declined from the 1950s to the 1970s, the vacated industrial premises became available for alternatives uses, including artists' lofts and cheap housing. In time artist presence stimulated real estate prices along with an international reputation for these districts. Many artists subsequently found their loft lifestyle unaffordable and shifted to cheaper premises.

This phenomenon is now occurring at pace in many of China's big cities. Spaces like the 798 Precinct in the Beijing's Chaoyang District, Hangzhou's Loft 49 on Hangyin Road in the north side of Hangzhou, Tianzifang in Shanghai's Luwan District, and the Tank Loft in the Chongqing Contemporary Art Centre showcase alternative art, performing arts, and music not permitted under previous political regimes.[1] Consumption is also a part of the revitalization of these former industrial precincts with the new pluralism and openness to international art communities drawing visitors in large numbers. Artists now pay premium prices in some of these precincts in exchange for exposure to the passing tourist trade.[2]

However, this story is being written on a larger canvas than isolated outbreaks of pluralism. The changes that are occurring in China are endorsed by central, provincial and municipal government. By 2006, there were 30 'clusters' in Shanghai. Beijing had 10 established clusters, with another 8 planned to begin development. Beijing's plans are even more ambitious than Shanghai's in terms of scale. In 2007, the Beijing Iron and Steel Factory in the western district of Shijingshan will reduce its operation allowing construction to commence on a new 'integrated services district' called the Capital Recreation District (CRD). The factory will be moved further outside Beijing in Hebei Province, and with it most of the pollution and most of its 10,000 workers. In Tongzhou in the north-east of Beijing plans are in development for another integrated services centre, the Cultural Creative Park, not far from the existing Songzhuang artists' community village. This 200-hectare Cultural Creative Park will have an emphasis on animation and will provide an incubation base for small and medium Chinese creative content companies. According to reports, the Cultural Creative Park will also include a university campus with a mission to produce the talent base that will accelerate China's competitive position in the creative economy.

In many ways China is following an international script. Former high-tech parks are being reclassified as creative clusters. However, there is a distinctively East Asian emphasis in this process. Michael Porter's idea of competitive advantage, although criticised in many places, provides a starting point. Porter (1990) initially sought to understand industrial environments, including fragmented industries, emerging industries, industries undergoing a transition to maturity, declining industries and global industries. As I discuss below in the case of Hong Kong, Porter's work on the determinants of industry cluster competitiveness has been influential in persuading regional governments of the need to focus more on the institutional factors of innovation policy.

Clusters, moreover, have become mandatory in debates about regional economic development (Amin and Thrift 1992; Scott 1988, 2006; Storper 1997; Storper and Christopherson 1987: Porter 1998). The economic logic of clustering is distilled into parks, bases, incubators, industrial districts, cities, regions – and even countries. As economies push towards increased specialisation in trade and seek out high-value markets, policy makers target agglomeration as a competitive growth strategy. An important benefit of clusters is the trade off between competition and cooperation. Firms locate in particular regions or centres to gain benefits of labour, knowledge and ideas. Firms, universities and enterprises create an excess of services and knowledge; the former is used in creating more specialised services (e.g. expansion) while knowledge is diffused, acquired by people working in the milieu.

Wu (2005: 3) argues that 'clusters mitigate the problems inherent in arms-length relationships without imposing the inflexibilities of vertical integration or the management challenges of maintaining formal linkages such as alliances and partnerships'. Yusuf (2003) points out that clusters have existed for some time in East Asia. Low-tech manufacturing clusters in Japan produce everything from auto parts to eyeglass frames, while high-tech clusters are often co-located close to universities. While most industrial parks are heavily invested in by government and business, other clusters are more organic in their evolution, drawing skills and capital because of their proximity to cosmopolitan urban centres, or to transport routes. As I discuss in Chapter 8, clusters are also embedded in regional growth, stimulated by the migration of cheap labour and preferential government policies.

Aside from the availability of excess cheap labour, an important ingredient for regions and cities looking for a distinctive edge in the global economy is research and development (R&D), the competitive advantage of large corporations. The success of Silicon Valley has led to regional high-technology clusters (Beijing's Zhongguancun, Taipei's Hsinchu, Korea's Taeduk). However, it needs to be noted that the factors that contribute to the success of East Asian high-tech clusters are in many ways different from the hub and spoke district built around one or more major corporations, or the satellite district model, which often contains branch plants of multinational corporations (Marshall 1920). While branch offices of multinationals frequently dominate in the early stages, government policy provides a helping hand to domestic enterprises through cheap land, labour training, recruitment subsidies and generous tax breaks (Chen 2006). The nature of manufacturing clusters in particular is often predetermined by advantages of low-cost production. In short, there is less emphasis on product innovation in China and more on process, mobilising specialised companies across many levels of an extended business process.

This occurs because major suppliers and assemblers work in tandem (Brown and Hagel 2006).

In terms of specific locations in East Asia, Tokyo, Hong Kong, Seoul and Taipei have relative advantages over China, including a mix of local creativity and international finance, a talent base drawn to urban centres or incubated in universities and colleges, greater interaction with international ideas and tastes, as well as a base of advertising and financial service industries. However, the recent shift to clustering, in both media groups and cultural creative industries edges China closer to the innovation frontier. Ideally, the co-location of firms, combined with spill-overs of knowledge, works to create a milieu of innovation. For example, Silicon Valley's proximity to Stanford University attracts research collaboration in addition to the Valley's internationalised human capital (Kenney, 2000). However, as Margaret O'Mara (2005) has argued, places like Silicon Valley and Boston's Route 128, 'are not simply high-tech regions that resulted from fortuitous combinations of capital and entrepreneurship' (2005: 1). The role of policy was instrumental in making and shaping these locations, and in providing the ideal environment for science to grow and prosper. Such 'knowledge cities' grew away from 'the distractions and disorders of the changing industrial city' (O'Mara 2005: 2). Elsewhere the term 'knowledge city' has been applied with less focus on science (Ergazakis *et al.* 2004; Carillo 2006). Ergazakis *et al.* (2006: 4) describe the knowledge city as 'a city that aims at a knowledge-based development, by encouraging the continuous creation, sharing, evaluation, renewal and update of knowledge. Examples of knowledge cities in this definition include Barcelona, Stockholm, Munich, Montreal and Dublin.

Media capital

Writing from the standpoint of media history and cultural geography, Michael Curtin (2007) has formulated the concept of 'media capital', in part to examine the recent East Asian cultural influence in Hollywood, typified by films such as *Crouching Tiger Hidden Dragon*, *Kung Fu Hustle* and *Hero*, but also as a provocation on the future of audio-visual media diversification. The term 'capital' has two points of reference: first as a geographical centre and second as a focus of finance. Curtin asks: 'Where and why do certain locations emerge as significant centres of media production? What is the extent of their geographical reach?' He looks at the recent history of centres such as Hollywood and Hong Kong and the operation of media capital through three frames of reference – logics of accumulation, trajectories of creative immigration, and forces of socio-cultural variation.

The idea of accumulation is not unique to media industries. Indeed, it is the core logic of capitalism as enterprises seek to extend markets. Concentration of resources and the integration of sites of production, both local studio and international co-production sites, allow more efficient production. In tandem with the systematisation of international distribution (see Miller *et al.* 2001), these forces have consolidated the centrality of locations like Hollywood and Hong Kong in the film and television industries. Curtin notes, 'By the end of the 1920s, Hollywood was such a dominant force that the only hope for fledgling competitors was to carve out parallel spheres of operation, ones that were often protected by government policies or cultural impediments that kept Hollywood at bay' (Curtin 2007: 14).

The second principle of media capital, 'trajectories of creative migration' has much to do with current debates in China. Specialised labour provides the necessary resources for film, television, animation, and video games production – industries that promise high returns on investment if the end result is a hit. It is not altogether surprising that media companies locate in cities. Curtin argues that whereas in the past artists would migrate to places where wealthy individuals provided patronage, in the modern era market dynamics prevail. Talent seeks out opportunity and this creates a virtuous circle. Mutual learning effects are enhanced as inter-related producers come together, generating 'traded' and 'untraded inter-dependencies'. Traded dependencies evolve from collective interactions, such as subcontracting and servicing relationships (Kong 2005). These relationships frequently flourish in clusters and communities, although, as Pratt (2000) observes, cultural producers rely heavily on their address books, in other words, their wider network of contacts. In contrast to such formal relationships, moreover, proximity frequently leads to a sense of sociability. Informal networking generates trust and cooperation (Kong 2005). Storper notes that these untraded dependencies 'take the form of conventions, informal rules, and habits that coordinate economic actors under conditions of uncertainty' and that 'these relations constitute region-specific assets in production' (Storper 1997: 5).

The third idea in the media capital argument is forces of socio-cultural variation. This refers as much to the efforts of policy makers and regulators over time to force production into national and culturally specific categories as strategies by media industries to break into new markets. Many countries have established forms of local content protection in the face of what is often perceived as the damaging effects of cultural globalisation (see Curran and Park 2000). China is no exception. Foreign content is assiduously screened; a limit of 20 is placed on the theatrical distribution of international films. Socio-cultural variation occurs in spite of this as the demand for international films drives the black market economy. Socio-cultural variation also occurs with non-mainstream production – from art house foreign language cinema, dubbed or subtitled, to amateur flash animation globally distributed, usually free, over the internet.

Allen J. Scott's work on 'production complexes' provides a theoretical base for Curtin's notion of media capital. Beginning with the seminal work of Piore and Sabel (1984) in *The Second Industrial Divide*, Scott has carried forward the idea of two models of capitalist production: the first is the very familiar large vertically and horizontally integrated corporate model – the target of much critique in the field of political economy of the media – while the second level comprises a host of small interdependent firms, often engaged in subcontracting (Scott 1986). Scott's work on Hollywood illustrates how this dual tier operates (Scott 2004; see also Rifkin 2000). Extending the analysis to locationally differentiated webs of production in subsequent work, Scott has coined the term 'creative field' to describe 'any system of social relationships that shapes or influences human ingenuity and inventiveness and that is the site of concomitant innovations (Scott 2006: 3). The creative field is similar to the innovative milieu (Camagni 1995), the learning region (Florida 1995), and regional innovation systems (Cooke and Morgan 1994). However, the key point that Scott advances through the creative field concept is that as agglomeration intensifies, for example in various forms of clusters, those individuals working within the creative field are well placed to observe emerging entrepreneurial opportunities. Innovation is enhanced in such environments. He writes:

> An additional ingredient in this rich creative mix of production networks and local labour markets is place itself, not only as a collection of industrial capabilities and skills, but also as a stockpile of traditions, memories, and images that function as sources of inspiration for designers and crafts workers, and that help to stamp final products with a unique aura.
>
> (Scott 2006: 13)

The concept of the innovative milieu is central to Scott's work, and certainly to Curtin and to others now working in the disciplinary field of creative industries (Cunningham 2006; Hartley 2005; Potts 2006; Wu 2005). The genesis of the concept, according to Hall (1999) comes from Philippe Aydalot (1986), and is in turn associated with the origins of the creative milieu, first developed in Sweden (Törnqvist 1983). Although his background was France, Aydalot's intervention is particularly informative as it captures the essence of what is now occurring in China. He nominates three different kinds of innovation: first, in-house corporate restructuring; second, the restructuring of an old industrial environment, usually with a creative synthesis of outmoded activities and new technologies; and third, the production of new knowledge and its application in research (Hall 1999). Of these, the most desired is the third; however, the most evident is the second.

The Chinese creative field

Can the idea of the creative field be extended to describe China? Certainly, maintaining competitive advantage is crucial in the face of emerging abundance and international competition. Broadly speaking, instead of a dual divide between large vertically and horizontally integrated capitalist firms and a second tier of small flexible businesses, the Chinese creative field bifurcates into a limited number of state-owned media and cultural organisations (in various sectors) and a multitude of small specialist micro-businesses, many of which operate on the borders of legality. By borders of legality I mean these enterprises often dispense with copyright, regularly engage in price-cutting, and trade on *guanxi* to a greater extent than in the larger more regulated sectors. The term *guanxi* refers to trust relationships and is generally understood as the oil of much economic exchange in China (Yang 1996; Guthrie 1999). In industries such as publishing and advertising, small enterprises proliferate. In the former, thousands of publishing studios (*gongzuoshi*) take work off state-owned publishing companies (see Chapter 12) while in the advertising industry over 60,000 companies compete for spoils.

In investigating this bifurcation as a creative field more closely it is obvious that a simple big and small division fails to capture how innovation occurs, or fails to occur. Situated within the 'big end' of the field we also find transnational enterprises. For example, in the advertising industry 4A companies have established joint ventures with Chinese companies since the 1980s.[3] Following WTO accession in 2001, advertising companies were progressively allowed to raise their level of joint venture equity, to up to 70 per cent by 2004, and, by the end of 2005, were allowed to establish wholly owned foreign enterprises. The fact that most advertising agencies have since maintained joint venture (JV) relationships with Chinese companies suggests that there is a great deal of synergy occurring. Jing Wang (2008: forthcoming) points out that nationalist concern with international companies taking over the field have transformed into a more pragmatic model of looking for partnerships and sharing knowledge. Wu Xiaobo, director of PCBP, the company that helped deliver Ningbo Bird increased market share (see Chapter 10), quotes Marcel Proust, 'The real act of discovery lies not in finding new lands but seeing with new eyes', to illustrate the creativity conundrum. He says, 'International companies have an edge in the knowledge base, particularly brand management and systems procedures to create value. Local companies have experience in executing in China, more flexibility, and understanding of local trends' (Wu Xiaobo interview with Michael Keane and Christina Spurgeon, World Trade Centre Hotel, Beijing, 15 September 2004).

In illustrating the inherent and often contradictory dynamism of the Chinese creative field Wu Xiaobo refers to a Chinese expression *kezhou qiujian* (literally, there is mark on the boat where the sword fell). This saying comes from a popular fable and means it is impossible to make a mark to indicate where something lies in the water when a boat is moving. Likewise, it is difficult to plan ahead using data collected half a year ago, or when policies change rapidly. Most domestic agencies therefore depend on intuition and not research. This idea is supported by Gilbert Yang of the Shanghai Adbay company who maintains that because the market is so big there are many opportunities for local creatives. The smaller companies maintain advantages over the larger transnational companies because 'creativity is outsourced'. Companies shop around for value in China more than in the West and are inclined to use multiple agencies (Gilbert Yang: interview with Michael Keane and Christina Spurgeon, Shanghai, 16 March 2004).

The creative field therefore is a contradictory mix of rigidity and flexibility. The larger institutions, including transnationals, are more hampered by bureaucracy, the necessity of adhering to policy; the smaller companies can often evade such restrictions. This evasion is illustrated by the fact that smaller companies swim in a different, and very large, pond. Most Chinese media industries service the domestic market in which networks of *guanxi* provide the means to remain competitive.

These strategies allow the smaller companies to stay footloose. However, on the other edge of the pond, the state's call to build national champions points towards enhanced agglomeration. The formation of media groupings (*jituan*), beginning in 1998, was meant to bring about national champions worthy of competing with the likes of News Corporation and Time Warner. The state policy of 'securing the big and letting go of the small' (*zhuada fangxiao*) was tested particularly in the audio-visual sectors (film, television and new media). As more and more provinces set up their own groupings, this strategy appears to be fundamentally flawed – a reversion to duplicate construction of resources (*chongfu jianshe*) rather than building an oligopoly of strong contenders. On one hand the establishment of media groups has been a state-led initiative, while the proliferation of small dispersed enterprises has been driven by demand. Can these two underperforming ends of the creative field come together?

The creative city

The answer to this question may lie in rethinking how clusters can contribute to enhancing the creative field. In effect, the focus on cluster strategy in China is an extension of the idea of media industry grouping, moving agglomeration to the next stage. The idea of the creative city is now pervasive and internationalised. Since 1995, when Landry and Bianchini used the term 'creative city', city policy makers – indeed 'city image makers' – have become increasingly predisposed to rezoning industrial space to accommodate new kinds of creative classes. In 2000, Landry published *A Toolkit for the Creative City*. In the first decade of the twenty-first century it seems that any city can become more creative with gentrification, more festivals and more enlightened policy – even cities already enjoying a reputation for tolerance. In this unfolding of a creative zeitgeist, the re-spatialisation of arts and culture becomes a selling point, which while not unique, certainly illustrates city government's attempts to claim urban regeneration. As Donald suggests (2006: 64), the branded city is a creative city in that it allows 'the folding over of place, stories, marketing and consumption'.

In 2006, for instance, the city of Amsterdam announced itself as 'a creative city'. A glossy advertisement in a publication called *The Amsterdam Index* announced the Media Wharf project as an international place for creative industries: 'Former industrial sheds are being transformed into contemporary buildings with their historical worth fully intact. The location? The banks of the river IJ. This is where art, culture and media meet and flourish'. A leading radio personality wrote 'Noord is becoming a place where people reinvent themselves, like California' (Jan Donkers, *Amsterdam Index* 2007: 101). Another architect enthused 'We're attracted to the rawness of an industrial district' (Barbara Kuit, *Amsterdam Index* 2007: 101).

In a post-industrial landscape where manufacturing is outsourced or relocated to developing countries – or in the case of China moved from the big coastal cities to inland locations – the creative city has become an expedient economic development strategy. Pragmatism drives the re-invention and re-branding of former industrial areas as 'cool' alternatives to sterile modern business centres. In Asia creative city visions are integrated into the language of international competition for creative talent and place competitiveness. Singapore, in the past regarded as a city-state governed by a technocratic vision of the future, began a rapprochement with creativity during the 1990s, substantially increasing investment in culture and the arts. The Renaissance City Report of 2000 and the ensuing Creative Industries Development Strategy produced by the Economic Review Committee (ECR 2002) reiterated Singaporean aspirations to have ownership of an international creative hub, in addition to its already acknowledged gateway role in international transport and services. Singapore has pinned its hopes on two ambitious clusters, Design Singapore and Media 21 (Kong *et al.* 2006). In addition to these deliberate governmental programmes Singapore has become the de facto gay capital of Asia, echoing Richard Florida's views on the role of alternative cultures in attracting talent. Yue has written of recent social changes in Singapore, where the People's Action Party (PAP) government is often stereotyped as resolutely homophobic. She argues that gay entrepreneurship, gay foreign talent and gay indexes are now actively wooed to fashion a creative city (Yue 2006: 24).

In Taiwan local manufacturing has increasingly chosen mainland China to outsource production. The island's creative economy discourse has followed largely in the wake of more well-publicised developments in Singapore and Hong Kong. The focus is national although Taipei – along with Singapore and Seoul – has revealed aspirations to transform into a new economy information hub. The creative industries have more recently found support. Competition for tourism from the Mainland, particularly with the Beijing Olympics approaching, has increased the urgency of redefining Taiwan as a destination for investment and (cultural) experience. The creative economy was first noted in the six-year national development plan initiated in 2002, named 'Challenge 2008'. The Cultural Policy White Paper created by the Council for Cultural Affairs subsequently adopted the strategy of cultural and creative industries, drawing primarily on British Government and UN definitions (Kong *et al.* 2006).

In north Asia Seoul is advancing construction for a Digital Media City, an area of 565,000 square metres (Wu 2005). This is expected to be completed in 2010. Again, the idea of a knowledge-creative cluster is used to justify the government investment: to 'develop a futuristic info-media industrial complex that will serve as a centre of information technology in northeast Asia'. The Digital Media City is described as an incubator for developing social capital (Seoul Digital Media City n.d). The Seoul Metropolitan Government has facilitated the project by providing the IT broadband and wireless networks, constructing infrastructure, and providing tax incentives and favourably-priced land for the most desirable tenants. The Korean national government has also located several key IT and cultural agencies within the Digital Media City.

In summary, the felicitous convergence of creative cities and clusters draws upon changes in the global economy as much as attempts to grow national and regional 'champions'. Ideally, clusters provide new and better ways of organising the production and marketing of products and services and they allow serendipitous innovations to occur through mixing of people and ideas. In addition, spatial proximity generates trust, common languages, and obviates the need for time consuming formal relationships. In doing so clusters can facilitate a 'learning economy' (Malmberg and Power 2005). Importantly, clusters provide advantages in industrial specialisation and specific skill-based activities, benefiting the creation of products and services that target export markets. These products have a global presence, brand recognition, and can command high prices, as demonstrated by Hollywood and Mumbai. On the other hand, clusters are generally the result of spontaneous market processes. In the current era of economic 'de-rationalisation', governments are increasingly disposed to find new clusters in as many regions and districts as possible. To straddle the boundary between reliance on government intervention and market forces thus becomes the new challenge for China's creative economy.

8   In search of China's new clusters

Creative, knowledge, entrepreneurial and world cities are all manifestations of a desire to internationalise, to attract capital and tourism and to capitalise on the kudos associated with events such as Olympics and World Expos. However, despite the fashionable buzz now associated with urban re-branding, China can claim a long tradition of creative cities. As I discussed in Chapter 3, over the past 2,000 years Chinese capital cities have nurtured markets in which diverse cultural commodities were exchanged. In the Tang and Song dynasties China was in a real sense the 'middle nation', drawing travellers and merchants to its inland capitals. The Silk Road from Samarkand (today's eastern Uzbekistan) to Chang'an (today's Xian) had been operating for several centuries since the Han dynasty. New habits of conspicuous consumption emerged, artists became entrepreneurs, travelling troupes came and went, and new forms of culture were incubated. From the Tang onwards, the Chang'an, Luoyang, Kaifeng, Hangzhou, and Beijing were commercial and political centres. During the first few decades of the twentieth century large Chinese port cities became cultural capitals. In the 1930s and 1940s, Shanghai was widely acknowledged as the 'Paris of the East'. It was brash, crowded, fashionable and decadent, a point not lost on the Communist revolutionaries under the leadership of Mao Zedong who condemned the bourgeois culture fermenting in the big coastal cities. By the 1950s, Hong Kong had taken much of the talent from Shanghai. It is to Hong Kong that I therefore turn as a way of illustrating how the discourse of creativity was reincarnated in China.

Hong Kong

In 1997, Hong Kong was 'reunited' with the motherland in an outpouring of nationalism. However, this compulsory reunion resulted in a great deal of self-reflection about Hong Kong's positioning in the global economy, debates that were further intensified by the East Asian economic crisis. Hong Kong was set to make a move to self-identify as a service centre. Current developments in China's large cities can be illustrated in the light of Hong Kong's shift from manufacturing to high-value services. Two commissioned reports in the mid 1990s were highly influential in this re-imagining and subsequent re-branding. The first report, by Harvard Business School consultants, titled *The Hong Kong Advantage*, drew heavily on Michael Porter's concept of competitive advantage to position Hong's Kong future as 'a business/service/financial centre' with 'hub functions' (Sum 2002: 76).

The second report, *Made by Hong Kong*, was sponsored by the local manufacturing sector and supported by the Hong Kong Government Industry Department and the Hong Kong Productivity Council. This report challenged the long-term viability of Hong Kong's offshoring strategies in Guangdong Province. The Pearl River Delta had become the preferred site for Hong Kong outsourcing. Mok writes that the shift from manufacturing in Hong Kong had ushered in a great demand for support services 'including trade finance, banking, insurance, communication services, transportation, and logistical support – so that manufacturers headquartered in Hong Kong could operate their business and command their industrial operations in Guangdong Province' (Mok 2006: 336). In sum, the verdict from both reports was that Hong Kong needed to 'climb the technology ladder' and produce more value added goods. In order to do this it was necessary to bring about institutional changes that would allow Hong Kong to be more competitive, such as acquiring more human capital (experts, technical knowledge) and promoting R&D through a range of agglomeration measures (universities, science parks, incubators etc.).

These reports helped to shape the consensus about where Hong Kong was heading, or should head, in the post-handover period. In addition, the acknowledgment of the importance of the arts to Hong Kong's future by the then Chief Executive Tung Chee-Hwa led to a further series of reports that imagined Hong Kong's role as a world city. Major projects including the Hong Kong Cyberport were borne out of this re-imagining. Designed by media magnate Richard Li and his company Pacific Century, the Cyberport's goal was to 'attract, nurture and retain the relevant innovative talent necessary to build a cyber-culture critical mass in Hong Kong' (Sum 2002: 83). Advertising itself as 'a healthy environment for creative talents', the Cyberport operates as a digital entertainment hub, holding symposia and media business events. At the same time as the Cyberport development was occurring, however, debates in the former colony were speculating as to the long term viability of Hong Kong as a service centre for outsourced manufacturing. The term 'neo-industrialisation' emerged, 'emphasising the production of high-value goods with design content, high technology, and service-enhanced industries' (Mok 2006: 336).

In 2002, Florida published *The Rise of the Creative Class* in which he argued that technology, tolerance and talent were the most important determinants of city competitiveness. In the same year the Hong Kong SAR Region Government had commissioned a team at the University of Hong Kong's Cultural Policy Centre to prepare 'a baseline report' on Kong Kong's Creative Industries, following the lead of the 1998 British Creative Industries Mapping Document (DCMS 1998). This comprehensive report was released in 2003. In contrast to the UK document, however, the Hong Kong report intimated that there were other dimensions to the creative industries: 'the term "creative industries" is better served as a *variegated notion* not only for describing the economic system of the creative sector, but at the same time for examining the cultural configuration in a society and its interactions with the public and socio-economic sector at large' (CCPR 2003: 13, italics in original). The Hong Kong Cultural Policy Centre Report nominated technology, skills, and cultural capital as the recipes for future growth (CCPR, 2003), adapting Florida's creative index and his prescription of technology, tolerance and talent. In 2004, this was extended to a Hong Kong Creativity Index, in which creative capital in various manifestations became a proxy for measuring Hong Kong's competitiveness (HKCI 2004). Further reports by the same team in 2006 have mapped the value of creative industries in the Pearl River delta (PRD) and its relationship to the viability of Hong Kong's own creative industries sectors, including film and television production (CCPR, 2006).

Shanghai's creative milieu

Shanghai's cultural centrality during the early decades of the twentieth century was built on the back of massive industrial growth. Shanghai transformed from a trading city in the nineteenth century to an open treaty port following the Treaty of Shimoneseki in 1895, which allowed foreigners to set up factories. Between 1910 and 1920 the population of Shanghai increased from 1 million to 2.5 million people (Fu 2002). By the 1940s, however, the countryside became the experimental site for socialist transformation and the urban centres became socialist 'productive' cities based upon a centrally planned economic model (Fu 2002). Shanghai's re-emergence as a creative city was put on hold until the 1990s, a decade in which the development of the new Pudong area, the construction of the Oriental Television tower, and the re-fashioning of Nanjing Road as a consumer mall gave the Shanghai city 'brand' a new lease of life.

As I mentioned in the previous chapter, the news of the Hong Kong Baseline Study reached China in 2004. Within a few months knowledge was exchanged between these two important centres. Policies were established to follow the lead set by Hong Kong, Singapore, and other international destinations. Shanghai was the first Chinese city to move with the idea of clusters, a key element of the revitalisation of urban space. Shanghai's world city aspirations had brought it into direct competition with Beijing and Hong Kong, the former positioned as the cultural capital of China and the latter the business services centre of Asia.

The Shanghai Creative Industry Centre (SCIC) was established on 6 November 2004 and began its operation on 8 January 2005. A month later the Shanghai Economic Commission (2005) published *Shanghai Creative Industry Clustering Parks*. The 14 clusters in this 'first wave' were mostly disused industrial spaces in high value commercial districts. Many were already operational and the term creative industries seemed appropriate to describe their activity. Meanwhile, the winds of change had been blowing in Beijing. The Chaoyang government in Beijing had commissioned a baseline report (see Chapter 6). In the heightened climate of world city competition between the two giants, Shanghai seized the moment. In August 2005, a delegation from Shanghai went to the UK to gather knowledge under the sponsorship of the British Council in Shanghai. The British

Council saw an opportunity to claim ownership of the idea creative industries and offer expert advice.[1] In November 2005, another Shanghai delegation visited Hong Kong to consult with Chinese experts. Following this, Shanghai published its strategic plan, identifying five key sectors: industrial design and design industry research and development, architectural design, culture and media industries, consumer fashion, and business consultation and planning services.

By the end of 2005, Shanghai had earmarked 36 creative industry parks. Old plant buildings, warehouses and disused building make up two-thirds of the clusters (see Table 8.1).

Of these clusters, a number are worth describing because they illustrate the post-industrial fervour of the city government and the adoption of the rhetoric of creativity within the city's Eleventh Five-Year Plan. Tianzifang is a mixed space cluster, located at Lane 210 on Taikang Road. It occupies an area previously used by the Shanghai Food Industry Machinery Factory and the Shanghai Clock Plastics Fittings Factory. The factories had closed down for several years. In 2000, the Luwan district government allowed these spaces to be refitted for a mix of artists' studios, design offices, photo studios, as well as a performance centre, fashion show room and ceramics hall. In 2006, there were 102 enterprises in Tianzifang of which up to 10 per cent come from international destinations. These include Australia, USA, France, Denmark, UK, Canada, Singapore, Japan, Ireland, Malaysia, Hong Kong and Taiwan (SCIC 2006).

Another renovated industrial space is M50, which is situated at number 50 Moganshan on the banks of the Suzhou Creek. The premises were previously occupied by the state-owned Shanghai No. 22 Cotton Mill, the No. 20 Wool Mill, and the Chunming Roving Mill. The makeover occurred in 2001. M50 now

Table 8.1 Creative clusters by district in Shanghai (October 2006)

District	No. of clusters	Development characteristics
Xuhui	7	Cartoon and comic design, digital applications design, handicraft design
Yangpu	5	Architectural planning, architectural design, industrial design
Hongkou	4	Cultural media, consumer culture
Changning	3	Software, costume and multimedia design
Luwan	3	Fashion events, architectural design, branding, media
Jing'an	3	Cartoon and comic design, media and advertising
Zhabei	3	Industrial design, architectural design, packing/printing design
Pudong	3	Software, technology consultation, cartoon and comic, exhibitions and conferences, tourism
Huangpu	2	Consultation and planning, advertising, visual arts, cartoon and comics
Putuo	2	Architectural design, visual arts, software design
Minhang	1	Arts

Source: SCIC (2006).

accommodates artists and design companies within an area of 41,000 square metres.

The Bridge 8 (*bahaoqiao*) is a much smaller piece of real estate, taking up a floor area of 15,000 square metres. Formerly the Shanghai Automobile Brake Company, it now has transformed into one of the most cosmopolitan of all the centres, generating consumer fashion products. Again the space is rented out to several international companies, presumably adding a greater focus on innovation. Other clusters that have reclaimed industrial space include the Shanghai Fashion Industry Park in Tianshan Road, Changning District (formerly the Shanghai Automobile Industry Clutch Factory); Zhuowei 701, now a 'creative centre' (following renovation of the Shanghai Knit Sock Factory); the Tianshan Software Park (formerly the Shanghai Shuanglu Refrigerator Plant); and the Leshan Software Park (formerly the Shanghai Xinfeng Yarn-dye Fabric Mill).

On 6 December 2005, the Shanghai Creative Window was formally instituted as the coordinating office of the Shanghai Creative Industry Centre's activities and enterprises. Situated on Huaihai Road in the Luwan District of Shanghai's CBD, the Window combines exhibition space with administration. It communicates information about local and international developments through its website. Together with the Shanghai Creative Industries Association, administered by the Shanghai Propaganda Department, the Creative Window assists in coordinating events such as the Shanghai International Creative Industry Expo, a yearly festival each November that features an 'avenue of creativity' – 'a space for experiencing creative life, including creative comics, hip-pop dance shows, creative food, creative furniture, creative clothes, publications, antiques and so on' (SCIC Publicity brochure).

Chongqing and the Ecology Business District

While Shanghai has established an international reputation for its business ethic, its entrepreneurial spirit and its cosmopolitanism, the city of Chongqing illustrates the aspirations of an industrial zone transforming into an international city. Chongqing is a massive metropolis in central south China. The world's largest city, counting 31.5 million people,[2] Chongqing is one of China's four municipalities (the others are Beijing, Shanghai and Tianjin). The city became an autonomous municipality in 1997, separating from Sichuan Province, whose capital is the smaller city of Chengdu. The economic 'growth pole' for Sichuan province and the gateway to the west, Chongqing city sprawls relentlessly along the intersection of the Yangzi (Yangtze) and Jialing rivers, providing a night panorama that rivals Shanghai, although less flamboyant in its high rise design.

Chongqing's history dates back to the mythical state of Ba from the eleventh century BC. In the Sui dynasty the city was named the Yu prefecture. Nowadays the term *bayu* culture describes the cultural heritage of the city. The current name, Chongqing, means double celebration, and is attributed to the Emperor Guangzong of the Southern Song dynasty, when China's economic centre moved from the northern Song capital of Kaifeng towards the south-west.

During the 1930s and 1940s war with Japan allowed Chongqing to transform into an industrial military complex. Factories moved inland from Shanghai and other coastal cities. The city was the stronghold of General Chiang Kai-Chek, who led the nationalist government (*guomindang*) against the Communists before his defeat and subsequent retreat to Taiwan in 1949. During the 1960s, Chongqing began its surge as a heavy industry centre. Important industries now include mining, iron and steel, aluminium, military, car and motorcycle production, chemical, textiles, machinery, electronics and building materials. Downstream from the epicentre of the Three Gorges project, Chongqing is also a beneficiary of the tourism industry although the ever-present haze, a combination of pollution and fog, diminishes the attractiveness of the city.[3]

Chongqing's makeover has proceeded on the back of high-tech infrastructure. In 1988, the national Torch Plan was instituted by the Ministry of Science and Technology, a move to establish a distribution of high-tech industrial parks. Chongqing established its first park in 1990, currently one of 29 national-level parks. In 2000, the municipal government established a new 130-square-kilometre district in northern Chongqing in response to the central government's Western development plan, a determination to link the underdeveloped western regions with the more prosperous coastal cities. Within this new high-tech development zone is located the Ecology Business District (EBD), spanning some 50 square kilometres. The EBD is promoted as an alternative to the central business district (CBD). In the glossy EBD publicity book published by the local district government the following rationale appears: 'The concept of the EBD is a turning point in which labour-intensive, resource-hungry industries turn into intellectually intensive and sustainable ones' (EBD 2005: 19). It further notes, 'Traditional CBDs have disadvantages such as overcrowded buildings, heavy transportation burdens, a poor environment, a "dead-city phenomenon, office illness etc"' (EBD 2005). In 2005, the three leading industries in the EBD were nominated as information technology, bio-pharmaceuticals and instrument design and manufacture.

In 2006, the Chongqing Municipal government announced plans to develop creative industries as part of its Eleventh Five-Year Plan. Chongqing was signalling its intent to embrace the new economy, citing the creative industries developments of Shanghai and Beijing, already under way. Chongqing's ambitions in these 'clean non-polluting' industries are underpinned by the 66503 Plan. In short, this plan estimates that by 2010 creative industries will contribute 6 per cent of GDP, provide 60,000 jobs, and account for 50 bases or clusters, three of which will be accredited as national bases. One of the major new research and development infrastructure projects will be a Creative Industries Port (*chuangyi chanye gang*) on the Yangzi River, an 'ideas incubator' incorporating a mixed model of education, research and business.[4]

The EBD was chosen as the location for a national animation base. One of the companies positioned within the EBD is the Chongqing Lele Xiong Cartoon and Animation Development Company. The company's successful product to date had been an animated character, the happy panda (*lele xiong*). When I spoke to the director of the company, she emphasised the challenge facing Chinese animation in changing children's perceptions of local content. The company was working on an animated story called *The Magic Box and Melodies* (*mohe yu gesheng*) that would be educational as well as entertaining, exactly in tune with the specifications of the government policies on ethnic harmony. According to the synopsis this was a tale of a princess whose mother had passed away leaving her a magic box. Once the magic box acquires a collection of 81 melodies from China's 56 minorities, the box would have the powers to defeat evil. Elsewhere in Chongqing, the Chongqing Shimei Animation Co. had set up a base with the support of the Chongqing Media Group and the Sichuan Fine Arts Institute with a brief to produce over 10,000 minutes of animation within two years.

The Chongqing creative industries model has six focal points, one more than Shanghai. Indeed, there is much similarity. All of Shanghai's sectors are represented, with the addition of software design. The policy language is also similar with an emphasis on use of old factories and buildings, and the development and attraction of creative talent – in particular drawing Chongqing expatriates back home. The sweeteners include a creative industries development fund, low-interest loans, rewards for outstanding innovations, tax deductions for R&D investment, and tax deductions for employees' education expenses. Animation businesses in particular are eligible for 3 per cent tax rebate, complying with national policy.

The creative industries strategy in Chongqing embraces the traditional cultural industries with an emphasis on the theme of Ba culture. 'Cultural experience areas' include Guotai opera theatre, the Three Gorges Museum, folk culture parks, and the Hongyadong baguo retail and consumer fashion district, an area adjacent to the Yangzi River with a range of shops selling local experiences, a range of handicrafts, as well as a modern theatre space. Also located in the Chongqing Fine Arts Institute is the Tank Loft, formerly a factory for the production of military personnel carriers. Now it sells itself as the Chongqing Contemporary Art Centre. Graduates of the Arts Institute receive preferential access to these studios which, according to director Yu Ke, act as a vehicle to promote local artists' work, without the dangers of over-commercialisation (interview with author, 15 October 2006).

Beijing: the Capital Recreation District and the Central Business District

Beijing's ambitions in the 'cultural creative industries' have closely followed developments in Shanghai. As I discussed in Chapter 6, the move to accommodate the international discourse of creative industries occurred more rapidly in Shanghai than elsewhere in mainland China. While the Chaoyang district government in Beijing had commissioned reports as early as 2004, the dissemination of the idea among Beijing's propaganda officials took longer. The fourth session of the Beijing Municipal Council, which followed the fourth session of the Twelfth Beijing Municipal People's Congress subsequently ratified Beijing's model as 'cultural creative industries'. This term was effectively a compromise. In order to green light some of the proposals earmarked for development it was necessary to receive endorsement from the Beijing Committee of the Chinese People's Consultative Conference. Many of the current proposals are already accommodated within the Beijing Urban Planning Scheme 2004–2020; others are initiated under the city's Eleventh Five-Year Plan.

By mid 2006, Beijing already had 10 established cultural industry clusters or bases; another eight are scheduled to begin development over the next four years. Established centres include the Zhongguancun Creative Industries Leading Base, the Deshengyuan Industrial Design and Creative Industries Base, the craft and antiques cluster at Panjiayuan market, artists' spaces and lofts at Dashanzi, the Songzhuang artist village in the eastern district of Tongzhou, as well as several leisure and cultural tourism theme parks.[5] Major proposed developments include the Capital Recreation District (CRD) in the western region of Beijing, the relocation of China Central TV, Phoenix TV and Beijing TV to the central Chaoyang District, and a Cultural Creative Park in Tongzhou District, headlined by the Sunchime Cartoon and Animation Company.

Of these developments it is worth noting a few. The relocation of China Cental Television (CCTV) to the eastern third ring road in Chaoyang is a massive project, only topped by the Beijing Olympics construction, significantly also in Chaoyang district. The new CCTV headquarters has been designed by the Dutch architect Rem Koolhaas, a 230-meter-high arch formed by two L-shaped towers containing over 400,000 square metres of floor space. Koolhaas himself is upbeat about China as a place of creativity, a place where international companies can design and experience 'new architecture', free from the restrictions placed on development in the Netherlands presumably. The relocation of CCTV will reshape Beijing's CBD, bringing the talents of media professionals closer into the business services milieu. Chaoyang is already the most clustered business centre in China, taking into account the high proportion of foreigners working in embassies and in businesses (Hui 2006). The district has 60 tourist hotels, 12 of which have 5- or 6-star ratings. However, the relocating of CCTV and the re-imagining of Chaoyang will also mean that thousands of people will be forced to relocate elsewhere. Real estate prices, already high, will escalate, making the district unaffordable for poorer Beijing residents.

One of the least visible landmarks of Chaoyang, at least for its residents, is the 798 artists' collective at Dashanzi. However, the name 798 is well known internationally and 798 is one of the top tourist attractions for many visitors to Beijing. For both artists and visitors alike 798 is a symbol of Beijing's new openness. The name refers to the electronics factory complex that pre-existed the current gentrification. The 798 is situated within a larger industrial cluster initially called Joint Factory 718 between ring roads 4 and 5 on Beijing's central north-east. The area originally contained multiple factories designed in the Bauhaus style by East German architects in the 1950s in the Dashanzi locality. It was the largest East German project in China. In 1964, the 718 Joint Factory was disbanded and six sub-factories took on their own lives. In 2001, the factories joined together under the name Seven Star China Electronic Corporation (*qixing huadian jituan*).

The area includes a power generation Factory 751 which is adjacent to the arts centre and currently remains under heavy security. The area was initially used for public art projects by the Beijing Central Academy of Fine Arts when it moved during its transitional period to a semi-conductor factory one block away from 798 in September 1995. However, the precinct was first made available for individual studios in 2000 when the Academy moved out. Within two years the area had transformed into an exhibition space featuring China's avant-garde. The design elements of 798 were further enhanced by Chinese artists who had experienced loft-style living overseas (He 2004). The future of 798 is currently under local government review. Urban planners have recommended extending the cultural tourism aspects to include the adjacent 751 factory and even turn one of the gas tanks into a boutique brewery, together with landscaping to beautify what is regarded as an eyesore. The 798 regularly utilises its space for international exhibitions, music events and performance.

The Cultural and Creative Park in Tongzhou District (formerly Tong County) is another ambitious project, the scale of which is difficult to imagine in developed countries. Tongzhou is the location of the Songzhuang artist village, a collective of contemporary artists, exhibiting in a new purpose built complex funded by the local government. In the Jin and Yuan Dynasties (twelfth and thirteenth centuries CE), the region was the northern axis of the Great Canal leading to Hangzhou. The district's economic success has been attributed to high-tech industries as well as manufacturing, food processing and garment production. The relocation of the Sunchime Cartoon and Animation Group's administration from Hunan Province to Beijing in 2006 provided the impetus for the rescaling of creative industry ambitions. Sunchime is the producer of China's most successful animation export, *The Blue Cat* (see Chapter 10). The Chairman of the Board of Directors at Sunchime, Sun Wenhua, is a person who has moved rapidly from Made in China to Created in China. Mr Sun was formerly responsible for the reconstruction of the new city of Wenzhou, deep in the heart of Zhejiang's boom manufacturing economy. Plans for the new Cultural Creative Park in Tongzhou include the Sunchime Cartoon and Online Game Industrial Base. The 34-hectare park is described as 'integrating cultural resources, technological innovation and artistic creativity to form an industrial cluster' (Sunchime: *Using Motion to Create Emotion* 2006).

The Zhongguancun Creative Industries Leading Base was established 5 May 2005. It occupies a total area of 9.89 hectares with a construction area of 7 hectares. The Haidian Book City currently occupies central position. The base is close to the Beijing University Science and Technology Park, the Tsinghua University Science and Technology Park, the People's University Cultural Industries Park, the Beitaipingzhuang Animation Design Centre and the Ganjiakou District Architectural Design zone. The Zhongguancun Creative Industries Base includes digital media technology, internet-based industries, and digital entertainment software enterprises, cartoon and animation incubators. Companies locating in the centre include Yahoo China and Tengxun and China Netcom.

Beijing's ambitions reflect the growing competition within China for investment and status. A range of policies offers incentives to those that qualify as 'cultural creative enterprises'. The Zhongguancun high-tech zone encourages enterprises that engage in high-technology and new media. Sweeteners include a two-year tax freeze.[6] Universities that engage in research and development that embodies technology transfer are exempt from operational taxes as well as receiving an income tax dispensation on fees earned from their consulting activities. Eligible creative enterprises in Beijing can claim 150 per cent deduction on technical development costs as well as 2.5 per cent of staff education costs. Generous management fee depreciation benefits also apply to enterprises depending on their level of investment. The Beijing Municipal government has also established an RMB 0.5 million 'cultural creative industries development fund' as well as similar 'cluster infrastructure fund'. In summary, these policies are broad and strategic, although the question always remains as to how transparent the governance of the schemes will be, taking into account the *guanxi* that inevitably seems to follow investment.

Of all the current and scheduled projects, however, perhaps the most ambitious is the Capital Recreation District. In 2007, the Beijing Iron and Steel Factory in the western district of Shijingshan will reduce its operation allowing construction to commence on a new 'integrated services district'. The factory will be moved further outside Beijing in Hebei Province, and with it most of the pollution and most of its 10,000 workers. The new modern district will accommodate members of China's creative class, to use Richard Florida's felicitous phrase. The CRD, with the support of the local government as part of the district's Eleventh Five-Year Plan, will offer relocation benefits to firms, including software developers, mobile communication, animation, and video games companies. The development will also lure creative talent by offering incentives including Beijing residency permits and rent-free apartments. The site is already being referred to as the Beijing Cyber Recreation Industry Base. There are hopes that spill-overs from Zhongguancun, sometimes referred to as China's Silicon Valley, will occur, especially as Zhongguancun rents are now increasing. As China edges closer to the innovation frontier, Zhongguancun is repositioning itself as more than just a massive high-tech agglomeration. A Shijingshan high-tech development space with the CRD will be administered by Zhongguancun district government. According to the pre-publicity, the registered population of the CRD is estimated to remain under 520,000 people with services industries accounting for 40 per cent of the economic output.

Concluding remarks: real estate or real innovation?

The idea of media and creative clusters makes good sense in today's China, given the legacy of collective production: the Peoples' Communes (1950s–1960s), the town and village enterprises (TVEs) (1980s–1990s), the science and technology parks (1990s–2000s), and the media conglomerates (instigated in the late 1990s–early 2000s). In differing ways these collective models responded to social and economic reforms. The common ingredients were a high degree of hierarchical management, favourable investment policies, and state supervision.

Table 8.2 Value of China's domestic cultural sector to GDP (comparison National, Beijing, Shanghai, Chongqing)

	GDP/local GDP (100 million yuan)	Added value of cultural industry (100 million yuan)	Added value of cultural industry to GDP/local GDP
2003			
National	135822.8	3577	2.6%
Beijing	5023.8	246.1	4.89%
Shanghai	6694.23	391.46	5.84%
Chongqing	2272.82		
2004			
National	159878.3	3440	2.15%
Beijing	6060	328.7	5.4%
Shanghai	8072.83	445.73	5.5%
Chongqing	2692.81	52.4	1.95%
2005			
National	183084.8		
Beijing	6814.5	388.4*	5.69%
Shanghai	9154.78	509.23	5.6%
Chongqing	3070.49	66.67	2.17%

Source: Chinese Academy of Social Science: data compiled from *Blue Book of China's Cultural Industries* series

*According to Beijing's new statistical standard for cultural creative industry, the added valued for Beijing 2005 is 700.4 billion yuan, or 10.2% of GDP (see http://www.beinet.net.cn/enews/200612/t146634.htm).

However, while the new clusters are favoured for their 'cultural economy' benefits and their capacity to attract talent, questions will remain: about whether this will lead to 'creative fields' within non-creative policy environments, whether they will produce innovation, and whether the emphasis on regional specialisation will impact upon spontaneously evolving diversity.

It would be quite easy to dismiss the breakout of such clusters, bases, parks and gardens in China as expediency. After all, this is a nation in which the cookie-cutter approach to policy making is widely regarded as normal practice. From such a perspective it is indeed 'fast policy' but underlying this is a deep-seated vision that these strategies will work. Some critics have suggested that parks are uncreative places. One of my respondents suggested that these were places for nerds; why did you need a park anyway in the virtual age?[7] Isn't it better to be close to business districts? Indeed, can you assume that creative inspiration will ferment in such places?

Indeed, these developments are more likely to produce the kinds of results intended if there is the right balance between hard and soft infrastructure. While the first term is fairly self-explanatory, the latter term refers to the enabling 'glue' that makes creative milieus and clusters work, that allows ideas and inventions to be incubated, and downstream applications to be commercialised. In China in the past, the practice has been to locate artists in places where their activities can be monitored and regulated. In order for these processes to occur, such places must remain open systems, and this means providing physical and mental space so that a critical mass of businesses, entrepreneurs, intellectuals, administrators and power brokers can share ideas.

The Chinese 'development script' reads that creative clusters will assist media and cultural industries to become more competitive. Clusters were given credibility by Harvard Business School's Michael Porter (1998). However, Porter's work was referring to places like Silicon Valley (California), Route 128 (Boston) and numerous other manufacturing districts from Denmark to Italy to Thailand and Japan. Porter argues that the geographical concentration of companies working within a particular field produces 'competitive advantage', which impacts upon the business, the area and even the wider economy. It needs to be established if these are in fact viable clusters, as discussed by Porter, Curtin and Scott, or just collectivism re-bottled in pseudo-economic jargon. One of the critical success factors is structures of governance. To put it bluntly: if we take Chinese 'independent innovation' at face value, these clusters ought to have a greater capacity to self-organize. Will they just be another extension of government? Will the heavy hand of government stifle innovation and constrain creativity? Will they generate real change?

9 Reality TV, post-collectivism and the long tail

In 2005, China's cultural trade deficit hit the news. Despite a massive domestic market China is a net importer of cultural products. A press conference convened in April by the State Council Information Office allowed Ding Wei, the assistant Minister of Culture, the platform to announce the nation's deficit in international cultural trade. This was what might be colloquially termed 'a wake-up call'. China needed to look outwards. Figures published in the *2004 Yearbook of China's Publishing Industry* revealed that the ratio of imports of cultural products to exports stood at 10.3 to 1. In 2003, China had imported 12,516 copyrighted books and had exported just 811 (see Table 9.1).[1]

Meanwhile, the Deputy Director of the Ministry of Culture's marketing department, Zhang Xinjian, admitted that the cultural share of Chinese cultural products in the USA was close to zero. In diagnosing the cause of the deficit, he pointed out how cultural products in overseas markets mostly target Chinese consumers. With distribution mainly occurring through Chinese communities rather than the international mainstream, these demographics currently represent lower value markets. A great deal of Chinese film and TV content is accessed through Chinese video shops located in Chinatown districts (Cunningham and Sinclair 2001). Citing the success of Zhang Yimou's *The House of Flying Daggers*, which recouped US$12.5 million in America and US$10 million in Japan, he said, 'Cultural trade dominates in today's international culture market. We have to adapt' (*The China Daily* 19 April 2005).

How does China adapt? How does it overcome its cultural trade deficit? Furthermore, to what extent is this cultural trade deficit linked to a creativity deficit? In August 2006, I asked one of China's leading media entrepreneurs about China's cultural trade deficit.[2] What did he think of the national debate? What was needed? He replied in two words: 'good content'.

What is good content? According to the TV Program Marketing Department of the China International TV Corporation, good Chinese content first and foremost reflects national culture and socialist ideology. The company's annual promotional brochure for trade fairs (2005–2006) lists 12 historical costume dramas, 11 contemporary and modern TV dramas, 22 documentaries, 5 game shows and 7 cartoons. Leaving aside the obvious fact that China is competitive in producing historical drama, mainly due to low production costs, the category where China

Table 9.1 China's copyright import and export statistics for 2003 and 2004

	Copyright import (items)	*Copyright export (items)*
China's copyright import and export statistics 2003[a]		
Total	15555	1427
Books	12516	811
Magazines	542	—
Music CDs	1068	473
Audio-visual disks	564	—
Electronic publications	180	35
Software	478	—
Film	132	—
TV programmes	10	108
Others	65	—
China's copyright import and export statistics 2004[b]		
Total	11746	1362
Books	10040	1314
Magazines	411	—
Audio productions	331	4
Visual productions	159	4
Electronic publications	143	39

Sources:
a *Statistics of China's cultural and creative industry 2004 in brief,* The State Statistics Bureau.
b *Report on development of China's cultural industry: (2006),* Chinese Academy of Social Sciences Publishing.

ought to compete – in contemporary and modern drama – is dominated by heavy political stories such as *Twenty Days to the Dawn of Shanghai (linjie 20 tian)*, *The Eighth Route Army (balu jun)*, and melodramatic tearjerkers such as *Chasing My Love (zhuigan wo keneng diule de aiqing)*, a story about a bungled vasoligation operation in which the main protagonist succumbs to lung cancer after finding that the daughter he rejected is in fact his biological offspring. The images of characters of the TV dramas advertised are sombre and joyless. In comparison, trade brochures of Korean broadcasters reach out to the market with positive youthful dynamism.[3]

Demand for ideological content is not high in international markets. However, there is an expectation among senior propaganda officials that ideology needs to be central to the Chinese export profile. Unfortunately, such kinds of drama ultimately diminish the profile and lower the value of Chinese content; these dramas are regarded by international viewers, many of whom are expatriates, as bearing the stigma of 'old China' (see Zhu *et al.* 2008). Animation, regarded as a growth market in China, is directed almost exclusively at children, in comparison with sophisticated Japanese, US, Korean and European animation content which targets both youth and adult audiences. Even when favourable investment and tax write-off policies and training initiatives are offered as a remedy for bland domestic production, the emphasis falls on pedagogy more than creativity. Can media content break free of the 'mouthpiece of the Chinese Communist Party and government' mould? Can public institutions learn to function as industries?

Certainly this strikes at the heart of the creativity paradox as we understand it in China. In order to produce 'good content' there needs to be more emphasis on original value creation, one of the core ingredients of the creative industries. However, the emphasis on novelty in China is low. Intellectual property is misunderstood and widely abused. Diversity of expression, and diversity of cultural forms, is constrained by national cultural policy, which in the recent past has served to protect the population from dangerous ideas. Certainly, the legacy of the recent past hinders 'creative destruction'. How do you promote risk taking in a nation where straying from accepted formulas is likely to result in criticism? How do you change the innovation ecology? How do you encourage businesses to spend resources developing original content in an environment where there is indeterminate reward for innovation?

Copyright is central to success in industries such as television, advertising and animation. Indeed, the UK definition of the creative industries is upfront about this: 'activities which have their origin in individual creativity, skill and talent and which have the potential for wealth and job creation through the generation and exploitation of intellectual property' (DCMS 1998). These industries are characterised by novelty, compared with manufacturing components or widgets. However, because of high sunk costs many media products are based on formats and genres. Consequently, under-capitalised media industries tend towards conservatism – following the leader, copying, making sequels, prequels, spin-offs and reversions.

When media is public funded, as in the case of public broadcasting, this is often justified as a mandate to take risks and be innovative. But, for a number of reasons more to do with ideology and national stability, the fundamental axioms of competition and risk do not carry as much importance in China. Until recently, China has valued content for its use value rather than its exchange value (to use a standard Marxist line). How does China break the mould? Will a greater focus on rights rectify the cultural trade deficit? Should China ascribe to John Howkin's (2001) formula for a creative economy ($CE = CP \times T$), where the creative product (CP) is linked to a transaction process (T). In order to facilitate such transactions, the processes by which profit and risk are shared need to be agreed. In China, there are multiple ways in which this agreement occurs, as I shall describe below.

The question of how money is made from creative content industries in China is convoluted. The black market strips away much of the available revenue. What does this mean for copyright? In most developed media economies content generation begins with the core intellectual property (IP), for instance the creative work of authors, journalists, producers, songwriters, or independent artists. These rights are then sold based on a variety of deals (up-front fee, share of revenue, licence fee, package deals and revenue sharing). The next stage is packaging, whereby the final product is produced (the book, magazine, TV programme etc). The pricing principle then determines how this is marketed. Options include cover price, free-to-air TV, subscription or free distribution. Finally, the delivery to the end user is mediated by distributors, marketing agencies and advertisers.

The content generation and distribution process in China is far removed from this model. First, the notion of exclusivity in relation to ownership of rights is widely ignored and often misunderstood by creators.[4] State agencies have been culpable in exploiting the intellectual property of artists. During a forum at the Chinese Communication University in October 2006, one of China's leading comedians gave an impassioned speech, detailing how television stations had 'stolen' his work. In the past, most performers would happily contribute their services to variety formats for an upfront fee, a fee which was minimal in special celebrations such as the nationally broadcast New Year's show (*chunjie lianhui*). Many of these performances have since been reformatted in VCD and DVD and used to generate further income. According to the aforementioned comedian, financial benefits have not been passed on to the performers.[5] Because artists, writers and journalists have been employed by the state, and because media institutions are state-owned, the 'work' belongs to the state in the absence of any rights distribution contract. Unsurprisingly, state ownership, combined with inefficient rights models, has acted as a disincentive to create original content. This is beginning to change. The emergence of the independent artist as entrepreneur is a recent phenomenon in China, along with new varieties of copyright regimes, royalty payments and licensing models. There have been a number of instances, particularly in book publishing where authors have sued, or attempted to sue over alleged copyright infringement.

The innovation ecology and the long tail

The conventional model through which the media has sold the value of its audience to advertisers, relying on big budget 'blockbusters', supplemented by industry accounting techniques is changing globally as subscription services, multi-channelling, concept programming (e.g. reality TV) and niche media products displace mass media. In particular, subscription has become an emergent viable business model. Access invites the user to enter a world of associated products and services, or the freedom to choose from a buffet of premium services. Since the early 1990s the viability of mass media (television, popular magazines and press) has relied primarily on income derived from advertising. In this changing environment China's low-cost media market provides some indicators for global media, which is struggling to deal with the demise of spot advertising. In Chinese television, ancillary merchandising is fast supplementing, and even replacing traditional spot advertising. In online news and entertainment media, subscription models are dominant.

As I have argued there are five layers in the innovation ecology. At one end is 'Made in China', the factories and workshops that provide fabrication services; at the other are the new planned clusters – the so-called creative parks – that will unlock potential value, train talent, and create strong Chinese cultural brands.

In between these layers new models of collective consumer behaviour are also emerging – the beginnings of China's long tail. The term 'long tail' was coined by Chris Anderson in 2004. It refers to how the economics of abundance – the increasing access to more varieties and genres of music, more television channels, and more books – has inverted the traditional reliance on experts and critics to ascribe value and determine taste (Anderson 2006). Increasingly users are influencing other users' consumer habits by sharing evaluations. The internet is the key platform for this peer-review network. One report even claims we are leaving the information age and entering into the 'recommendation age' (in Anderson 2006: 107). In China, where producers of media have not taken account of demand, mainly due to the absence of strong competition and restrictive cross-media policies, the long-tail effect becomes an important element of the innovation ecology.

The shift from mass to niche has important implications for how creative products are distributed. China is not insulated from global disruptive technologies despite its highly organised propaganda system. To illustrate this point, I want to return briefly to the orthodox model of cultural production in China. The quota model that prevailed in China during the periods of high socialism (from the 1940s to the end of the 1970s) was an industrial approach. The party-state placed a premium on standardised production. It sought to eliminate the idiosyncratic character of artistic activities and individual competences. In this top-down model there was no feedback loop, and no need for one; there were no consumers, only masses in need of education and the Chinese Communist Party was the ultimate source of truth. All recommendations emanated from one source. While there were alternative channels of distribution, there were risks associated with disseminating alternative truths. Effectively a closed systems model, this scientific management of the cultural sphere maximised propaganda efficiencies. Chinese artists, along with teachers, were 'engineers of the soul' and their tasks were to help build the nation, not to provoke the conscience of the nation.

The transition, beginning in the early 1980s, from a planned socialist production model towards a competitive enterprise model led many cultural producers directly into the Made in China layer; that is, they gravitated towards the bottom segment of the ecology. While not exactly a 'race to the bottom', it did lead to increased competition to provide services for foreign companies. Perhaps this was a legacy of cultural producers responding to direction or being unwilling to produce new ideas for fear of criticism. In the bottom layer of the ecology the creative execution occurs at a distance. Fashion products are designed in Japan and made in China, TV dramas are scripted in Taiwan and shot in China, and animation is conceptualised in the USA and rendered in China.

The cultural implications of imitation

As markets emerged for cultural products during the 1980s, fabrication, duplication, and copying became dominant business models. This is the second layer. Globalisation, while facilitating the cross-border movement of intermediate products, notably technology, leads to the widespread replication of products.

The propensity to imitate in China, however, can not be simply blamed on global-isation. The problem is much deeper in the national psyche. On a more fundamental level, it is the legacy of an education system based on memorisation; it is the inher-itance of a political regime that has sought to systematise production; and it is a consequence of state ownership of media institutions.

The strategic business model of the market has been mimetic isomorphism, a desire to succeed while avoiding political criticism. In China the predisposition to imitate brings with it advantages of speed to market without the outlay of resources in testing (R&D). It is also a form of quality assurance; it assures that the prod-uct passes regulatory barriers that are intended to normalise and often standardise cultural expression, for instance, the periodic edicts from the Chinese Propaganda Department prohibiting Chinese television personalities using Western slang. This standardisation applies to the cultural sector as much as the industrial sector. Isomorphism, imitation and 'localisation' have prevailed because the regulatory system has until recently prevented media businesses from operating outside their regional or provincial markets. In an environment of such 'duplicate construction' (*chongfu jianshe*) it is easier to copy success than invest time and scarce resources in creating intellectual property that will probably be 'exploited' by someone else. A vicious circle prevails.

The problem becomes one of dependency – dependency on other peoples' creativity, and on other nations' innovation. This cloning culture hinders the incu-bation of good content, which as I was reminded, is so essential to overcoming China's cultural trade deficit. However, the positive news is that integration into the regional creative economy is slowly changing the mindset and moving the ecological benchmarks from imitation to innovation. In addition, China's new long tail, illustrated by a generation of bloggers, online gamers and music down-loaders, is transforming the ecology from within at the same time as clustering policies are regulating production. In this dynamic ecology, the Chinese Commu-nist Party is no longer the epicentre of truth. Instead of being peer reviewed by committees, ideas and content are peer reviewed by communities. Indeed, it could be said that China is moving through a stage of arrested development, an era of post-collectivism.

In the following sections I show how China is gradually breaking out of the non-creative unproductive patterns of the past and is moving upwards in the value chain. State intervention is playing a role, as is international expertise. I first look at successes in reality television programming. The examples are *Supergirl* (*chaoji nüsheng*), *Into Shangrila* (*zouru xianggelila*), and *Win in China* (*ying zai Zhongguo*) – three variations on the theme of elimination. Following this, I show how television drama co-productions have brokered greater awareness of revenue sharing models.

Reality TV

The genesis of reality television (*zhenren xiu*) in China provides interesting insights into the emerging innovation ecology. Much of the reality television that has appeared on television screens in China since 2001 has not been original. In other words, they are imitations of successful programmes created elsewhere. Producers' claims of serendipitous discovery have faded into confessions of cloning. From a copyright infringement perspective successful litigation depends on the degree of 'substantial similarity' (see Keane *et al.* 2007). However, leaving aside the issue of originality and similarity for the moment, the reality show has provided the vehicle for the evolution of the Chinese long tail. Nowhere is this more evident than in the Idol show copy, *Supergirl*. This is a talent format in which amateur singers compete for an ultimate prize. *Supergirl* was produced by Hunan Satellite Television, first in 2004 with a male version, and then with a female show in 2005 (literally translated as 'super female voice').

Supergirl took south China by storm with huge numbers of applicants registering in Changsha (16,000), Nanjing (11,000), and Wuhan and Chengdu (each 10,000). Like the franchised international versions of *Idol*, the three judges in *Supergirl* are strong personalities, are often rude, and refrain from expressing emotions. Also like the international versions, interactivity adds value through internet sites and is accounted for by SMS voting. Cross-platform collaboration with internet service providers helped *Supergirl* to maintain consistent high ratings. The production company likewise followed the international practice of using such talent shows to sign successful participants to recording contracts. In short, the process generates a relatively low-cost form of talent scouting. The director admitted that the programme took similar overseas programmes as 'reference models', but he was quick to claim that the producers tried every possible means to differentiate the formula (Keane *et al.* 2007). This localisation included a more complex system of adjudication in which selected audience members get to pass comments directly to the three judges, including adjudication on the judge's own performance (Duan and Deng 2006).

In the context of Chinese TV history the economic dividends from *Supergirl* were astonishing. The cost of voting was one yuan RMB (eight yuan equal one US dollar). In the semi-finals, each contestant received an average of three million votes despite an imposed limit of 15 votes per day for each phone number. Fans overcame this ruling by multiple voting on their parents and friends' phones. The company responsible for marketing the performers and aggregating ancillary rights such as merchandising, concerts, and CDs – the aptly named *Entertainment Package Company* (*yule baozhuang gongsi*) – accrued RMB 78 million in revenue. Telecom carriers associated with the show recouped RMB 9 million, receiving 15 per cent of each SMS call. The other 85 per cent from SMS was apportioned among Hunan Satellite TV, the producers, and other interests. Altogether, Hunan Satellite Television earned RMB 68 million while the producer Shanghai Tianyu reaped RMB 27.5 million. Other big winners were the internet service providers, which provided constant updates and gossip to SMS subscribers. They recouped RMB 21 million. A further one million was earned by companies who advertised on dedicated *Supergirl* web and chat sites (Duan and Deng 2006). The biggest winner, however, may well have been the show's sponsor, the Mongolian Cow Yoghurt company, whose income from its products associated with the TV show totalled RMB 550 million.

Tie-ins, product placements, and the numerous merchandising activities of the stars during, and since the show finished, are important landmark developments in the commercialisation of the Chinese media. The programme was also noteworthy because it generated alternative models of collectivism. Initially, it involved the masses directly as willing participants; they were viewers but they were also subjects of the programme. The audience were able to cast votes and in doing this they quickly and spontaneously formed coalitions of support for the various finalists, communicating and organising online. In the process, the show also created a new surge in fan culture in China. The transliterated term *fensi*, literally meaning vermicelli, was coined to replace the standard word for fan, *mi*, which had the connotation of a lost and confused follower. The fans of the eventual winner, Li Yuchun, self-identified as *yumi* (corn), cleverly inverting the word *mi* (second tone pronunciation) to the culinary (third tone) *mi*. Other finalists had fan groupings and these would hold up placards in the audience (Duan and Deng 2006; Keane *et al.* 2007). With three contestants originating from Chengdu, loyal fans formed the 'Snack Food Federation of Chengdu'. Other smaller 'federations' were founded to support contestants of various geo-cultural linguistic origins – for instance, lychee, milk powder, honey, chicken wings and cashew nuts. In a nation where products of television were hitherto regarded as 'spiritual food', fans' self-identification with tasty food rather than passive masses (*guanzhong*) is evidence of both agency and audience segmentation. Zhong and Wang (2006) points to the scale of collective activity – arguably the largest legitimate display of non-governmental organization in modern China. This was a visible demonstration of the long tail.

Into Shangrila

Supergirl was not the first Chinese reality show, but it was a breakthrough media event. A lesser known precedent was *Into Shangrila* (*zouru xianggelila*), produced in 2002 by the Beijing Weihan Cultural Production Company. The format used was 'substantially' similar to the international *Survivor* (CBS). According to producer Chen Qiang, the show was a totally new concept in China.

> You asked if this (programming) was influenced by the international formats. Without doubt, it was. However I had not seen *Survivor* when we were starting to plan our programming in October the year before last year. But I had heard that there was such programming in Britain and Europe.
>
> (Interview with author, 15 October 2003)

Into Shangrila was filmed in Sichuan province in the foothills of the Himalayas. Similarities were evident in the wilderness 'reality' and in the competitive endeavours of amateur participants. Two groups, the sun and moon teams, tested their survival skills in a series of challenges, against the elements and against themselves. The promotional material closely echoed its international cousins. The opening credits even saw the word 'China' burning across the ground, a branding strategy reminiscent of the opening credits of the Western versions.

Into Shangrila attempted to generate publicity through its novelty, using similar promotional strategies as *Survivor*. The preparations for the adventure were linked to web-sites and people could follow the events unfold. The programme was sufficiently differentiated from *Survivor* (and sufficiently unsuccessful) to make litigation futile. In the US version there was a visible host; in the Chinese version there was a documentary style voice-over. The US version was shot in open spaces as well as on a purpose-built *Survivor* set, while the Chinese version had no corresponding *Shangrila* set. The emphatic difference, according to the producer, consisted of *before* and *after* visits by producers to each of the 18 contestants' home towns, wrapping the event in the respectable cloak of social documentary.

What is perhaps more interesting than claims of imitation is the vision of using a reality show to break out of geographically bounded media space. The show's contestants had been chosen from 18 different provinces. The producer was even contemplating what the future of Chinese international television could be:

> What will the second generation look like? It will have greater interactivity and it will support and operate more tacitly across other media. What will the third generation look like? It will allow the audiences to interact and communicate more widely, even globally. Our programming can cover a global mediasphere via satellite and represent Chinese ideas as they are being debated. Everyone who can speak mandarin will be able to take part. Maybe we will choose 10 volunteers and 10 honoured guests for our next programme. They might come from all over the world or be drawn from families that speaks mandarin. It can also become internationalised if suitable translating software is available.
>
> (Interview with author, 15 October 2003)

Win in China

Within a couple of years the reality television vehicle had moved on, achieving legitimacy, and in the example of *Supergirl*, some notoriety. In May 2006, China Central Television's economic channel (CCTV Channel 2) launched a programme called *Win in China* (*ying zai Zhongguo*). The developer of the concept was Wang Yifen, previously the host of the popular CCTV talk show *Dialogue* (*duihua*). During a visit to the USA, Wang had witnessed the reality game show *The Apprentice* in which a group of young wanna-be business entrepreneurs pitch their ideas and skills to a panel headed by the US tycoon Donald Trump. As Wang recounts, '*The Apprentice* inspired me. I wanted to use the television medium to select creative innovative talent. *Win in China*'s initial conceptualisation came about this way; the theme idea of innovative start-up accords with the national project and popular sentiment through the government's promotion of the policy of independent innovation' (Chun 2006: 30).

The show advertised for talented participants and unsurprisingly in the context of the *Supergirl* inspired reality TV fever of 2005 there were 120,000 online applicants. From these 3,000 were randomly selected to answer 100 questions; a further cull brought the numbers to 108 candidates (incidentally the number of members of the outlaw brethren in the well-known Ming Dynasty popular classic *The Water Margin*). These 108 were brought to Beijing to undertake an MBA-devised simulation game, following which the field was reduced to 36. The contestants then confront judges including Ma Yun, the CEO of Alibaba.com, Zhang Chaoyang of SOHU, and Xiong Xiaoge from IDG, the show's main sponsor. The top five 'winners' get an opportunity to start up a dream business, including a business operation registration valued at RMB10 million for the winner and ownership of up to 20 per cent of company shares; the next four runners-up also receive lesser but still substantial business registrations.

While the show is ostensibly an imitation of *The Apprentice*, the process of refining is a work-in-progress. The show's producer/editor Hu Bin confided that the *Win in China* format was capable of further adaptation, arguing that it was not fixed and required further modification. Formatting of this kind is widespread in Chinese television; it is always easier to build on someone else ideas than create a new idea. Adaptation is an expedient term in China. Likewise the use of the description 'emulation' to deny copy-catting invokes a Confucian heritage. In effect, whether adaptation or emulation, the process is more about innovation than creativity: here innovation is a downstream activity refining someone else's (upstream) intellectual property without paying a fee. Copying extends to other industry sectors in China including advertising, video games, design, and publishing. The incidence of cloning is itself due to the size and fragmentation of the market; small operators are quick to copy, outrunning the industries' attempts to bring legal action (see Keane *et al.* 2007).

The question of whether such format cloning is progressive or regressive, creative or opportunistic turns on the understanding of original authorship, often an immaterial concept in the Chinese media landscape. Widespread non-compliance to copyright law can to some extent be attributed to historical events and cultural differences. Confucianism emphasised learning by copying while the ideal of communal property has been the dominant ethic for most of the socialist period. However, copyright is a means of regulating supply according to value: that is, if a programme has value, it is in the interest of the producer to restrict its broadcast so that it obtains a higher value. The obverse is that if the producer (copyright owner) is unable to control the distribution of copies, the price of the work will inevitably collapse.

Korea in the regional innovation ecology

In recent years Chinese cultural producers have begun to recognise and learn from the experiences of their East Asian neighbours. China's shift from Made in China to Created in China in some ways replicates the history of the East Asian creative economy. In his book *Created in Japan: from Imitators to World-Class*

Innovators Sheridan Tatsuno (1990) tells of Japan's transition. Following years of imitating and mastering quality, Japan began to emphasise basic research and creative products. Tatsuno was writing in 1990, some 12 years after the creation of the Sony Walkman. He notes that 'during the 1950s and 1960s, Japanese companies produced low-cost imitations; by the end of the 1960s, however, they had achieved the manufacturing quality and product and product reliability that are now acknowledged as global standards' (Tatsuno 1990: 5).

Imitation has been a core strategy of China's other near neighbours. The Republic of Taiwan, and more recently South Korea, found ways to unlock the door to regional and global success in film, animation, video games, and software. Over the past two decades media content in these countries has evolved from being largely imitative of Japanese, and international formats, to becoming innovative and distinctive. Producers and writers in these countries have acknowledged the increasing role of intellectual property as their content has moved from domestic to international markets. Perhaps the most telling example is that of South Korea, which has generated substantial profit from its content industries since the mid 1990s. In the early 1990s the Korean government was alerted to a report that estimated that the box-office value in Korea of the Hollywood blockbuster *Jurassic Park* was equivalent to the sales value of 1.5 million Hyundai (Shim 2006). Not only did this compel *chaebol* such as Hyundai and Samsung to invest in the cable television and movie business, but it brought with it increased awareness of business processes. The *chaebol* lost money during the mid 1990s, mostly in cable TV, and were eventually forced to divest their interests in 'non-core' cultural assets as a condition of the International Monetary Fund Asian crisis 'bail out' in 1997 (Shim 2006). However, corporate management of creative assets had served to increase professionalism. This had important consequences, notably a greater awareness of internationalisation and a preparedness to export culture. The Korean Wave was further stimulated by government support through the Korean Cultural Content Agency (KOCCA), which actively promoted Korea creativity: film, TV drama, animation and music.

The best model of facilitating cultural export success in television content also comes from South Korea. Prior to Korean television dramas achieving breakthrough success in the late 1990s, the Broadcasting Act Enforcement Ordinance of 1991 had mandated that an independent production sector be established to increase efficiency. The major terrestrial broadcasters subsequently set up departments to oversee copyright and international sales. The production funds came from the broadcasters who subsequently claimed the major share of the rights. The export profits of Korean dramas such as *Winter Sonata* in Japan in 2003 and *The Jewel in the Palace* in China in 2005 stimulated greater awareness of copyright and forced the independent production sector to attempt to renegotiate the share of rights with the broadcasters. The broadcasters subsequently refused to compromise, leading the production companies to seek out new marketing strategies and funding mechanisms to ensure greater autonomy. Lee (2008: in press) writes: 'The expanding market has contributed to the concurrent transformation of the local drama production structure, which used to be dominated by the domestic broadcasting industry'.

In short, Korean drama producers became increasingly concerned about international marketing, investment and co-production strategies. Since 2001, co-productions with Korean companies have become more common in China. Early forms of co-production featured Korean stars including Jae Wook Ahn and Na Ra Jang in Chinese dramas. Lee (2008) suggests that these were highly limited forms of collaboration; the programmes were produced in China with Chinese investment and personnel.[6] Other forms of collaboration have since involved extensive use of Korean investment and personnel. With the Chinese government anxious about the dominance of Korean dramas, these co-productions are a way of 'claiming' the production as local content. In addition to this, there are the obvious benefits of cheap production in China, particularly at locations such as the Hengdian World studios in Zhejiang (see Chapter 11).

Taiwanese dramas have also taken advantage of the low-cost location and the access to Chinese markets. In 1998, the most popular drama in mainland China was *Princess Huanzhu* (*Huanzhu gege*), a co-production with Hunan Television based on a script by the Taiwanese writer Qiong Yao, and directed by the Taiwanese Sun Shu-Pei. Since then there have been a number of successful co-productions, as well as a number of ventures that have run into political trouble due to the vexed cross-strait relations between the mainland and Taiwan (see Chen 2008: in press).

Despite many difficulties in negotiating policies, there are good reasons why international companies continue to seek out co-productions and joint ventures. Companies may be seeking to enter the Chinese market and gain a position by which they can enter into future relationships; in other words, absorbing losses in order to gain a foothold. A number of market entry options exist in international media markets: sale of finished content, licensing, joint venture agreements and wholly owned operations or subsidiaries. The first and the last are the most problematic in China's sensitive content industries. Ownership of media companies is off limits to 'foreigners' although a number of strategies exist that allow Chinese media companies to have significant degrees of foreign investment.[7]

Production of programming, in particular co-productions with foreign partners, is constrained by the time-consuming process of submitting programmes to the regulatory bureaus: the SARFT (State Administration of Radio, Film and TV) in film and TV and the SAPP (State Administration of Press and Publishing in the case of publishing: see Appendix).[8] Licensing (including formatting and franchising) means giving over or sharing production and distribution rights, or as seen in the examples above, coping with copy-cats. Finally, joint ventures, mergers, and in particular film, animation and TV co-productions allow greater degrees of revenue sharing based upon tradable rights. Co-productions in particular allow the sharing of expensive production costs and access to markets in both countries. In most instances, co-productions can be counted as local content, thereby increasing opportunities for prime time broadcast. On the negative side, there are often difficulties in shared decision making, lost of control and the risk of opportunistic behaviour (Hoskins *et al.* 2003). In China, moreover, access to local expertise includes knowledge of how to get scripts past the pre-production censorship barriers, and how to encode culturally specific ideas, thus increasing marketability.

These examples of co-production demonstrate how sharing resources has the capacity to reinvigorate production. Whereas adaptation is a limited form of creativity by definition, collaboration in its various manifestations brings with it opportunities to break out of duplicative practices and target multiple markets. Of course, as the examples above also illustrate, collaborations often involve greater financial and political risk. But risk is a fundamental and necessary ingredient of China's engagement with the creative economy (see Caves 2000; Howkins 2001).

10 Joint ventures, franchising and licensing

One way of understanding change in China's media industries is to focus on the nature of linkages, alliances and networks. Perhaps the key development post-2001 is the shift to cross-geographical and cross-platform alliances. The media and creative industries are entering into new forms of associations, including mergers and licensing arrangements with other media and telecommunications providers, as well as joint ventures with international companies.

In this chapter I look at examples of joint ventures and innovative forms of content distribution. I begin with the example of Ningbo Bird, perhaps the most successful Chinese mobile handset producer. Bird's success in climbing the value chain involved a number of key international joint ventures, which were in turn incorporated into successful advertising campaigns. Following this I turn to the Taiwan-based art licensing company Artkey and the popular Mainland children's animation *Blue Cat* (*lan mao*) to demonstrate how intellectual property can operate through licensing and franchising in China. Broadly speaking, licensing refers to a business arrangement in which one company or individual grants another company or individual the right to exhibit or sell its product in return for a specified fee. In contrast, franchising is based on an arrangement between the owner of a concept (the franchisor) who enters into a contract with an independent actor (the franchisee) to sell goods of services under the former's trademark. As Karin Fladmoe-Lindquist notes, 'This approach to franchising involves a set of procedures, designs, management approaches, and services that are to be delivered exactly as specified by the franchisor' (Fladmoe-Lindquist 2000: 198). In addition to these success stories, I examine how Moli Media, a digital content aggregator, formed a partnership of convenience with government in order to secure a revenue stream from the Internet. Such partnerships might seem unusual to many Western critics of China's media, who see the Internet as a mechanism of control. However, the partnership is also strategic in growing the creative content base. The final example illustrates the potential of the Internet to generate instant success stories: this is a tale of 'the long tail', illustrated by Zhou Xixi, China's first ringtone king.

Ningbo Bird

In her book *Brand New China*, Jing Wang considers the Chinese 'blue collar' (*langling shangji*) demographic as evidence of the Chinese long tail. While the affluent managerial stratum, the 'gold-collar', is inclined to conspicuous consumption, the blues are moderately affluent, well-educated and discriminating. They consume less conspicuously than the 'golds'. In short, they look for value and variety, particularly in their choice of mobile phones (Wang 2008).

The growth rate of the Chinese mobile phone market is redefining business models in digital content industries. In addition to generic growth factors associated with economic reforms, mobile telephony has allowed Chinese consumers to bypass fixed-line services connection costs and queues. In a very short period of time, China has emerged as both the global centre of mobile phone manufacturing and the world's largest mass consumer market for mobile handsets and services. China claimed 334 million mobile subscribers by 2004 (MII figures: see SMH 2005). In early 2006, the number was reported in excess of 400 million.

Many features of the Chinese mobile phone market are common the world over. Global brands such as Motorola (USA), Nokia (Finland), Siemens (Germany) and Samsung (Korea) are popular with affluent consumers. China, however, has a highly competitive and crowded market in which over 40 local and international brands tout hundreds of handset models. Businesses are increasingly forced to compete for market share on price. While Chinese branded phones have performed well in these circumstances and account for up to 40 per cent of total Chinese mobile phone sales, such success is not explained away by the resilience of the local industry to competing on the basis of price alone. The case of Ningbo Bird illustrates the learning process; within four years of entering the mobile phone market in 1999, Bird had matched and exceeded its major local competitor, TCL, with a 10 per cent market share by 2003. From being a compositor of components for foreign-branded handsets, by 2002 Ningbo Bird was designing one in seven of the phones it was manufacturing and selling in China.

Ningbo Bird was listed on the Shanghai stock exchange in 2000, the same year that it secured a licence to manufacture mobile telephone handsets. The state-owned conglomerate China Putian was its largest shareholder (Rose 2004). While a beneficiary of state investment, Bird does not have a history of state ownership and in this respect it differs from other Chinese mobile handset manufacturers such as its domestic competitor TCL (Einhorn 2003). Bird was started in the early 1990s by a group of four young engineers to manufacture Chinese-developed pagers. The English name 'Bird' was apparently chosen because the connotations of a small, fast and unfettered entity appealed to the founders (Rose 2004). Likewise, the Chinese name *bodao* translates felicitously as 'leader in communications'. The company became the leading local brand of Chinese pagers, second only to the USA-based electronics manufacturer, Motorola, one of the first communications companies to enter China in the late 1980s. Critical to Bird's success in pagers was the national network of call centres it developed to support the paging service and which also doubled as customer support and retail outlets.

This logistical network also gave Bird a major advantage when it started to move into mobile phone manufacturing in the late 1990s.

The opportunity for Bird to move into manufacturing mobile handsets arrived when French defence communications technology company Sagem was looking for a way to enter the Chinese market. Sagem provided the basic components for mobile phones and Bird provided manufacturing, distribution and customer service. Bird went on to establish partnerships with Korean and Taiwanese components manufacturers and designers, and also began to invest in its own R&D effort, which informed handset design as well as marketing decisions (Einhorn 2003).

In the first year of market entry Bird relied upon advertising developed by a Taiwanese agency to compete with the global brands that dominated the domestic market. This campaign featured a well-known Taiwanese pop star, CoCo Lee. By the end of 2000, Bird had sold about 700,000 handsets. In the Chinese market context, this performance failed to satisfy its ambitions. Bird aimed to improve its position and it achieved this by changing its marketing and communication strategies.

Bird continued to use CoCo Lee as Taiwanese popular culture retains strong appeal in mainland China. But the range of advertising appeals was quickly diversified to take account of a more varied range of market segments. In 2000, Bird switched to a mainland advertising and market research firm, PCBP. This company is unusual in the Chinese advertising landscape because it is one of a very few domestic integrated marketing communication firms. Although there are estimated to be 70,000 advertising agencies in China, most only sell media, for example outdoor advertising space, and provide very few other services to advertisers.

Following the switch to PCBP, and the incorporation of systematic market research into communication strategies, Bird achieved exponential growth, increasing to 2.5 million handsets in 2001, and then 7 million in 2002. By 2003, it was vying with TCL for the title of leading local brand. While international brands such as Motorola and Nokia still dominate in international as well as Chinese domestic markets, the Bird success in carving out a 10 per cent market share is now legendary.

Each year PCBP executed three to four campaigns that relied on different types of appeals to communicate these product attributes and brand values to different market segments in a variety of media. One campaign used a 'global' appeal to convey the luxury status of Bird handsets (Zhou and Belk 2004). Other campaigns emphasised the use of 'advanced' European communications components in two distinct ways: to associate Bird with leading-edge developments in science and technology; and to support youthful appeals to global cosmopolitanism. PCBP also pursued opportunities for high-impact product placement. In a high-profile advertising campaign Bird was a sponsor of the Chinese television coverage of the Sydney 2000 Olympic Games. Journalists involved in the live coverage were provided with Bird handsets to hand to winners so that they could call home from the winners' dais. According to PCBP Director Wu Xiaobo, this campaign associated Bird, a national champion in the technological sector, with 'national champions' in the sporting arena, costing approximately RMB 700,000 (Interview 15 September 2004). In addition, the company gave away 100,000 handsets in 2000.

The Bird success story illustrates the value of joint ventures in creating synergy. The Bird phone maintained its national appeal while inheriting strong technology partners. These strategic alliances were creatively deployed in advertising to enhance the company's profile and brand.

Licensing (Artkey)

The joint venture and co-production model provides advantages of pooling of resources and access to shared knowledge of markets and distribution. Another business model that directly exploits traditional cultural heritage and unique design is licensing and is illustrated by the Taiwanese company Artkey, now operating successfully in China.

Founded in 1997, Artkey is an aggregator of fine art content with rights to over 60,000 artworks from 700 Chinese artists, including artefacts from Taipei's National Palace Museum and the National Taiwan Museum of Fine Arts. Products included in the Artkey repertoire include posters, porcelain, mobile phone greeting cards, fashion accessory designs, home textiles and furnishings and stationery. In April 2006, Artkey launched an exhibition of digital art in the exhibition space of the Shanghai Creative Window. The images were drawn from the work of painters including Qi Baishi and Liu Guosheng. According to CEO Guo Yicheng, 'Artkey provides a way for Asian artists to exploit their intellectual property in international markets' (Interview with author August 2006).

By using the designs of artists on contemporary products and services a process of cultural re-conversion takes place. In the past, according to García Canclini (1992), traditionalists had sought to preserve culture from industrialisation, urbanisation and foreign influence with the result that cultural products and institutions were divided. Artworks were found in museums and biennials while crafts were located in traditional museums and popular fairs. With the growth of electronic cultures, the process of re-conversion has prolonged the existence of cultural capital and facilitated the dissemination of products into new formats – digitised art, multimedia messaging service (MMS) enabled mobile content and contemporary design. With a strong emphasis on indigenous design evident in China, for instance calligraphy, licensing has become the core of Artkey's business model. Products are licensed in galleries and museums and returns are passed on to the artists. Artkey has also ongoing projects with licensees in various industries currently, such as Nokia, Allposter, Plus Licens, Museum Masters International, China Airlines, EVA Air and Sheraton Hotel. Alex Guo considers China's ancient culture to be its most valued resource. The question is how to find the best way of converting these traditional asserts into products that can be licensed, accruing intellectual property rents for the creators. Guo is optimistic of China's creative future and argues that creativity is not the core problem. The answer is how to transform it into an industry and create sustainability.

The Blue Cat

As I discussed in Chapter 8, Sunchime (Sanchen) Cartoon and Animation Company is China's most successful animation company. Its rise to prominence, however, demonstrates the vicissitudes of China's often chaotic copyright system. In the mid 1990s, the Sanchen Cultural Development Company responded to central government policy targeted to develop youth programming in the face of perceived threats to the morals of Chinese youth from international media including Disney (see Table 10.1). Quotas were set to fast track appropriate content and limit the amount of non-Chinese animation. By 2006, these policies had extended to banning 'foreign' animation from Chinese peak hour programming slots.

In 1998, the Sanchen Audio-visual Product Network had been established to operate an online audio-visual product hire service. The company compiled a catalogue called *The New China Stage: Selections of Audio-visual Art* (*xin zhongguo wutai - yingshi yishu jingpin xuan*), which was eventually edited into the Sanchen Audio-visual Archive. In 2000, Sanchen and Hunan Eastern Cartoon Cultural Company established the Hunan Sunchime Cartoon Archive Development Limited Company,[1] and entered into the animated cartoon production business. Their product was *The 3000 Whys of Blue Cat and Naughty Mouse* (*Lanmao Taoji 3000 wen*). This product had the approval of the government ministries as it functioned as an educational content provider, and was used as a teaching aid in primary schools.[2] For instance, questions answered by the animated blue cat

Table 10.1 Top 15 animated cartoon: broadcast time (2004)

No.	Animated cartoon	Country of origin	Broadcasting time (seconds)
1	*3000 Whys of Blue Cat and Naughty Mouse*	China	684,028
2	*Detective Conan* also known as *Case Closed* in America	Japan	505,984
3	*Bomberman B-Daman Bakugaiden*	Japan	328,283
4	*Bakusou Kyoudai Let's & Go* also known as *The Racing Brothers, Lets & Go*	Japan	310,770
5	*Doraemon*	Japan	263,503
6	*Biker Mice from Mars*	America	256,451
7	*Hamutaro*	Japan	231,545
8	*Magical DoReMi* also known as *Ojamajo Doremi*	Japan	225,269
9	*Rantarou the Ninja Boy*	Japan	224,234
10	*The Legned of Nezha*	China	219,769
11	*Astro Boy*	Japan	218,304
12	*Captain Tsubasa*	Japan	218,098
13	*Journey to the West*	China	209,552
14	*Chibi Maruko-chan*	Japan	200,041
15	*Rave Master*	Japan	189,895

Source: *Report on China's Development of Cultural Industry* (*2006*)

ranged from the mysteries of physics to the laws of social conduct. With the distribution support of television stations on the lookout for content approved by the national government the 'blue cat' soon became a household name. The Sunchime Cartoon Group became one of the leading youth programming content providers in China.

Media industries operate in three markets: the content market, the advertising market, and the end-user market. In the first of these markets producers offer their content to stations. In the case of Sunchime, their content was the 'blue cat' and the 'buyers' were hundreds of TV stations in China. The end users were initially the consumers of the programme – the youth of China. However, having exploited China's television stations to build a loyal fan base for the cartoon character, Sunchime then experienced difficulty forcing stations to pay license fees to broadcast. Production costs were between RMB 6000 and 8,000 per minute while the average fee paid by stations was between 5 and 10 yuan per minute (Zhou 2005). There were claims that Chinese TV stations were willing to pay licence fees and observe legitimate industry practices with international animation companies while undercutting the value of Chinese champions such as the *Blue Cat* franchise.

The alternative revenue source was advertising. Stations would allow Sunchime to promote *Blue Cat* merchandise in the programme. This proved a much more lucrative model and the Blue Cat logo was quickly patented. However, an inability on the part of Sunchime to control the practice known as 'zapping' – replacing the company's product advertising with local advertisements – led to recriminations. Having advertising spots (*suipian guanggao*) in lieu of programme licence fees was beneficial in so far as it promoted ancillary product lines. The company expanded their merchandising operations, extending the brand from audio-visual products to books, stationery, toys, clothing, shoes, hats, food products, beverages, cosmetics, bicycles and household electronic goods.

Altogether more than 6,000 items carried the 'blue cat' logo and the company quickly set up 14 specialist companies and 11 regional franchise companies to administer more than 2400 'blue cat' outlets (Zhou 2005). This success established a new financial model for China's cartoon and animation industry. By February 2003, the company had earned RMB 60 million, but this success brought with it imitation of its brand and numerous fake 'blue cat' products. The company's business plan of diversifying without necessarily differentiating further reduced their brand equity and focus. In addition, Chinese regulations did not allow the *Blue Cat* franchises to license other popular children's products such as those of the Disney Corporation. In spite of these market restrictions, Sunchime has established itself as the best known, if not the most successful Chinese animation company, with heavy investment in the Tongzhou Cultural Creative Park development in east Beijing (see Chapter 8).

Digital content: Moli Media and Goyoo

Digital content industries such as video games, interactive media, and digital television production are expensive. Due to the untested nature of the digital content industries there are very few established business models. Reliance on cash flows has led to the collapse of many digital companies in China as well as globally. An important problem for business is digital rights management (DRM). In China the government recognises the importance of intellectual property but as far as international digital content companies are concerned the protection regime is still undeveloped. This deters investors, but more importantly it inhibits the development of Chinese creative content. Just as international businesses are reluctant to invest in China because of piracy concerns, local producers find that their ideas are copied before they can achieve return on investment.

Digital content industries therefore provide interesting contrasts with the advertising business models that have helped to sustain film and TV industries. The cases of Moli Media and Goyoo are instructive. Moli Media began as a Beijing-based digital content company. It was established by Jerry Wang, a young entrepreneur with experience working with international companies in 2003. By 2005, the company had 20 staff with an average age of 25. Shortly after founding the company, Wang set up an annual event supported by the US company Intel. This was initially known as the Intel Creativity contest. In 2004, this became the *Diggi Awards*. Jerry Wang was at the time cultivating relationships with the Chinese Ministry of Culture and in 2005 the National Diggi Awards were officially recognised. In effect, from a commercial venture initiated by Intel in order to scout new talent and ideas within China, the Diggi Awards turned into a government-supported digital film and animation competition.

This enterprise model shows that government can play an enabling role in creative industries, even in China. The model is not dissimilar to the international pop *Idol* format that has made handsome profits for Hunan Satellite Television. The difference, however, is that Hunan were in effect copy-cats, evading the costs of paying licence fees. Moli established a network of relationships with talented developers who provided a stream of local content. While the company could have followed the normal Chinese practice of using in-house developers, it chose to aggregate content though an agency model and in doing this helped to facilitate the Chinese developer's community. Each winner of the contest signed a contract and contributed content, which was then redistributed through Internet, broadband and mobile channels to consumers. In effect, the company provided infrastructure and expertise, and established e-payment channels to assist individuals to recoup financial gain for their creative labour.

Despite these ambitions to create a community the returns were not significant. Jerry Wang attributed this to the problem of the free internet: users in China, as in most countries, had become habituated to seeing the net as a source of free content. Added to this were problems of copyright and piracy. The solution might at first seem strange to most observers of China's media. In 2006, Moli Media was folded into another company called iMotion Film, which took on the task of aggregating content such as short film and animation while another company was established to work with the Ministry of Culture to provide a buffet of content and services to Chinese internet cafes. The rationale for this partnership was based more on establishing a viable digital content business model than any desire to work hand in hand with a regulatory body. In China the internet is probably the best means to draw revenue out of digital content industries, but because the payment mechanism for content from home computers is still undeveloped, and because most home computers are relatively slow, internet cafes have become a viable platform for providing content and assuring revenue. According to the Eighteenth CNNIC report data (2006), there are 112,264 registered i-Cafés in China (although there are undoubtedly many more that are unregistered). While it is hard to estimate how many people actually use i-Cafés, estimates stand at between 20 and 30 million, the great majority of whom are between the ages of 18 to 25. Of these, 70 per cent play games and 20 per cent watch movies or videos. The company that is now working with the Ministry of Culture is called Goyoo (*guangyin*). It provides registered internet cafes with a buffet of refreshable contact, including casual games, animation, and mini-clips of animation and TV drama entertainment content, often Korean and Japanese. The café owners pay a monthly fee while the end users have access for free.

The advantage of i-Cafés is performance. Most ADSL home computers are not equipped to deliver high speed access with the result that i-Cafés attract gamers. In addition, the i-Café environment allows greater monitoring of content. From a Western perspective, this might seem a disincentive but for serious gamers in China it is not a problem. Home users are more interested in searching and chatting while café users play multi-role playing games such as *Legend of Mir* (Korea) and the *World of Legend* (China), or watch film and video. Monitoring of content also means that the content is legal, thus ensuring that there is a rights revenue stream – in contrast to black-market DVD and free-download domains in which no money finds its way back to the creators.

The long tail effect

As these examples illustrate the innovation ecology in China is increasingly dynamic yet at the same time fundamentally unstable. This instability is central to the viability of media and creative content industries globally. The proposition that consumers anxiously anticipate the next big thing has long driven promotional culture – the magazines, the video hits, radio play lists, and the professional critics. Hundreds of millions of dollars are spent each year in pushing products and services. But beneath the machinery of record and movie industries the online media has changed the relationship between producers and consumers. By 2006, China had more than 100 million registered Internet users, most aged under 30 years.

In 2005, one of these netizens was to become very rich in a very short space of time. Zhou Zhiyou was a native of south China's Jiangxi province. Although graduating in computer technology in the Beijing Post and Telecommunications University, his first love was music. While studying, he spent time working in bars in Beijing listening to music. One day he found himself engaging in a conversation on the QQ online chat site with Li Fan, who was at that time CEO of the Longle Cultural Company. The topic of the conversation was ringtones. Zhou convinced

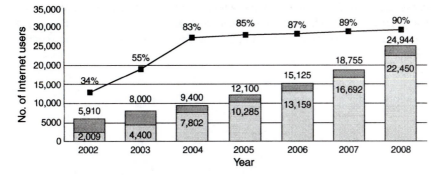

Figure 10.1 Statistics (2002–2005) and Forecast (2006–2007) for China's Online music
users. Dark grey: Internet users (×10,000); light grey: online music users
(×10,000); line graph: percentage of online users accessing music downloads.
Source: *Report on China's Development of Cultural Industry (2007)*.

Li that he had a new line in musical ringtones and he was quickly signed up as
one of China's first ringtone composers. *Wait Till I'm Rich (deng zan you qian le)*,
the first of Zhou's ringtones, was released online in November 2004. Using the
pen name of Zhou Xixi (literally thin porridge), Zhou's quirky satirical lyrics
and rap-inspired style soon struck a rich online vein. At a cost of RMB 2–3 each
download, and with over 1 million downloads of *Wait Till I'm Rich* in the first
three months, Zhou was on his way from working in bars to riches. China's first
'ringtone king' soon released an album of original ringtones which included such
tracks as *Dinosaurs Crawling over the Campus (xuexiao konglong mandi pao)*,
Conditions for Marriage (jiehun de tiaojian), and *Boss, Give me a Rise in Salary
(laoban jiaxin ba)*. In a country where communication is dominated by mobile
phones and text messaging, and where the value of the ring tone industry exceeds
the CD market, these customised ring tones, with their humorous twists, were a
recipe for success. The copyright for the album was purchased for RMB 1 million
by a Shenzhen company (Zhou and Jiang 2006).

The rise of Zhou Xixi is paralleled in a different content universe by *A Murder
Triggered by a Steam Bun (yige mantou yinfa de xue'an)*. This remix spoof of *The
Promise (Wuji)*, a film by celebrated art house director Chen Kaige, was produced
on a mini budget; the 'creator' Hu Ge, admitted he made it in 10 days for less than
RMB 200, which included RMB 6 for the black-market purchase of a DVD of
The Promise. The other RMB 194 he reckoned was depreciation on his computer
(Zhou and Jiang 2006). The spoof, which included quotes from Chairman Mao
and others, was sent to a few friends; it was then posted online, becoming an
online sensation, and accruing hundreds of thousands of downloads within two
weeks, much to the consternation of Chen Kaige who threatened legal action.
The success of *Mantou* illustrates the power of the internet to produce a feeding
frenzy, especially when content is free and satirical. Following this, two companies

in Suzhou raced to register the name Hu Ge as a brand of mantou, dim sim, and drinks, a total of 30 categories in all (Zhou 2006: 20). The rights to produce the newly named commodity were then licensed to a famous tea house, as well as a restaurant in Suzhou. On 23 February 2006, the first Hu Ge mantou rolled out of the steamer.

11 Re-branding the dragon

Culture as resource

Beijing celebrated its First Cultural Creative Industries Expo from 10 to 14 December 2006. It was a spectacular and diverse event, launched with great ceremony at the Great Hall of the People adjacent to Tiananmen Square, concluding in the Sheraton Great Wall Hotel where propaganda officials spoke enthusiastically of creative excellence and the shift from 'Made in China' to 'Created in China'. Beijing's 10 designated cultural creative clusters were announced in the final ceremony. Following a flurry of contract signing to demonstrate the success of the occasion, a throng of photographers recorded the presentation of large-size silver plaques. This was an auspicious time. Even though Shanghai had already celebrated its second Annual International Creative Industries Week a month earlier, Beijing's coming of age in the creative economy signified a deepening of the creative zeitgeist. However, this was not an auspicious occasion for those who had built their reputation on promoting the cultural industries concept. The cultural industries 'school' now had to accept a weakening of their position in the queue for government patronage as independent and enterprising entrepreneurs moved forward to validate the state's call for independent innovation.

In this chapter I trace the confluence of cultural *and* creative industries. I examine the Chinese dragon mythology and its embedding in the iconography of historical imagination. Two questions are central to this investigation. First, how can national culture be converted, or re-converted into national products? Second, how can culture be used to produce ideas that are valuable both nationally and internationally? I begin my investigation at Badaling, a key tourist site on the Great Wall outside Beijing and finish at the 'Forbidden Palace' in Zhejiang Province's Hengdian World Studios. The journey into China's past takes me through Henan Province, where the ancient capitals of Kaifeng and Luoyang draw on history to produce prosperity. Just south of the Yellow River, the Shaolin Temple fuses Buddhist tradition and kung-fu fighting. This fortuitous commercialisation brings younger audiences into contact with heritage and provides much needed employment for locals.

Writing about 'cultural re-conversion', Néstor García Canclini (1992) notes 'There have never been so many artisans and popular musicians nor such diffusion of folklore' (30). Re-conversion prolongs the existence of tradition, an abiding concern of China's cultural conservatives. Yet as a propaganda director from China's National Museum notes, speaking of the capacity of new technological formats to reinvigorate tradition, 'Creative inspiration is needed for contemporary artworks, but creativity also brings about the re-creation of ancient cultural and artistic products' (ICCIE 2006: 17). Suddenly, creativity has become the key to unlock the door of prosperity. For the Ministry of Culture, the State Administration of Radio, Film and TV (SARFT), the State Administration of Press and Publications (SAPP) and the Beijing City Government, 'the opening up of creative thinking' entails a triangulation of creativity, technology and culture. The official verdict on cultural and creative industries borders on transcendence: 'creative intelligence is the light, which incorporates the power of technology to radiate the enchantment of culture creating wealth and value' (ICCIE 2006: 17).

'Re-creation' and 'cultural re-conversion' are powerful themes. Disused factories rediscover the life-force of artists while districts, regions and locales look for new cultural solutions to economic stagnation. In the contemporary age of media-assisted cultural regeneration, globalisation has increased the potential to transform culture into 'resource'. George Yúdice (2003) argues that if nature is a resource, culture can be viewed in the same way: something to be maintained and invested in, not so much from a sense of residual value – as in the case of the preservation of cultural traditions and relics – or as a public good, but for its usefulness in assuring the governability of populations. In bringing to the fore the idea of management there is a sense of 'expediency', a link to the Chinese past in which culture was closely tied to government. But in the current age of Chinese cultural creative industries, the government role has moved from engineer to architect and facilitator. In addition, the creative economy momentum has emerged not from the central government, but from municipal, district and county governments.

The Great Wall: not yet in ruins

The Great Wall is an enduring symbol. For Chinese people it is a national icon. For many living in the proximity, the Great Wall brings sightseers in droves who pay good money for old artefacts and new experiences. For international visitors, the Great Wall mostly conjures up stereotypes: for tourists, it is a must-see site; for journalists and writers, it provides a ready-made symbol of China's xenophobia and isolation; for others, the Great Wall is a potent symbol of a long civilisation.

On 13 December 2006, the day before the closing ceremony of the First Beijing Cultural and Creative Industries Expo, I contacted an international news correspondent in Beijing and suggested that the event might be a newsworthy moment demonstrating the rollout of a major initiative – the 'Created in China' project. Although based in Beijing, the 'foreign correspondent' was unaware of this event and the government's 'cultural and creative industries' concept. After I explained the background, he added that while it sounded 'quite interesting', he would be at the Great Wall on the day making a report about some structural damage that had become visible at Badaling.

I wondered: was the Great Wall in danger of collapse? At the time I was en route to the Badaling area to participate in a forum called 'The Great Wall Cultural Creative Industries International Collaboration Planning Framework', organised by the Creative China Industrial Alliance. The venue for the event was a location called the Commune on the Great Wall, a meeting place during the period of enforced commune-style clustering in the late 1950s. The meeting this day took place in a rectangular-shaped conference space called 'the suitcase'. The attendees included editors of business magazines, local government officials, artists, academics and creative industries lobbyists, most aged between 20 and 40.

The project was an exercise in brainstorming and in redesigning the identity of the region surrounding Badaling in Yanqing county. The theme of the key presentation was 'Creative Great Wall: Reclaim the Name of the Dragon'. This linking of the two icons underpinned a strategy to revitalise the areas further away from the key tourist attraction of Badaling. Yanqing county is under the administration of the Beijing Municipal Government and is attempting to respond to the call for ecological sustainable development, as articulated in the Beijing Municipal Government Plan 2004–2020.

The ecological elements of the revitalisation plan include natural and historical resources. The area surrounding Badaling contains numerous defence watchtowers (*fenghuotai*) that were deployed in the skirmishes between the Northern Song Dynasty and the Jurchen Jin in 1126 CE, when the Song emperor was captured by the northerners. Other ingredients listed in the sustainable re-imagining of Yanqing county include river marshes, grasslands, deserts, ancient cliff dwellings, virgin forests, wetlands, valleys and canyons, historical towns, courier stations for mail during the dynastic past and ancient historic battlefields.

The addition of the dragon to the promotional campaign was an attempt to reclaim its true nature, as well as represent the Great Wall as a positive symbol of strength rather than a negative symbol of isolation. According to organiser of the event, Su Tong, from the Creative China Industrial Alliance, the Chinese dragon has been misrepresented. In comparison with the Western fire-breathing dragon, the dragon in China mythology was one of four magical benevolent animals (the others were the phoenix, the tortoise and the unicorn). In many representations the Chinese dragon holds an enormous magical pearl, which has the power to multiply whatever it touches. The ancients believed the pearl symbolised wisdom. Furthermore, dragons are considered to bring abundance, prosperity and good fortune.[1] Chinese dragons are also associated with waterways, lakes, rivers and seas, and for this reason the dragon is reclaimed as a positive auspicious symbol, unifying urban and rural areas, and the county's two rivers, the Yongdian River and the Chaobai River. One presentation at the meeting compared the potential for the underdeveloped tourist region with Route 66 in the USA. Through a combination of creative 'cultural re-conversion', combined with some judicious value adding, Yanqing county could reclaim its identity in time for the 2008 Olympics. Even as an 'outsider' I sensed this was grass-roots activism of a kind only imaginable in China. A new generation of writers, thinkers and scholars were taking the concept of cultural creative industries and diffusing it before it could be registered and diluted by the propaganda apparatus.

The cradle of Chinese Civilisation

Henan Province is located in the middle and lower reaches of the Yellow River. The name translates directly as 'south river'. In the Warring States period Henan was known as Central State (*zhongzhou*). It claims three of China's ancient capitals: Anyang (Yin and Shang dynasties), Luoyang (Han, Wei, Sui and Tang dynasties) and Kaifeng (Northern Song dynasty). The core resource is tradition, in particular the celebration of Buddhist and Daoist legacies. Henan is a poor province, compared to more coastal regions. According to national statistics, Henanese consume far below the national average of cultural and recreational goods and services, exceeding only Guizhou, Tibet, Qinghai and Xinjiang (National Bureau of Statistics of China 2005). Sofield and Li (1998: 362) note that 'a unifying theme throughout China's long history of tourism is the place of culture and the traditions of heritage tourism and pilgrimage'. World famous cultural relics reflect the region's role in the introduction of Buddhism and Daoism. The so-called birthplace of Daoism is Fuxi Mountain, which has some 108 peaks, 108 caves and over 200 temples. However, Buddhism is the key ingredient of the heritage industry. The Longmen Grottos outside Luoyang is a classified World Heritage site. Thousands of Buddha statues and frescos were carved in caves during the Tang Dynasty. The Shaolin Temple in Mt Songshan is the home of Chan Buddhism. The province claims philosophers from the golden age of the Zhou Dynasty as well as the ancient Yin Ruins from the Xia Dynasty near Anyang where oracle inscriptions on bones and tortoise shells were found.

Tradition drives economic development in Henan. The Province's Tenth Five-Year Plan established the transportation infrastructure to capitalise on the past, including upgrades to the Xinzheng International Airport in Zhengzhou, the Kaifeng-Luoyang expressway, and the Anyang-Luoyang Expressway. The province of Henan has invested heavily in tourism, branding five historic sites: the Ancient Capital Tour, the Yellow River Tour, the Root-seeking Tour, the Kung-fu (*gongfu*) Tour, and the Flower Appreciation Tour (the peony festival at Luoyang; the chrysanthemum festival at Kaifeng). Furthermore, Zhengzhou is said by some to be the birthplace of the legendary Yellow Emperor, Xuanyuan, and the site of his capital in the Xia Dynasty.

The Shaolin Temple

Buddhism embraces kung-fu at the Shaolin Temple. The temple is situated in the Western foothills of the Songshan Mountains, 13 kilometres northwest of Dengfeng city. The Shaolin Temple was established in 495 CE during the Northern Wei Dynasty. Emperor Xiaowen was an ardent believer in Buddhism and encouraged an Indian monk called Batuo, who was living in Luoyang, to take up residence in the Shaoshi Mountains at a forest location that would become the

Shaolin Temple. However, the Shaolin Temple owes much of its legacy to another Indian monk, Bodhidharma, who lived there for nine years and founded the Chinese Chan sect in the sixth century.

The road to the Shaolin Temple is well maintained. Factories producing coal and cement dot the countryside. At the Shaolin temple the head abbot, Shi Yongxin, has concreted a series of plans to commercialise Buddhism, plans which led to critical exposure in 2006 in the *Southern People Weekly Review* (*nanfang renwu zhoukan*). The lead article, entitled 'CEO of Buddhism' (21 September 2006), drew attention to what was perceived by many true believers as an unhealthy attachment to worldly concerns. A 2002 Discovery Channel documentary on the abbot and the temple's relationship with the kung-fu tradition had previously fanned unrest among China's large Buddhist community, while another report in 2004 in the influential English-language *China Daily* opined that the temple was exploiting the Shaolin myth on an industrial scale: 'Shaolin, famous as the birthplace of China's martial arts, has emerged as a well-oiled money-making machine servicing hordes of tourists attracted to the scene of countless kungfu novels and movies' (*The China Daily* 22 November 2004).[2]

The abbot's entrepreneurial motives had been directly associated with the term 'kung-fu economy' (*gongfu jingji*). Rumours circulated about apparent discontent among monks – 'bewildered and unhappy strangers in their own homes', asked 'to hawk RMB 60 yuan T-shirts' (*China Daily* 22 November 2004). Adding to the generalised displeasure in 2006 was the abbot's endorsement of a TV programme called *Kungfu Star* (*gongfu zhixing*) in which participants compete in a '*Supergirl*' style elimination format. The Shaolin Temple also sponsors a travelling kung-fu performance troupe managed by a local Henan cultural organisation. The link between kung-fu and Buddhism is what business entrepreneurs might term 'synergy'. The abbot himself claims to have come to the Shaolin Temple in 1982 as a 17-year-old after seeing the Hong Kong film star Jet Li in *The Shaolin Temple*. Prior to this, David Carradine had recreated the Shaolin myth in the long-running cult TV serial *Kung Fu*, in which a humble itinerant Shaolin monk roamed the mid-west saving innocent people from injustice. The series contained flashbacks to the Shaolin Temple's desecration by warlords. Tradition 're-converted' into popular culture provides a powerful connection. On the day that I visited most of the temple's visitors were under the age of 30.

Seven hundred metres west of the Shaolin Temple itself is the Far East International Martial Arts Training Centre, which was jointly constructed by the National Tourism Administration and the Henan Provincial People's Government. Students are taught the skills of Shaolin kung-fu. Altogether there are more than 200 kung-fu schools and over 40,000 students. According to the annals of this school of martial arts, its adherents develop superhuman skills. According to my guide, these superhuman skills are mostly sought after for employment in the security industry, rather than in historical TV dramas and kung-fu movies.

The CEO of Buddhism moves easily between the world of popular culture, kung-fu ceremony and his pastoral duties. He engages in a busy daily schedule, pressing the flesh, attending to ceremonies, and regularly meeting with VIPs.

Abbot Shi Yongxin has undertaken more than 60 overseas trips since 1987. It is this active engagement with the material world that offends some members of China's Buddhist community who regard the ideals of Buddhism as inward-looking. In 2002, the Chinese President Jiang Zemin made an important visit to the temple and symbolically burnt first incense of the day, thus opening up the right for 'outsiders' to burn incense at premium prices. In most temples in China this ritual is free. Defending the commercialisation of religion, Shi draws attention to the self-sufficient Buddhist tradition. He claims that in Buddhism if you don't work you don't eat: 'Our cultural subsistence relies on tourism; and for this we need to use both hands. It doesn't rely on the government nor does it rely on the faithful; it relies on us cultivating the dharma and being self-reliant. We don't have to worry about cultivating face to ensure our future' (Interview *Southern People Weekly* 21 September 2006).

In the nearby city of Dengfeng the blessings of the dharma are evident. The standard of living for locals is manifestly higher than in the large crowded cities of Luoyang, Zhengzhou and Kaifeng. Business entrepreneurs advertise Shaolin noodles, foot massage and souvenirs. The Shaolin Wushu Hotel and the Shaolin International Hotel offer three-star service. Currently in China 54 Shaolin trade-marks have been authorised covering hotels, seafood hotpot, beer, cars, tyres, furniture, wine and cigarettes. But according to the State Administration of Indus-try and Commerce (SAIC) none of these has any connection with the Shaolin Temple. Many of these local brands were established before the Shaolin Temple applied for trademark protection. Recently, the Temple has attempted to pre-vent further 'abuse' of the tradition by establishing the Henan Shaolin Industrial Development Co. Ltd., which has acted to claim unregistered intellectual property territory, in particular to prevent international organisations registering Shaolin trademarks. According to Shi Yongxin, 'We cannot perform Shaolin *gongfu* when going abroad for cultural exchanges. Otherwise, the holder of the Shaolin *gongfu* trademark in the local place would accuse us of violation, unless we get permission from the holder' (*China View* 29 June 2004).

Among Henan's many attractions is Kaifeng, the capital of China in the Northern Song Dynasty. At that time it was called Bianjing and numbered a million inhab-itants. As I discussed in Chapter 3, cultural markets proliferated in Bianjing; theatres (*goulan*) and performance spaces (*washe*) brought the new forms of pop-ular literature, art and poetry to people. The most famous cultural artefact of the Song Dynasty, the Qingming tapestry (*qingming shanghe tu*), is recreated in a theme park established by the city government in 1998 and suitably entitled The Millennium Park. It reflects the height of Kaifeng's glory. In stark contrast to the youth market of the Shaolin Temple, mostly visitors to the park are middle-aged or elderly. The experience allows people to purchase handicrafts of the regions, participate in tea ceremonies, dress up in period costumes, and travel in a replica boat along the Bian River. In 2005, there were 740,000 visitors with gate receipts totalling RMB 22 million.

The Millennium Park is rated as a national class 4A scenic site. In addi-tion to re-enactments of the contents of the *qingming* tapestry, performers offer recreations of *The Water Margin*, the famous epic story in Chinese popular literature based on resistance struggles against corrupt officials during the Northern Song. The Qingming tapestry is available for purchase in the park, miniaturised and commoditised for the cultural tourism market. These formats vary from cheap mass-produced copies to highly priced 'authentic' versions, the latter strategically placed in the artefact shops of tourist hotels. These are cultural industries – more about tradition and craft than the fashionable design-oriented creative industries in the new industrial clusters of Beijing, Shanghai and Shenzhen. The products sold are invariably cheap replicas. The major consumer is the Chinese and Asian tourist whose expectation is that the artefact or souvenir reflects traditional iconography at an affordable price. Aside from variation in the kind of formats (key rings, toys, postcards), there is very little creativity on display.

Chinawood

In August 2006, I visited Zhejiang Province's renowned film and TV production centre, Hengdian World Studios. The studios have achieved recognition in recent years for major productions including *The Opium War* (1997), *The Emperor and the Assassin* (1998) and *Hero* (2002), together with a slate of East Asia's historical and kung-fu television dramas.

The World Studios are the largest television drama and film production facilities in China, occupying 3.1 million square metres of territory outside of the city of Dongyang. Four hours by car from Shanghai, and midway between Hangzhou and Wenzhou, Hengdian World Studios have been occasionally described as 'Chinawood'. Of course, the differences are considerable. Whereas Hollywood is the epicentre of high value global film production, Hengdian is currently a low-cost production centre competing with several other Chinese studios and staking its claim in the historical costume drama genre. It is, however, attempting to establish itself as more than just Made in China by luring investors, and putting together strategic plans for an integrated audio-visual service centre, augmented by cultural tourism.

These expansion plans are an attempt to position Hengdian as China's largest film backlot, in addition to becoming a film exhibition and trading centre; in short China's Hollywood. In the meantime, however, the Hengdian World Studios is cashing in on its low-cost advantage at a time when a wave of creative real estate parks is mushrooming in Beijing, Shanghai, Shenzhen, Chongqing and other large cities. Goldsmith and O'Regan point out that such global international studio complexes like Hengdian World Studios are essentially about the 'contracting out' of audiovisual production. The emergence of Hengdian World Studios follows the contracting model, combining location, film services infrastructure, and an 'international-production-friendly context' (Goldsmith and O'Regan 2005: 41).

The location of the World Studios in central Zhejiang provides an interesting variation on the Made in China phenomenon. The population of Dongyang and Hengdian combined numbers approximately 70,000 people in the midst of China's boom manufacturing belt. Hengdian is somewhat of an enigma. The term *hengpiao* (literally floating to Hengdian) describes a transient population, a combination of film and TV industry production teams, extras, cleaners and associated service industry workers. According to my model of China's rise up the creative value chain, the 'Made in China' segment was absorbing a significant proportion of China's cultural workers. These are not Florida's restless creative class but people willing to engage in labour intensive rendering for Japanese and Korean animation companies, or fabricate fashion apparel consigned by US, Japanese and European designers. But Hengdian was a Chinese film and TV drama studio complex. In term of the innovation ecology, Hengdian occupies all positions simultaneously. It is obviously a cluster: it is receiving business from East Asia, many projects are joint ventures and co-productions, much is imitative and much production is straight outsourcing. This was a chance to test the proposition that the high value 'Created in China' model could exist alongside the low-cost model.

The road from Shanghai to Hengdian traverses the most dynamic region of China's boom economy. A driver arrived at my hotel at 5.30 p.m.; by 6.30 p.m. we had finally managed to exit Shanghai. Slow roads turned into four lane toll-ways as we accelerated towards the city of Hangzhou, weaving past hundreds of slow-moving trucks transporting pipes, machinery, electrical equipment and textiles. An endless display of billboards provided a rich commentary on Zhejiang's boom economy. This is the most prosperous province in China, if measured by the density of private enterprises. The so-called 'Zhejiang model' refers to the proliferation of self-reliant small-scale enterprises. Economists regard the entrepreneurial productivity of Zhejiang as a type of organic industrial cluster. Thousands of factories engage in basic manufacturing, as well as providing low-end components for new economy industries. In 2002, private enterprise output in Zhejiang was RMB 366.7 billion, some 47.1 per cent of the total provincial output, surpassing even Shanghai (38.1 per cent) (Kanamori and Zhao 2004: 30). While Guangdong Province had more private enterprises in 2002 (54.3 per cent), much of this figure was absorbed by foreign invested companies. Furthermore, the Zhejiang region is characterised by small-size enterprises, often working together to produce complementary goods. These enterprises do not require high technology. Entry barriers are relatively low and as high quality labour is not needed, these enterprises are well-positioned to absorb the region's excess labour force.

This is China's industrial revolution. The links to Manchester in 1835 are striking. On a visit to Manchester in that year Alexis de Tocqueville wrote 'Thirty or forty factories rise on the top of hills...Their six stories tower up; their huge enclosures give notice from afar of the centralisation of industry' (De Toqueville 1958: 106; cited in Hall 1999: 310). Such an observation might be made of Yiwu, which proudly announces itself as the small household goods capital of the world. About 30 kilometres from Hengdian, Yiwu is the centre of the 'Made in China' universe. Chances are that much of what turns up in the budget marts in the developed world are Made in Yiwu products: calculators, sports goods, telephone handsets, lamps, kitchen utensils, office equipment, toys, tents, jackets, shoes, socks, clocks, cigarette lighters, zippers and all kinds of household kitsch.

Paralleling Richard Florida's argument about creative environments acting as attracters for business, Yiwu's so-called 'small dog cluster economy' attracted the Zipper Industry Association of China to relocate from Shanghai in 2005. Yiwu now produces 30 per cent of China's zippers.

In less than three hours I arrived at Hengdian and was met by the Hong Kong television serial director Lee Kwok Lap. Lee's Tangren Production Company has a base at Hengdian, pushing out a string of high quality martial arts dramas aimed primarily at the mainland market. Lee has been working at Hengdian since 1999 and maintains that cost advantage is the reason he works in Hengdian. He brings his creative team with him. As well as savings of labour costs compared with Hong Kong, there is an added advantage provided by local knowledge, that is, knowledge of how to comply with regulations. One of Lee's latest productions is a new version of the Chinese classic *Generals of the Yang Family (Yangjia jun)* set in the Song Dynasty.

That night I stayed at a hotel that doubled as a set. In the morning Lee introduced me to Zhang Xianchun, the production designer of many highly successful Chinese productions. Zhang is best known for *The Opium War*, which was directed by Xie Jin and released in 1997 to coincide with the return of Hong Kong to the motherland. Zhang also received an Oscar for his role in the production design of Bernardo Bertolucci's *The Last Emperor* (1987). Most of Hengdian's 13 film backlots were designed by Zhang Xianchun. My tour of China's past began in the late Qing Dynasty, entering into Canton Street adjacent to the same era's Hong Kong Street. The set is meticulously crafted, replicating a mix of colonial monuments and Chinese shops. Tourists nearby were experiencing a re-enactment of a scene from *The Opium War*. As police on jet skis pursued foreign opium dealers, a gunboat opened fire over the masses of spectators. The riposte was a return of fire and a spectacular boarding scene which culminated in the arrest of the foreign barbarians. Chinese nationalism was the message as the events of the opium wars were narrated over loudspeakers and celebrated with enthusiasm by the spectators, many drenched by the spray of the jet skis.

The company that has financed the studios is the Hengdian Group, more known for its factories than its creativity. *The Opium War* was the Hengdian Group's CEO Xu Wenrong's first venture into the creative industries and this successful production was followed two years later in 1998 by Chen Kaige's *Emperor and the Assassin*, which was bankrolled by the Hengdian Group. In 1999, with the Chinese film industry deep in recession, Hengdian Studios lost RMB 50 million (Tang Yuankai 2005: *Beijing Review*). However, the success of *The Opium War* combined with generous location sweeteners brought other film makers and actors to Hengdian – names like Chen Kaige, Zhang Yimou, Gong Li, Maggie Cheung, Zhang Ziyi, Norika Fujiwara and Kim Hee Sun.

The set of the Palace of the Emperor of Qin, a feature of both *Emperor and the Assassin* and *Hero*, is a full-scale replica, authentic even as far as the number of steps leading from the courtyard to the great hall. Tour leaders provide historical commentary mixed with anecdotes about actors, directors and film production. Significant parts of Zhang Yimou's *Hero* were filmed here, requiring adjustments to the set used by Chen Kaige in *The Emperor and the Assassin*. However, the bread and butter of Hengdian World Studios remains television drama and more than a third of China's costume dramas are 'made in Hengdian'. In addition to the Qin Dynasty set there are dedicated Ming and Qing sets – and a full scale replica of the Forbidden City, including all of the emperor's official and nuptial chambers.[3] Meticulous care has been taken to ensure authenticity, as much to entice audio-visual production as for the cultural tourism trade. Indeed, the tourism market is more likely to provide the added value that is craved by the creative industries in China. Song Dynasty sets provide the backdrop for renderings of much-loved classic tales such as *The Water Margin*. Kaifeng's Millennium Park is also faithfully recreated, although on a smaller scale than in Kaifeng while the Southern Song sets are a hybrid of Hangzhou and Suzhou vistas. Plans are in place to extend the backlots to include Shanghai Bund and Tang Dynasty as well as develop more theme park elements, including the nearby Bamian Mountain and a Movie Fantasy Land project, based on similar movie theme parks developments by Warner Brothers and Disney internationally.

In order to attract film makers and drama producers to Hengdian, the Zhejiang Hengdian Audio-Visual Experimental Area Service Co. Ltd. advertises a range of favourable policies, ratified by the SARFT in 2003, and supplemented by the Zhejiang provincial government and the Dongyang city government the following year. Altogether 16 preferential policies are available to eligible new enterprises, mainly related to tax concessions, fee structures, land usage tax waivers, loss write-offs, and cultural export investment subsidies.

Despite the scale of Hengdian World Studios, its competitive advantage remains cost. Hengdian Studios founder, Xu Wenrong, an entrepreneur with deep pockets, has pointed out the value offered by locating in Zhejiang as opposed to more expensive studio locations in Shanghai, Beijing and Xian, 'A project that needs RMB 100 million elsewhere only needs RMB 20 million in Hengdian' (*Beijing Review* 2005). Xu also adds, 'Zhang Yimou spent RMB 4 million shooting in Hengdian but he spent over RMB 8 million in post production'. However, *Hero* was filmed in three different locations and the post-production took place in Sydney, Australia. Zhang was attracted to Animal Logic, the company responsible for many of the special effects in *The Matrix*. What does this say about China's post-production capacity? Is this a reverse outsourcing model – high-cost overseas post-production offset by low-cost local production at Hengdian Studios? Or is it a search for a distinctive aesthetic that could only be 'created *outside* China'?

Indeed, the future of Hengdian is ultimately linked to the East Asian penchant for consuming costume dramas. The problem, however, is that unless the 'park' transforms into an integrated services district and attracts highly skilled personnel, cost advantage is likely to remain the only real motivation for Hengdian. Added to this, there is uncertainty about the glut of historical dramas that are reducing the value of the genre. Recent SARFT policies restricting the number of histori-cal costume dramas allowed to be broadcast have not exactly helped to promote Hengdian's brand image. Much of what is 'created' in the genre is repetitive, new versions of old stories albeit with more special effects and more kung-fu action.

The promotion documents for Hengdian include mention of future plans to develop an environment in which creative talent will be incubated. According to the publicity new scripts will emerge: 'with numerous film production teams in Hengdian World Studios there is a foreseeable bright future, which is a virtuous cycle of script writing from "made in Hengdian" to "created in Hengdian"'. However, for Lee Kwok Lap and many other visitors to Hengdian, creativity resides outside Hengdian, not inside.

There are two possibilities for Hengdian and these lie at either end of the innovation ecology. The Made in China option means that Hengdian will need to continue to pitch its services at the most competitive prices. Presently, the studios service a productive genre, that of historical TV and film production. In many countries historical content has become niche; but in China it remains mainstream, sustained by the relative ease of production of such epics and viewer tolerance of remakes of history. The stories exist and they reflect common meaning systems: it is a matter of rewriting and adding more effects, and even more political nuance to resonate with contemporary events. Elsewhere in Asia the focus is on contemporary stories of modern life. These scripts demand different inputs – the ability to deal with more sensitive issues and to write for younger audiences. The second option for Hengdian is to grow its talent base by stepping outside of the safe waters of historical TV drama. This is an option that locals are reluctant to consider.

Resource as development: prosperity as management

Increasingly, provincial governments are looking to the idea of the creative economy as a development template. Tim Oakes has written about the town of Maotai in Guizhou Province where an 800-metre 'liquor culture street' has been constructed with wine shops and halls from different dynasties (Oakes 2005). The re-branding of Henan Province as the heart of China's cultural heritage, together with upgrading of transport facilities, is an example of local government policy. Another successful example of cultural re-conversion is the city of Taiyuan where the Creative China Industrial Alliance conducted a branding campaign in 2003 to develop the local wheaten festival. According to the CCIA director Su Tong,

> As the core manufacturing industries shift to coastal cities, most of the corresponding industries in the inner regions are facing bankruptcy. The policy direction of local governments in these areas is attempting to reshape the new industrial structure. We designed a campaign called 'China's wheaten food road' together with the idea of 'cultural Jin (golden) meal' for Shanxi's biggest restaurant. We utilized the idea of creative industries in this program, integrating local food and local performance through the creative application of local culture.
>
> (Interview with author, 23 July 2005, Beijing)

For other regions outside the big cities, however cultural maintenance has a deeper significance than selective branding. George Yúdice's notion of 'culture as resource' captures the mood of the times; resource reflects global debates on cultural policy which have led government officials, agencies, lobbyists, activists, non-governmental organisations (NGOs) and consultants to advocate a role for culture in the regulation of economic development, the alleviation of social inequality, identity formation and re-formation, and in promoting cultural diversity. The developments taking place outside the major centres in China are important elements in the Created in China project and need to be evaluated accordingly. Jing Wang has written of the importance of negotiating meaning transfers 'between seemingly contradictory scales and subject positions (the local, the national, the global, the regional, the urban and rural, the Centre and the frontiers …)' (Wang 2005: 7). It is easy to be overcome by the hyper-modernism of big city architecture, superhighways, and franchised capitalism. The problem, however, is that the urban rural divide is likely to increase. Cultural tourism is an inexhaustible resource and perhaps for this reason a never-ending supply of historical films and TV dramas are needed.

12   The great new leap forward?

Imagine this: the year is 2012. Rupert Murdoch's Eastern News Corporation is convening its annual general meeting in the Beijing Creative Cultural Park in Tongzhou District. In Shanghai's Zhangjiang Cultural and Technological Creative Industry Base in Pudong Bill Gates announces Microsoft's venture with the Double Happiness Software Company to distribute the next Windows operating system. Meanwhile, the former state-owned Xinhua News Agency follows its listing on the stock exchange by mounting a corporate raid on *The New York Times*. In California, Mayor Tom Cruise greets Chinese investors who promise to provide film industry jobs by offshoring production of a series of kung-fu action epics in Los Angeles. In Malaysia, political leaders urge restrictions on the availability of Chinese video games, which are said to be having detrimental effects on youth.

Of course, none of these scenarios are likely to happen, at least not in the next decade. But as I have shown Chinese aspirations of success in international and regional content markets are building in momentum. Further success is to be expected unless the Chinese Communist Party's zealous management of content conspires to destroy creative ambitions. A massive diasporic audience is assured if the focus on propagandistic content is relaxed. In contrast to culturally specific content that brings rewards in domestic markets, export content negotiates with tastes and expectations of foreign cultures. Export competitiveness builds on strengths in domestic production; it is valued – not solely for economic dividends – but because international success contributes to a sense of national identity. International success counters the rhetoric of protectionism and it facilitates national industry development.

In this final chapter I reconsider the conditions of possibility for the Created in China project. Currently, creativity is presented as a solution to cultural trade deficits, stagnant production, copy-catting, duplication of resources – and even environmental pollution. Creativity is a super-sign imported into the Chinese lexicon. It points the way forward for an education system tied to rote memorisation practices. However, can path dependency, in particular, the enduring legacy of conformity and conservatism, be overcome? Will the clustering of new industries produce rewards for investors or simply create new real estate value? What are the options for development outside of the new clusters? Will authoritarianism and information control prevent China from realising its ambitions to be a leader in the region? Will China's creative visionaries overcome rigidities built into the system? What role can the international community play in this transformation? Will 'Created in China' ever become a reality?

As I have already noted, the development of the creative industries in China induces a transformational rhetoric that is often ungrounded in solid research. Policy makers believe that turning high-technology parks into creative incubators or constructing new creative districts will force new ideas to spring to life. But in the new age of the Chinese creative economy, perhaps people are asking the wrong kind of question. It is all too often about *what China needs*. The usual short shopping list included incubators, more creative parks and lofts, more university courses on cultural management and creative thinking and, importantly, more investment. The harder question – the one seldom asked – is: *what is possible*? What does 'Created in China' really entail?

Creativity reconsidered

To answer this I want to reframe my discussion of creativity in Chapter 6 by asking: what models of creative development are right for China, and what benefits might the enhancing of creativity in China provide for the international community? Indeed, we might anticipate greater social liberalisation, which has its own 'multiplier effects' – more democratisation, greater openness to ideas, deeper institutional reform, and increased transparency in business transactions. The conventional approach to understanding creativity in most liberal democracies derives from the myth of the heroic artist who taps into society's collective anxiety. Often characterised as Western individualism, and borne out of civil society, this model of creativity is frail in China. The individual approach privileges basic research, discovery, breakthroughs and great insights. The rewards are Oscars, patents, international bestsellers and Nobel Prizes. The individual artist is often unconventional and irrational, challenges conventional thinking, but needs to be rationalised or developed by (non-creative) management bureaucrats. These intermediaries might be specialist/experts (e.g. the agent system, promoters, and psychologists). Rationalisation may be required to make the person work more productively, to realize their economic or creative potential or work within a team. According to cognitive psychology such individual creativity is embedded in a domain (visual arts, literature) and monitored or regulated by a (creative) field (judges, critics, censors) (Gardner 1993).

The conventional liberal view, moreover, is that creativity is a natural talent and this resonates with much arts policy. It also supports Richard Florida's arguments that cities and regions need to attract more creative individuals, however defined, and to do so must provide the stimulating open environment that these individuals need. In this Western liberal sense, the key intangibles of the creative economy are novelty and invention. Nurturing individual creative talent maximises social and economic outcomes and lends itself to the ideal of intellectual property enforcement, as defined in the UK creative industries model and championed by organisations such as WIPO (World Intellectual Property Organisation).

If creativity implies producing something new, valuable or original, then we might expect outbreaks in times of openness to new ideas, and in times when social conditions favour free expression, and in times when there is a market for creative ideas. Alternatively, can creative industries prosper without these conditions? Can you have 'limited creative' industries, for instance? As I have discussed in Chapter 3, the Tang dynasty was China's golden age of invention and liberal thinking. In the ensuing dynasties cultural markets prospered but creative breakthroughs were less widespread. In the modern period, many of China's greatest writers advocated the creative spirit (*jingshen*) and were critical of the nation's inability to innovate. Some, like the great early twentieth-century writer Lu Xun, actually advocated deliberate 'taking' (*nalai zhuyi*) as a bridge to develop China. Creativity enjoyed a brief period of intellectual uptake during the 1920s, when the literary school known as the Creation Society (*chuangzao she*) championed the superiority of the Western Romantic canon, the ideal of 'art for art's sake', and decried the creative poverty of much Chinese literature. In Chapter 4 I showed how this celebration of individualism spirit was nipped in the bud by political expediency. One of the leading proponents of 'art for art's sake' and co-founder of the Creation Society, Guo Moruo, later became a leading Communist official, endorsing the Party's negative rulings on bourgeois culture. With revolutionary mass culture the default setting from the 1940s to the late 1970s, there was no room for individualist sentiment, except if this was expressed as undying commitment to revolutionary goals and the Chinese Communist Party. There was plenty of evidence of this in film and literature throughout the 1950s and 1960s (see Goldman 1967).

As I discussed in Chapter 5, the mid 1980s witnessed a revival of the creative imperative in the rarefied domain of literary culture with its emphasis on rediscovering Chinese identity. A second wave occurred in so-called 'creativity societies'. These were organisations attached to university departments, often supported by 'industrial' bodies outside the humanities. For instance, the Hunan Creativity Society was set up in the mid 1980s by the Hunan Institute of Scientific and Technological Research, while a short-lived Invention and Creativity Society was formed in Hangzhou in 1985 under the auspices of the Department of Management Engineering at Zhejiang University (Xu and Xu 1997). However, these were marginal associations with no real hope of gaining mainstream support. By 1987, creativity research had bottomed out. According to one report, 'some people lost their courage to carry out further work' (Xu and Xu 1997: 252).

From the brief flurry of creativity societies, however, it is possible to glimpse an evolution of thinking about creativity; that is, it is not just about aesthetics and excellence; it is reflected in and across multiple disciplines. To take this argument back to the core bedrock of culture from where creativity emerges, the cultural domain is not the unproductive superstructure but rather contributes to the innovation system of the economy generally speaking. Herein resides the promise of the creative industries for some of its proponents in China. For this broadening of creativity to take root, however, there needs to be a fundamental shift in thinking. Certainly, one of the criticisms levelled at post-socialist nations in the former

Soviet Union is that decades of cadre-driven supervision resulted in unwillingness on the part of many intellectuals 'to think out of the box', the ingredient so central to competitive modern economies.

Why is this important?

During the course of my research into this book I had the opportunity to present a work-in-progress paper to some colleagues within the field of China studies. At the end of one presentation, the first question I fielded was: 'But, why is this impor- tant? Why should we, as scholars, be concerned about whether China becomes a creative nation?' While this took me by surprise, it remains a valid question. There are many important social issues that conventionally organise research into China: democratisation, information control, human rights, economic reform, environ- mental degradation, rule of law, nationalism, to name but a few. These are cate- gories that have conventionally framed the field. As I have argued in the beginning, however, much research in the field is predicated on a static image of China.

The arrival of the super-sign of creativity and the even more upbeat 'creative economy' signals a dynamic transformation, which I have called a great new leap forward. The creative economy is more than simply goods and services. It is about institutional change. What will this mean for China? Already the indications of change are manifest. Creativity institutes have reappeared: what was marginal is now mainstream as Chinese media groups and companies finance the new vision outlined in the Eleventh Five-Year Plan. In September 2006, the Beijing Centre for Creativity in Dongcheng District was inaugurated. Supported by the Gehua Group, a company with extensive investment in cable television, the Centre's objectives 'are to exhibit, extend and exchange the newest international research achieve- ments in the field of arts, culture, science and technology; to carry out education and research on related knowledge and technology; and to provide services such as market research, promotion, product development, investment consultancy and copyright services to enterprises and independence artists in creative industries' (Beijing Centre for Creativity, *Promotional Brochure*).

It is important to reiterate that such developments are not driven by Western transnational media companies, the 'usual suspects' of political economy of the media scholars. Where do these changes in the creative field leave international investors? Significantly, the championing of local creative content industries flies in the face of China's moral obligations under the WTO. Can international (Western) companies compete for preferential policies on a level playing field? Chinese-invested projects that qualify receive provincial, municipal and district government support; many also draw supplementary investment from Korean, Japanese and Taiwanese entrepreneurs. This is state-assisted industry support and it is carefully targeted at growing the domestic base.

Although international similarities are evident in the language – the emphasis on value adding, revitalisation of urban space, enterprise, and clustering – the genesis of creative industries in China does not blindly follow the Western tem- plate. In many countries the creative industries have become the target of virulent criticism from the left. Some of this criticism is well-founded, in particular a tendency to collapse the value of the IT industries into the cultural sector in order to make the creative economy appear more robust (Garnham 2005). Another constant criticism in the West is that creative industries policy is a product of neo-liberalism. The traditional and performing arts struggle to survive; they are asked to relocate to disused industrial spaces, become more 'enterprising', and reach out to new audiences. Indeed, for many working in the traditional arts – in museums, galleries and the performing arts – the term creative industries provides little comfort, save for its use in boosting the total value of the cultural sphere. Whether this translates into public support in the longer term is a moot point.

Florida's creative class idea has also divided international opinion as 'Cool Cities' programmes attempt to reshape urban environments, turning dilapidated factories into arts centres (Peck 2005). The tendency to legislate into existence creative quarters reflects what has been called a 'cookie-cutter approach' to urban development (Oakley 2004). Others have criticised the creative industries for their use of non-unionised casualised labour, arguing that workers are more precarious in these industries (Rossiter 2006; Ross 2006). Disintermediation changes the creative field, although this is more an effect of industry and technological convergence. Many artists have adopted self-management processes, cutting out intermediaries such as agents and distributors. Critics have targeted the escalating real estate values in new precincts. Flew (2006) suggests that while new wealth and jobs are created by industrialisation, including new middle-class managers and professionals, this inevitably brings with it rising inequality, overcrowded urban centres and discontent among 'excluded' classes. Fault lines also appear among the creative classes. Comparing Russia with the UK and China, O'Connor points to the resistance from supporters of St Petersburg's high modernist culture to the more commercially focused cultural and creative industries (O'Connor 2005).

Yet when these arguments are applied to China, they find less traction. China is still following a developmental path in which the kinds of relationships that mediate government and civil society in Western society are lacking. Labour unions are conspicuous by the absence not only in the creative occupations but across all occupations, and particularly in manufacturing. People are frequently asked to move their place of residence in the name of progress and development. Moreover, while the convergence of science, technology and culture may appear to be expedient from a Western critical perspective, this has a longer legacy in China. Nor is the emergence of creative industries policy a sudden leap of faith. Policy making in China is an extremely complex process, passing through multiple iterations before implementation. While the outbreak of creative parks, precinct and clusters may appear to be a 'cookie-cutter' approach, it reflects a Chinese socialist model of planning and duplication of resources.

Cultural creative industries: the great compromise

The emphasis on 'cultural creative industries' is the latest stage of reconciliation with the super-sign of creativity. Rather than downgrading the 'spiritual' component of great works, fine art, and historical sites, however, culture is retained as the leading term. The cultural creative industries model embodies artefacts of value, produced from tradition, celebrated as cultural and political identity, and packaged for international consumption. Internationalisation has become an imperative as Chinese artists and producers look for success. Does the super-sign need more superstars? National pride is at stake. Does China need another Zhang Yimou or does it need to find culture heroes more in tune with local nuances? Is Zhang creative or is he just a fantastic cinematographer? In a review of Zhang Yimou's *Curse of the Golden Flower* (*mancheng jindai huangjinjia*) entitled 'Curse of the epic', Raymond Zhou writes, 'The golden hues are so pervasive and saturated that they tend to smother any human subtleties as if they were the white powders caked on the faces of French aristocrats living in opulent palaces'. As if this is not damning enough, he goes on, 'I fear the opening ceremony of the 2008 Olympics, of which Zhang is the principal helmsman, may march to the same martial tune' (*China Daily* 15 December 2006: 13).

How is creativity now understood in China? Indeed, there is a rush to fill the void with the latest ideas and theories. There is frequently a conflation of innovation and creativity, of style and substance. The focus on creative clusters in China's urban centres is intended to broker efficiency and better use of available cultural resources and supply networks so as to maximize available skill sets and processes. In many of these clusters division of labour remains central to efficiency. Production remains relatively standardised while comparative advantage guides choices of clusters. The benefits of this model of creative industries development are associated with the question: what is needed? China needs growth and the industrial cluster provides this, whether high-tech or 'creative industry'.

Harvesting ideas from a wide array of sources may be China's competitive advantage. Certainly this is evident in the search for international models. But can the silo model that has prevailed under socialist administration be re-invented? Cultural mixing promotes a greater chance of useful hybridity and serendipitous insights. The question becomes more than just what is needed; it is 'what is possible?' As I demonstrated in Chapter 3 in the example of The Silk Road, innovation occurs on the edges of cultures. Likewise, sharing of knowledge and insights across disciplines can provide rewards. The incubator model allows project teams to mix skills-sets, and harvest various knowledges and talents with a view to breakthrough innovations. Combinations of different types of thinking and different cultural backgrounds bring surprising results. This model, however, takes time to fine-tune; it is simply not a case of throwing resources together. Creative human capital is the essential glue.

Re-framing East Asian dominance and Chinese catch-up

Cultural heritage parks, new technology zones, five-year plans, networks of finance and *guanxi*, preferential policies, and post-industrial restructuring: how do all these diverse elements of the cultural and creative economies fit together? And what do these developments mean for re-theorising the fields of media and communication studies?

While Taiwan, South Korea, and Hong Kong derive more than 70 per cent of GDP from services, the Chinese mainland remains tied to manufacturing. The current embrace of creativity at a governmental level is an attempt to bring together already well established ideas such as national innovation systems, the knowledge-based society and advanced productive forces.[1] At the level of economic reform, it is about changing the kinds of path dependencies that have led to massive duplication of resources and imitation. At the social level is about harnessing the power of digital technology, in particular the long tail – without allowing Western-style democracy.

Global and regional integration is transforming China and changing practices. China is looking to move up the global value chain by investing in knowledge. In this sense, it is following the lead of its near neighbours. But in other important respects China is exceptional and different from Japan, Taiwan and South Korea. Politically, it is still a one-party state; economically it is a manufacturing powerhouse; geographically it has several distinct regions and 22 provinces;[2] and socially it is experiencing unprecedented unemployment and class fragmentation. All these factors are important in the China puzzle.

Reform in education is an essential ingredient of catch-up, not just extending basic education, but in renovating long established attitudes towards the process of acquiring knowledge. The former Chinese vice-premier Li Lanqing, who was responsible for education reform under the Deng Xiaoping regime, has argued that 'theoretical and conceptual innovation is the precursor of innovation in education'. He says, 'If we want higher education to develop further, those of us involved in it must further free up our thinking, update our concepts, be pragmatic, keep up with the time, and make new breakthroughs in our outlook' (Li 2004: 227). The current vice-minister of education, Wu Qidi, is even more insistent on the prescription for success. In 2006, she said, 'The Ministry of Education strongly supports the development of qualified personnel relevant to creative industries and the training of qualified personnel by promoting cross-disciplinary integration and multi-disciplinary interactions in arts, engineering technology, marketing and psychology etc.' (Wu 2006: 266). In the Shanghai Personnel Bureau's 2005 annual survey of professional development expertise, the focus was how to nurture and attract high-level creative and management professionals over the next three to five years. At the top of the list was 'arts and culture' professionals. This is perhaps the best window of opportunity for international business and consultants. The training of China's creative workforce needs internationalisation. The international media companies are struggling, and will continue to struggle to sell content to China. The market for selling ideas and expertise, however, is still wide open.

Accounting for the value

Aside from the obvious rapid growth of its near neighbours' creative industries, epitomised by the high-profile Korean Wave, the evidence base for a

Chinese cultural renaissance has yet to be established. Areas of economic activity such as services and culture have not been adequately accounted for in existing metrics. Despite reports purporting to measure the value of China's media and cultural sector, the reality is that much of the value of China's creative economy is under-reported. For instance, how does one accurately measure the value of branding and marketing? This is even more problematic in China where media industry ratings are inclined to be a mixture of fact and fiction, generated to impress would-be advertisers (Keane and Spurgeon 2005). Indeed, national accounting for culture in China is fraught by problems of classification and measurement.

A lack of rigorous statistical scrutiny of the intangible nature of cultural services is not, however, only applicable to China. It is a general observation of cultural development globally that the intangible benefits of creativity have been under-represented. The highly flawed UNESCO (2005) (United Nations Educational, Scientific and Cultural Organization) report *International Flows of Selected Cultural Goods and Services* underlines the danger of trying to compare data without a robust system of categorisation. According to this report the UK is the biggest cultural exporter (US$8.5 billion), topping the USA (US$7.6 billion), with China a relatively close third (US$5.2 billion). For China's Ministry of Culture, concerned with the 'cultural trade deficit' this news is somewhat comforting. Likewise UNCTAD's announcement at the First Beijing Cultural and Creative Industries Expo that China's creative industry accounted for 6 per cent of its GDP, ranking it alongside the USA and the UK, made news in *The China Daily*. Confounding the UNESCO figures, UNCTAD (United Nations Conference on Science and Technology for Development) estimated China's cultural exports in 2004 as a mere US$1.35 billion (*The China Daily* 15 December 2006: 14). The fluctuation of claims about China's creative economy needs to be taken with extreme caution. Chinese statistics are probably more realistic, estimating the value as about 2.5 per cent of GDP.

The fault lines in statistics within China can be seen most clearly in media industries. According to official statistics, revenue from media in China comes primarily from advertising (newspapers, TV, periodicals, radio), advertising companies, cable TV subscriptions, book, newspaper and magazine publishing, movie box office, audio-visual products, SMS messages, Internet access fees and gaming fees. According to the *2005 Blue Book of China's Media*, the most authoritative source of information, in 2004 the total recorded revenue from these segments was RMB 327 billion, of which almost a third (RMB 11 billion) was attributed to book publishing (Cui *et al.* 2005). Two points need to be made in relation to these figures. First, they do not contain robust aggregated data from licensing of rights: most of the value is box office and subscription. Second, as I discuss below, there is incredible elasticity even in the most profitable sector, book publishing, where much activity is unrecorded. The same can be said for audio-visual products. Within these figures audio-visual products (CDs and DVDs) account for just 0.8 per cent of revenue, which is not altogether surprising considering that black-market transactions account for as much as 90 per cent of the market. How do

Chinese statistics account for the losses to piracy and under-reporting of profits? The short answer is, they don't.

While cinema, particularly US big-budget productions, is saleable across cultural boundaries in Asia, profits in China are undermined by rampant piracy. The Motion Pictures Association asserts that its members reportedly lost US$718 million in revenue due to illegal piracy in 2003.[3] Again these figures are extremely difficult to verify. Widespread discrepancies in the amounts of piracy parallel the high incidence of programme boosting that is evident in the ratings practices of Chinese media organisations; in other words, there is a palpable lack of transparent audited media research. The result is that international companies are often as culpable as Chinese companies of misrepresenting truth when it comes to reporting. Chinese media companies shy away from boosting their profit estimates for fear of falling foul of taxation, while international companies are inclined to under-report for fear of being seen as exploiting the Chinese market.

The common area where there is unanimity in relation to leaked profit is the black market. In drawing attention to the issue of the black market, I should also note that piracy of DVD and other electronic media retards Chinese domestic industry development to a greater extent than it does the Hollywood 'majors', who have the capacity to absorb the damage of illegal copying.[4] For domestic industries, piracy is poisoning their business models and their competitiveness (Montgomery and Keane 2006). Stevenson-Yang and DeWoskin (2005: 9) have put a sharper focus on the problem, arguing that the Beijing political leadership cannot quite decide what to think about the intellectual property 'paradigm'. They conflate 'legal commitments and prosecutorial energy with resentment of foreign IP and royalty claims'. In the creative content industries, however, the leakage of value has become critical. According to Cai Rong, while annual sales of TV drama on the audio-visual market in recent years topped RMB 2.7 billion, sales from pirate copies are estimated at 10 times the value of legal transactions. In particular, the new HDVD format (called the super DVD) allows up to 10 hours of video to be transferred onto one disk. This has become the technology of choice for DVD sellers (Cai 2008: in press).

Even taking into account massive piracy, China represents a huge market. While attempts to account for industry economics in China are hampered by a lack of robust data, international trade journals and business journalism are equally complicit in misrepresenting value. Reports usually register activities of large media companies. There is very little reporting in the English press of the influence of domestic programmes, genres and titles, unless these represent some form of international co-production or content licensing arrangement. Reports in the financial press also concern breaking stories and seldom provide a broader context.

Contradictions in the system

How then do the pieces fit together to make sense? What might be the new role for culture as it moves to become an economic resource, rather than a means of exemplifying socialist morality and monitoring conduct? In the past the Chinese

Communist Party purposively deployed culture as a mechanism to manage society. Cultural works expressed the contradictions in society: oppositions such as modern/backward, progressive/reactionary, and scientific/feudal. Mao Zedong's recognition of such 'contradictions', and their resolution, formed the basis of policy.[5] In January 1957, Mao announced:

> Everything in society is a unity of opposites. Socialist society is likewise a unity of opposites; this unity of opposites exists both within the ranks of the people and between ourselves and the enemy. The basic reason why small numbers of people still create disturbances in our country is that all kinds of opposing aspects, positive and negative, still exist in society, as do opposing classes and opposing views.
>
> (Mao 1977: 371–372)

The mechanism of dialectics, as a trajectory of development, was rewired on to the existing template of traditional Chinese philosophy and offered to the Chinese masses as a science of progress. This new science explained the materialist view of history and justified class struggle, according to which humankind progressed through a series of stages of production eventually arriving at Communism. In the 'creative harmonious society' of the twenty-first century, the template is further readjusted to account for stages of development – the knowledge-based society – and catch-up. However, in order to manage the transition, there needs to be a balance between new contradictory elements resulting from global integration.

The first contradiction concerns city and country. The transformation of abandoned industrial space in China's cities into new clusters and centres brings with it social disruption as residents are forced to relocate. Rents and land values rise.

Creative industries are predominantly located in the big cities with cultural consumption functioning as a key indicator of urban development: in other words, as incomes rise in cities people consume more cultural services, further drawing foreign investment and new services industries. In this equation, the poorer regions will remain disadvantaged in the creative economy. Traditional culture remains the key resource for most regions in China. Do the creative industries speak to the countryside? Can creative branding strategies promote and export local traditions?

The second contradiction is the relationship between commercialisation and public culture. The transition from the state institutional model – a kind of a 'cultural public service unit' (Zhang 2006) – to a commercial industrial model is not straightforward, particularly in 'sensitive' content industries such as broadcasting, journalism and publishing where the state is reluctant to cede ownership to the market. An example of the marketisation dilemma is publishing. Production costs are relatively cheap and China has best sellers and popular magazines. Nevertheless, most publishing ventures lose money due to the necessity of distribution through state outlets. As in the music publishing sector there are constraints imposed by the need to obtain a book number (licence) in order to publish. These are allocated by the State Administration of Press and Publications with the result that publishing is at best a quasi-commercial activity. At present, publishing is a controlled economy that is regulated by the book number system. Research by the Chinese Academy of Social Sciences has estimated that reform of the book licence system would allow a massive amount of private capital to pour into the publishing industries with the result that many of the large publishing houses would splinter into small and medium enterprises (Zhang 2006).

However, fragmentation currently occurs informally in a way that undermines attempts to calculate how much value is produced, or indeed lost. A publishing house in China generally has several studios (*gongzuoshi*) in which editors work. These editorial studios have an internal commercial relationship with the publishing house. In effect, the studios are not autonomous from publishing houses; they often venture into the marketplace under their own imprint – a kind of semi-commercial arrangement. This occurs when a publishing house sells a book number to a studio (*mai shuhao*), allowing the latter the right to publish. Because publishing houses need to deliver a certain amount of revenue per year, many achieve this quota by simply selling book numbers to the studio editors, who in turn take over publishing and distribution functions, often bringing in 'second channel' distributors. This is where value leaks out, evading attempts to quantify.

Greater financial autonomy exists in the magazine market although a proprietor of an independent magazine needs to be associated with a publishing company to obtain a licence. While foreign investment in content publishing is prohibited there are a number of models to circumvent this bottleneck. A foreign publisher may not invest directly in a Chinese magazine start-up although it may obtain a licence to form a joint venture and distribute a Chinese version in China after content has been vetted (for instance *Elle* and *Cosmopolitan* magazines). Alternatively, money is made available to magazine proprietors by informal investment mechanisms, that is, where the magazine proprietor has *guanxi* (relationship of trust) with a foreigner investor. Another model of publishing that typifies a model of disintermediation is online publishing whereby the author sells the rights to an online content provider linked to an Internet portal.

A third contradiction is the relationship between copyright and knowledge dissemination. Lack of copyright protection in film, television, and Interactive software constrains investment. Investors in these industries are likely to see their profits dispersed via DVD pirates, or in the case of television their programme ideas are copied without permission (Keane *et al.* 2007). For international companies the TRIPS (trade-related aspects of intellectual property rights) agreement, part of the WTO accession, offered some hope for the protection of copyrights. Yet as Wang (2003) points out, regardless of how far-reaching TRIPS or WIPO (World Intellectual Property Organization) agreements are, it is the effectiveness of national laws and enforcement that is crucial; in this regard, China has been slow to recognise the danger of piracy and the importance of rights to the sustainability of its own industries. Complaints in relation to infringement can be dealt with in two ways, through administrative or court proceedings. As the examples from animation and television drama co-production have illustrated, revenue from rights management is yet to be systematically regulated although leading directors and film industry producers such as Zhang Yimou and Chen Kaige are leading the call to develop workable copyright regimes and raise awareness of piracy.

Stevenson-Yang and DeWoskin (2005) are pessimistic, arguing that the state has a stake in managing a slow transition to international best practice. They write: 'China, meanwhile, wavers between accepting the Western model and claiming special, developing-country exemptions. Some Chinese believe the Western model of strong patent protection and vigilant litigation can actually work to China's benefit, but many are interested in using IP law as one more tool for strategically advancing the interests of chosen companies' (Stevenson-yang and DeWoskin 2005: 16).

The most appropriate model for China's intellectual property regime, particularly in the creative sector, may lie somewhere between exclusive property rights and open source approach. One of the advantages that creative industries discourse currently offers to China is that it can foster more flexible and sustainable projects than earlier state-funded cultural policy projects. Liao (2006) suggests that the new discourse can act as a 'translation project' for state policies and services. He uses the notion of creative *datong* (great harmony) to express the idea of 'an ecosystem of creative small and medium enterprises, flourishing around platforms and brands, and restructuring the industrial value chain' (Liao 2006: 402). This model is the obverse of the US intellectual property template, enshrined in the TRIPS, that favours the majors at the expense of smaller players in the creative ecology. In fact, the exclusive rights model favoured by the USA is likely to create rigidities and excessive transaction costs in China; it may enrich some large players but it does not encourage distributed innovation or creativity. A creative commons system with different templates of agreements for the most frequent types of usage and repurposing situations – such as for non-commercial re-use by educators and commercial use by film makers – will allow both government and private companies to unlock the richness of its cultural archives and make them available more efficiently and where appropriate share licensing revenues that may be generated. A digitisation strategy based around standards including rights templates creates stronger cultural and commercial opportunities than does a centralist copyright exclusivity approach.

As cultural creative industries inevitably respond to benchmarks of excellence mandated by propaganda officials, how do we differentiate technique, imitation and innovation? In Confucian societies technique and imitation were highly valued, constituting a bridge for novices to emulate the master before forging one's own style. The mentoring tradition (both Western and Eastern) accepts imitation as a process; this model deliberately takes from other cultures, and brings with it a transfer of knowledge. In the economics of creative or cultural industries, however, imitation is usually associated with low risk-taking and opportunistic market behaviour. As I have argued, in China's media industries during the past decade, copying other's originality has been a de-facto model of development and value-maximising, at least in short-term strategies; in turn, this model has become dominant because there is little effective copyright enforcement.

Does this tradition of transmission devalue creativity or just shift its focus? Sheridan Tatsuno (1990) refers to the idea of 'adaptive creativity', a model that favours harmonisation of the creative process through brainstorming and consensus. Adaptive creativity puts emphasis on idea refinement and recycling of ideas. The problem is that original 'out of the box' ideas may be stifled by consensus; some have argued that the failure to reward the individual within the group locks in creativity (Helm 2001). Nevertheless, the instrumental role of adaptive creativity is central to 'cultural re-conversion'. García Canclini (1992) shows how existing forms of culture might be revitalised; for instance, putting traditional culture in new applications such as mobile digital media. In a sense, cultural re-conversion is a form of adaptive creativity, suited to applications more than breakthroughs and producing useful outcomes. Entailing less risk, adaptation and imitation are roads frequently travelled.

A fourth contradiction is the relationship between risk and openness to ideas. The risk-taking role of the artist is de-emphasised in traditions where the artist is a transmitter. For China's innovation ecology to function effectively creativity needs to be distributed, not contained within 'creative classes'. Indeed, the Richard Florida development model is viewed with some suspicion within China. There is a limit to how much bohemianism the state will tolerate. The challenge will lie in new communication technologies which the state seeks to control, for instance by blocking foreign search engines and web-sites. Internationally, the Internet has led to the phenomenon of the long tail, shifting the balance of creative power from producer to user (Anderson 2006). While e-commerce is retarded by a lack of trusted online purchasing protection, China's nascent long tail continues to develop as more access the Internet. This is leading to what I call the 'post-collective recommendation ecology'. As successful media events like *Supergirl* have demonstrated, people can demonstrate their solidarity to pop idols by forming online collectives. Elsewhere coalitions willing to voice opinion form around nationalistic concerns – US military aggression, Japanese past aggression, and cultural imperialism.

The shift to the post-collective recommendation economy is acknowledged by China's power structures. When I discussed long tail 'theory' (*changwei lilun*) with a senior propaganda chief in the Beijing government, he demonstrated awareness of its potential for creative industries development. Of course, as long as the tail is not disruptive, it will be tolerated. If it produces more innovation it will be championed. However, the long tail is largely unpredictable. The progression to generating 'good content' for export is enhanced by better understanding of business processes and international best practices. Debates currently ensue over the importance of content versus channel. China now has more TV channels and more print media publications than any time in the past. In comparison to oligopoly models that characterise media systems in developed economies, the Chinese media industry model under socialism has emphasised the propaganda message, which in turn has led to duplication of channels. In this model, supply is abundant; but good content has been lacking because there are few effective distribution and revenue models.

Final remarks

International organisations, rather than undermining China's emergence, are contributing to the great new leap forward. Over the past decade many international media companies, notably News Corporation and Time Warner, have sought success in China. Many have tried, but most have failed, or settled for regional or niche markets. Many foreign companies have demonstrated poor understandings of the value, and the tastes, of the fragmented Chinese market. As many 'foreign' businesses regularly testify, the regulatory system that oversees particular creative industries sectors is archaic and impedes innovation. In new and potentially profitable industries such as streaming content firms need to obtain multiple licences in order to operate. Bureaucratisation hampers implementation of long-term business models. The necessity of obtaining multiple permits to produce creative content, often from different industry regulators (Ministry of Culture, The State Administration of Industry and Commerce, The State Administration of Radio, Film, and Television, Ministry of Information Industry), acts as a deterrent to entry into creative industries. This entry barrier is further exacerbated by the necessity of relationship maintenance as a means of achieving success. *Guanxi* is important in industries where ad hoc decisions can be made on the basis of an interpretation of government policy. This leads to uncertainty and in the case of the film industry fosters a grey market where green lighting is not required. The content is unlikely to pass the censors and finds its way instead into the 'second channel', where it supplements the stock of pirated videos for sale on street corners.

China's move 'from Made in China to Created in China' is now official policy. It will require more institution reform, more openness, and more transparency, if it is to live up to the great expectations. In this book I have traced the beginnings of this project, showing how ideas have transferred among key thinkers and through a delicate process of municipal government lobbying have finally reached into the higher levels of government. On a more pragmatic level more research is needed in mapping and accounting for creative inputs into the Chinese economy. As well as systematising standards for collecting data, there needs to be better understanding of linkages within the creative innovation system and these elements need to be identified and measured for their effectiveness. In addition, grassroots creativity and greater democratisation are beneficial to growing the creative ecology. These are harder issues to resolve in a one-party state system. The question remains: will China be a contender in the international creative economy or will the fruit wither on the vine?

Appendix: China's cultural and creative industries: table of regulatory powers and functions

Principal regulatory Bodies	Licensing and policy	Content supervision/sectors	Related regulatory bureau and industry organisations
State Council	Promulgates and rubber stamps all major national policy related to the cultural and creative industries[a]	—	—
Propaganda Department	Grants final applications for new periodicals; advises and guides central government bodies under State Council in policy formulation related to issues of national security (unhealthy content)	Content of national news broadcasts on CCTV and Xinhua news agency;	Ministry of Culture, State Administration of Radio, Film and Television, State Administration of Press and Publications
State Administration of Radio, Film and Television (SARFT) and SARFT bureaus at provincial level	Approves the establishment of cable channels; manages the day-to-day operation of the national broadcaster CCTV and CETV; licenses the establishment of TV productions, notably television drama; approves licences for foreign documentaries; licenses radio stations, oversees film production and distribution. Submits recommendations to State Council in relation to the management of Chinese terrestrial,	Overall responsibility for radio, television, audio-visual and film content (issues Film Public Screening Permits); can impose sanctions through Bureau of Disciplinary Inspection. This may involve revoking licences or imposing a	TV and Film Censorship Committees and Review Committees); Ministry of Education; Ministry of Culture, China Film Co-production Corporation, China International Film and TV Export Corporation, China

Table A.1 continued

Table A.1 continued

Principal regulatory Bodies	Licensing and policy	Content supervision/sectors	Related regulatory bureau and industry organisations
	cable, satellite, film and radio services. Authorises landing rights for foreign channels; regulates and approves permits for broadcast of foreign material	financial penalty between RMB 100,000 and 1,000,000	International Television Corporation (CITV)
Ministry of Information Industry (MII)	Licenses Internet service providers and domain names, Internet content providers, Internet entertainment industries, news/ information services, SMS and related providers, manages spectrum allocation, telecommunication services, mobile services. Policies, plans, regulations and technical standards for the information industry; policies for commercial applications of wireless, fixed-line and satellite networks	—	Central Propaganda Department, State Administration of Radio, Film and Television, Bureau of Public Security
State General Administration of Press and Publications	Overall regulation of press and news services. Administers publication licences for production and reproduction of book, newspaper and periodical publishing, audio-visual publishing; electronic and online publishing, software publishing. Advises on copyright cooperation between Chinese magazines and foreign publishers	Monitors content related to print media (including advertising)	Central Propaganda, State Council Information Office, Ministry of Culture, State Administration of Film, Radio and Television, Ministry of Education
Ministry of Culture (MoC)	Overall management of live performances, broadcasting (incl. film and TV) audio-visual	Supervision and administration of import, wholesale, retail	Public Security Bureau, Ministry of Health, State

Principal regulatory Bodies	Licensing and policy	Content supervision/sectors	Related regulatory bureau and industry organisations
	industries (incl. music), book and periodical publishing, cultural tourism, cultural entertainment industries, Internet culture-related content, cultural artefacts, arts training industries	and rental of audio-visual products; Monitors China Copyright Association	Administration of Radio, Film and Television, State General Administration of Press and Publications, National Tourism Bureau
State Administration of Industry and Commerce (SAIC)	Issues policies relating to advertising industries	Investigates copyright and trademark infringements in tandem with the National Copyright Administration (NCA) and customs (where appropriate)	—
Ministry of Commerce (MOFCOM) Ministry of Foreign Trade and Economic Cooperation (MOFTEC)	Jointly approves publishing and advertising ventures with foreign capital. Promulgates policies re foreign-invested advertising enterprises	—	—
State Council Information Office (SCIO)	Approves all foreign activities in publishing and print media	—	—

Note:

a The most important regulations (*fagui, guizhang*) pertaining to media are subsequently ratified by the State Council (the primary executive body of the government) and issued by the SARFT, SAPP, SAIC. However, there is a degree of overlap of personnel between party and government. Many secondary and locally specific regulations of a more administrative nature are delegated to regional and local government bureaus of the SARFT.

Notes

Introduction

1 For a discussion of restrictions see Lin (2004). In particular, foreign investment is prohibited in (a) publishing, distributing or importing books, newspapers or magazines; (b) publishing, manufacturing, distributing or importing audio-visual products and electronic publication; (c) news service; (d) radio station, TV station, radio and TV transmission network at any level; (e) companies for producing, publishing, distributing or projecting radio and television programs; (f) film and production ad distribution companies (Lin 2004: 183).

1 The Innovation ecology

1 The CRD also refers to Cyber Recreation District, the digital content base supported by the Beijing government.
2 For example see the work of Nelson (1993; 2005); Lundvall (1992) and Edquist (1997).
3 For example, consider this statement, 'If more researchers are doing more science, with ever more powerful computers, this increases the likelihood of meeting the global scientific challenges we face: from low carbon innovation to vaccines against pandemics. More brains, working on more ideas, in more places around the world, are good news for innovation. Out of that may come new fields of science, such as synthetic biology, and new methods that transform how science is done' (Leadbeater and Wilson 2007: 11).
4 *China Inc.: How the Rise of the Next Superpower Challenges America and the World* (Fishman 2005). *The Chinese Century: The Rising Chinese Economy and its Impact on the Global Economy, the Balance of Power and Your Job* (Shenkar 2005); and *China Shakes the World: The Rise of a Hungry Nation* (Kynge 2006).
5 *Billions: Selling to the New Chinese Consumer* (Doctoroff 2005); *One Billion Customers: Lessons from the Front Lines of Doing Business in China* (McGregor 2005).
6 This is a genre of publishing that epitomizes 'success stories'. *Billions: Selling to the New Chinese Consumer* is described on the back cover as 'The must-have guide to selling to the new Chinese consumer'. The author's unabashed self-promotion epitomizes a can-do American approach, one that self-deprecating Confucian traditions normally abstain from.
7 The online discussion group Chinese Internet Research chineseinternetresearch@ yahoogroups.com is an example of Western scholarship's fascination with the propaganda state. Rather than investigate the role of the internet in propagating China's long tail (and prompting diversity) more than 90 per cent of the posts concern condemnation of China's media controls.

2 Territory, technology and taste

1 For example, see Hobson (2004), Marks (2002) and Frank (1998).
2 The field of economic history is complex. For instance, economists such as Baumol (2002) have entered the debate about China's lack of innovation by arguing that in medieval China productive activity, for instance commerce, was regarded as disgraceful, in comparison to acquiring wealth and prestige through military expansion. The power of capitalism, in this view, is predicated on wealth, power and prestige, but in so far as this is achieved through entrepreneurship and innovation, attributes of progress in this view were conspicuously absent in China.
3 The Warring States period culminated in the ascent to power of China's first emperor.

3 The culture-knowledge economy of traditional China

1 The statement 'By observing Heaven's adorners, the changes of the seasons are examined, and by observing human perfection, the world is reformed' (*guanhu renwen yi hua cheng tianxia*) appears in the *Yijing*. See McClatchie (1973: 110).
2 The five Confucian classics were *The Book of Changes, The Book of History, The Book of Poetry, The Book of Rituals*, and *The Spring and Autumn Annals*.

4 Revolution, reform and culture in modern China

1 *Songs of the Red Flag*, compiled by Zhou Yang and Guo Moruo, Beijing 1961, cited in Goldman 1967: 246.
2 Wang Gungwu 1991: 146, 'The Chinese urge to civilise'. Wang notes that according to *Nihon shisoshi gairon*, ed. Ishida Ichiro, Tokyo, 1963, Kanda Takahira was the first to use *bunmei* to translate 'civilisation' in 1867 (quoted in Thomas R. H. Havens 1970: 83).
3 The May Fourth Movement, took its name from an anti-Japanese demonstration that occurred in Beijing on May 4, 1919. This was a period of heightened nationalism, following in the wake of the New Culture Movement, a groundswell of intellectual fervour which began a few years earlier. See Lee and Nathan (1985).
4 Maurice Meisner notes that this fable, retold by Mao Zedong in a speech to the Seventh National Congress of the CCP in 1945, and represented in 1966, became one of 'the three constantly read articles' which summed up the essence of Maoist wisdom. Maurice Meisner 1982: 119.

5 Cultural fever, critical theory and cultural industries

1 For a discussion of the Foucauldian notion of governmentality see Gordon (1991) and Bennett (1998), and in relation to China. See Keane and Donald (2002).
2 For the influence of Claude Levi-Strauss see Ye (1987). E. B. Tylor's name can be found in a number of recent publications. See Li (1988) and Hu and Zhang (1991).
3 This refers to recreational reading practices as opposed to politicised forms of literature. Examples are romantic stories, kung-fu stories and detective fiction.
4 *Zhongguo dangdai qikan zonglan* (List of Contemporary Chinese Periodicals), Heilongjiang renmin chubanshe, Harbin, 1987.
5 (*wenhuabu guanyu wenhua shiye ruogan jingji zhengce yijian de baogao*).
6 *Zhongda zhanlüe juece – jiakuai fazhan disan chanye* (Significant strategic policy – rapidly develop the tertiary industries).
7 The most significant demotion was that of the hard-line propaganda chief, Deng Liqun. Also losing endorsement in internal party elections in 1992 were Gao Di, Director of *The Peoples Daily* (*Renmin Ribao*), Wang Renzhi, head of the Propaganda Department, and deputy Xu Weicheng.
8 'Book kings' were private entrepreneurs who were involved in distribution networks and who often had contacts with underground presses. Often these people were poorly educated. When I was studying in China in 1993 I had the opportunity to meet several of

these 'book kings'. One particular gentleman would do the rounds of the university, taking orders and displaying a range of titles unobtainable through Xinhua (official) agencies. For a discussion of book kings and informal cultural networks in the late eighties, see Schell (1995).

9 The actual derivation of this term is uncertain. According to a Chinese dictionary of neologisms, xia hai referred to 'going to Hainan', a new Special Economic Zone (SEZ) of the mid 1980s where many opportunities existed to make money. See Xiong (1992).

10 The 'second channel' is a term used to refer to the informal, usually illegal underground publishers and distributors. See Schell 1995: 293.

11 For a discussion of Jin Yong (Louis Cha) see Minford and Cha (1994).

6 Innovation systems, creative economy and catch-up

1 *Cihai* (*Sea of Words*), Shanghai cihai chubanshe, Shanghai, 1989: 1731.

2 For examples of creativity research in the field of cognitive psychology see the work of Gardner (1993), in the field of management see Gardner (2004), Feinstein (2006) and Bilton (2007).

3 The etymology of the term *chuangyi* comes from Taiwan in the late 1980s. See http://3q. creativity.edu.tw/docs/write.php. In Hong Kong the alternative term industry *gonye* was originally used instead of *chanye*.

4 The '*Zhonggong zhongyang guanyu shiwu guihua de jianyi*' advocated 'perfecting cultural industries policy, strengthening the establishment and regulation of the cultural market and promoting the development of cultural industries' (Zhang *et al.* 2004: 2).

5 In addition to these national bases, by January 2007 a number of national cultural industry research centres had been established at six universities: Tsinghua University, Nanjing University, Ocean University of China, the Nanjing University of Aeronautics and Astronautics, Central China Normal University, and Yunan University.

6 China has 55 minorities or nationalities; however, the term can be used to include the Han majority, hence 56.

7 'Pearl River Delta: from "Made in China to Created in China"', *Chinese Business (Zhongguo gongshang)* June 2003; 'Call for "Created in China"', *Modern Business Education (xiandai qiye jiaoyu)*, June 2003.

8 See especially Chapter 5 for a discussion of China's creative value chain.

9 The conference was initiated by John Hartley, then Dean of the Creative Industries Faculty at Queensland University of Technology. The conference organisation team included myself, Zhang Xiaoming (CASS), Jin Yuanpu (Renmin University) and Su Tong (conference design). It was supported in China by CASS (Humanities Research Centre), Renmin University (Humanistic Olympics Research Centre, the Chaoyang government and the Tsinghua University Science and Technology Park.

10 Other experts and scholar consultants included Philip Dodd (UK), Justin O'Connor (UK), Kate Oakley (UK), Andy Pratt, Charles Landry (UK), Lily Kong (Singapore) and Richard Florida (USA).

7 Cities and the creative field

1 Previously many artists had congregated in the environs of Yuanmingyuan, the old Summer Palace, near Tsinghua and Peking Universities in the north-west Haidian District. The Yuanmingyuan Artists' Village was eventually closed down in the 1990s and many artists relocated to the north-east of Beijing, in particular 798 and Songzhuang.

2 In Beijing's 798 the rental fee is between RMB 1.5 and 2.5 per square metre. This price is equivalent to nearby office space.

3 4A stands for American Association of Advertising Association; 4A companies with a longstanding presence in China include J. Walter Thompson, Ogilvy & Mather, and Leo Burnett.

8 In search of China's new clusters

1 In 2006 I had a meeting with a representative of the British Council who confirmed that their advice to the Chinese in Shanghai was that the British model of the creative industries was world's best practice. It was also apparent that the British Council was determined to keep 'creative industries' as a home brand, backed up by British expertise. My impression at the time was that the SCIC was open to various international interpretations of creative industries.
2 This is the aggregate population of the Chongqing Municipality.
3 According to the Mayor of Chongqing Municipality, Wang Hongyu, the city has reduced its number of smog intense days from 110 to 52 in the past four years, demonstrating that the environmental movement is having an effect. See http://www.softpow.com/page/homepage/hot/20070227/2078.html
4 This development is influenced by The Creative Industries Precinct at Queensland University of Technology. In October 2006 I had the occasion to speak to the Chongqing Municipal government about 'the Queensland Model'.
5 Other bases include Shishanhai Cultural Tourism District, the Beijing Happy Valley Theme Park, the Gaobeidian Folk Culture Industrial Park, the Baigongfang Art and Craft Base (Mok 2006).
6 Following which a 15 per cent tax threshold applies.
7 Jerry Wang, Moli Media.

9 Reality TV, post-collectivism and the long tail

1 These figures may be conservative estimates given the Chinese government's penchant to over-estimate national productivity. In comparison UNESCO's highly problematic report *International Trade in Selected Cultural Goods and Services, 1994–2003* (2005) lists China as the third largest cultural exporter following Great Britain (first) and US (second). According to UNESCO the USA exports US$7.6 billion, even factoring in cultural services. In another report, not accounting for cultural services, Canada alone imported $Can3.1 billion in culture goods from the United States. See http://www.statcan.ca/Daily/English/060612/d060612b.htm
2 Bruno Wu, Chairman of Sun Media, Australia China Business Forum, 4–6 August, Brisbane, Australia.
3 *Chinese TV Programs 2005–2006*, distributed by the China International TV Corp., Beijing; *Drama, Documentaries, Variety Shows MBC* Chinese version. MBC Audio-visual Production Company. Korea. The efforts made by these publicity materials confirm the importance of the East Asian audio-visual market. By mid-2007 the Korean Wave had begun to diminish with Chinese TV drama and film hoping to fill a vacuum, in effect trading on a 'flying geese effect'. See Keane (2008) for more discussion of this.
4 China passed the Copyright Law of the Peoples Republic of China in 1990 at the fifteenth Meeting of the seventh National People's Congress (7 September 1990). China had the previous year become a member of the World Intellectual Property Organization (WIPO). See Zhang Yonghua (2006). Despite these laws, however, implementation of copyright remains under-resourced.
5 The comedian was Chen Peise.
6 The regulations for Sino-Foreign co-productions nominate three types: (1) *Joint production* where both parties contribute capital and undertake production activities. Profits and losses are apportioned according to investment; (2) *Assisted production*, where the foreign party provides capital and principal production personnel and the Chinese party provides resources such as equipment, sites and crew; (3) *Commissioned production*, where the foreign party entrusts capital to the Chinese company, which produces the drama on behalf of the foreign company (Article 9 of the Sino-foreign Television

Production Rules released by the State Administration of Radio, Film and Television; see Chang *et al*. 2003:11).

7 In the past a Chinese content producing company would link to a non-media company which would be associated with a 'foreign' company, ostensibly in a non-media field.

8 Prior to approval the partners in a television drama co-production must submit the following to the SARFT: an application form; the Chinese script of the programme in its entirety or a summary of each episode that is no longer than 1,500 words per episode; the resumes of the producer, director and scriptwriter, and a list of the actors/actresses and production staff; a production plan specifying which scenes are to be filmed in Mainland China and a detailed filming schedule; a letter of intent regarding the cooperation between the parties; a copy of the Chinese party's license to produce TV dramas; the registration certificate of the foreign party and a bank reference letter for the foreign party (Article 9 of the Sino-foreign Television Production Rules released by the State Administration of Radio, Film and Television; see Chang *et al*. 2003:11).

10 Joint ventures, franchising and licensing

1 Sunchime is the English business name for Sanchen.
2 Interview with Vincent Hsieh, Vice-director Sunchime 22 October 2006.

11 Re-branding the dragon: culture as resource

1 See http://www.crystalinks.com/dragons.html
2 The documentary was called *Xin Shaolin fangzhang* (*The new Shaolin Abbot*). See *Southern People Weekly* 21 September: 26.
3 See http://www.hengdianworld.com/english/park/

12 The great new leap forward?

1 Advanced productive forces are one of the three elements of Jiang Zemin's 'three represents' (*san ge diaobiao*). The others are China's advanced culture and the fundamental interests of the masses.
2 The Chinese government counts Taiwan as its 23rd province; in addition to four municipalities, five autonomous regions and two special administrative zones (Hong Kong and Macau).
3 See http://www.mpaaa.org/press_releases/2006_03_03.pdf
4 Jake Vanderkamp in *South China Morning Post* 5 August 2006 notes that total losses of piracy including Internet within North America accounted for 6.5 times as much as losses in China, or 2.5 times as much as losses in all of East Asia; losses in North America and Europe combined were 12 times as great as losses in China, or 4.6 times as great as losses in all of East Asia.
5 The 'science' of dialectical materialism was derived from the work of Marx and Engels, particularly the latter's *Anti-Duhring*.It was popularised by Plekanov and became the official philosophy of the Soviet Union. According to the *Fontana Dictionary of Modern Thought*, it was Engels who 'extended the scope of the dialectic to the natural world and proclaimed a series of completely general scientific laws which governed nature and society alike. These fundamental laws were: the transformation of quantity into quality whereby gradual quantitative change culminated in a revolutionary change of quality; the interpenetration of opposites whereby any entity is constituted by an unstable unity of contradictions; and the negation of the negation whereby any negative force is in its turn negated in a process of historical development which conserves something of the negated elements. See Bullock *et al*. 1988: 225.

References

Adorno, T. and Horkheimer, M. (1997) [1947] *Dialectic of Enlightenment*. London: Verso.

Adshead S.A.M (2004) *T'ang China: The Rise of the East in World History*. Basingstoke: Palgrave Macmillan.

Amin, A. and Thrift, N. (1992) 'Neo-Marshallian Nodes in Global Networks', *International Journal of Urban and Regional Research* 16 (4): 571–587.

Anagnost, A. (1997) *National Past-Times: Narrative, Representation and Power in Modern China*. Durham: Duke University Press.

Anderson, B. (1983) *Imagined Communities: Reflections on the Origin and Spread of Nationalism*. London: Verso.

Anderson, C. (2006) *The Long Tail: How Endless Choice is Creating Unlimited Demand*. London: Random House Business Books.

Anderson, J. (2005) 'The End of the China Love Affair', *Far Eastern Economic Review*. 168 (5): 20–26.

APEC (2001) *Executive Report on APEC*, Shanghai: APEC.

Appadurai, A. (2001) 'Grassroots globalization and the research imagination', in Arjun Appadurai (ed.), *Globalization*. Durham and NY: Duke University Press, 1–21.

Appadurai, A. (1990) 'Disjuncture and difference in the global cultural economy', *Public Culture* 2 (2): 1–24.

Armstrong, K. (2006) *The Great Transformation: The Beginning of Our Religious Tradition*. New York/Toronto: Alfred A. Knopf.

Ayaldot, P. (1986) 'Trajectoires technologiques et milieux innovateurs', in P. Ayaldot (ed.), *Mileieux Innovateurs en Europe*. Paris: GREMI.

Bai Haijun (2006) *Believe China 2049* (*xiangxin Zhongguo 2049*), Beijing: Zhongguo dangan chubanshe.

Baldwin R. (2006) 'Globalisation: the great unbundling(s)', Economic Council of Finland, available at http://www.tinyurl.com/2ol2n8

Barmé, G. (2005) 'Towards a new sinology' Available at http://www.csaa.org.au/news05.05.html#ESSAY

Barmé, G. and Jaivin, L. (1992) *New Ghosts, Old Dreams: Chinese Rebel Voices*. New York: Random House.

Barshefsky, C. (2000) *US Trade Policy 2000 Agenda*, available at http://www.ustr.gov/pdf/2000tpa_i.pdf

Baumol, W. J. (2002) *The Free-Market Innovation Machine: Analysing the Growth Miracle of Capitalism*. Princeton and Oxford: Princeton University Press.

Bell, D. (1974) *The Coming of Post-Industrial Society: a Venture in Social Forecasting*. London: Heinemann.

Bell, D. (1978) *The Cultural Contradictions of Capitalism*. New York: Basic Books.

Benn, C. (2004) *China's Golden Age: Everyday Life in the Tang Dynasty*. New York: Oxford University Press.

Bennett, T. (1998) *Culture: a Reformer's Science*. Sydney: Allen & Unwin.

Bilton, C. (2007) *Management and Creativity: from Creative Industries to Creative Management*. Malden MA: Blackwell.

Boden, M. (2004) *The Creative Mind: Myths and Mechanisms*. 2nd edition. London: Routledge.

Bourdieu, P. (1984) *Distinction : a Social Critique of the Judgement of Taste*, translated by Richard Nice. Cambridge MA: Harvard University Press.

Braithwaite, J. and Drahos, P. (2000) *Global Business Regulation*. Cambridge: Cambridge University Press.

Brown, J. S. and Hagel, J. III (2006) 'Innovation blowback: disruptive management practices from Asia', *The McKinsey Quarterly* 1: 35–45.

Brugger, B. and Kelly, D. (1990) *Chinese Marxism in the Post-Mao Era*. Berkeley: Stanford University Press.

Bullock, A., Stallybrass, O. and Trombley, S. (eds), (1998) *Fontana Dictionary of Modern Thought*, Revised edition. London: Fontana.

Buruma, I. (2003) 'Asia World', *The New York Review*, 12 July, 2003.

Cai, Rong (2008) 'Carnivalesque pleasure: the audio-visual market and the consumption of television drama', in Ying Zhu, M. Keane and Ruoyun Bai (eds), *TV Drama in China: Unfolding Narratives of Tradition, Political Transformation and Cosmopolitan Identity*. Hong Kong: Hong Kong University Press (in press).

Camagni, R. P. (1995) 'The concept of innovative milieu and its relevance for public policies in European lagging regions', *Papers in Regional Science* 74 (4): 317–340.

Can Bai (1994) 'Lishi changjuan zhong de yige xiao huamian' (A small canvas in the long sweep of history), *Dianshi yishu* (*Television Arts*) 1: 4–6.

Carillo, F. J. (ed.) (2006) *Knowledge Cities: Approaches, Experiences and Perspectives*. Burlington MA: Butterworth-Heinemann.

Caves, R. (2000) *Creative Industries: Contracts between Art and Commerce*. Cambridge, MA: Harvard University Press.

CCPR (2003) *Baseline Study of Hong Kong's Creative Industries*. Centre for Cultural Policy Research, The University of Hong Kong: Hong Kong SAR.

CCPR (2006) *Study on the Relationship between Hong Kong's Cultural & Creative Industries and the Pearl River Delta*. Centre for Cultural Policy Research, The University of Hong Kong: Hong Kong SAR.

Chan, J. Man (1994), 'Media internationalization in China: processes and tensions', *Journal of Communications* 44 (3): 70–88.

Chang, J. (1997) 'The mechanics of state propaganda in the People's Republic of China and the Soviet Union in the 1950s', in T. Cheek & T. Saitch (eds), *New Perspectives on State Socialism in China*. New York: M. E. Sharpe.

Chang Jesse, T. H., Wan, Isabelle and Qu, Philip (2003) *China's Media and Entertainment Law (Vol. 1)*. Hong Kong: TransAsia Publishing.

Chen, Gang (1996) *Dazhong Wenhua yu Wutuobang* (*Mass Culture and Utopia*) Beijing: Zuozhe chubanshe.

Chen, Yi-Hsiang (2008) 'Looking for Taiwan's Competitive Edge: the Production and Circulation of Taiwanese TV drama', in Ying Zhu, Michael Keane and Ruoyun Bai (eds),

TV Drama in China: Unfolding Narratives of Tradition, Political Transformation and Cosmopolitan Identity. Hong Kong: Hong Kong University Press (in press).

Chen, S. (2006) 'How much does urban location matter? A comparison of three science parks in China', in F. J. Carillo (ed.), *Knowledge Cities: Approaches, Experiences and Perspectives*. Burlington MA: Butterworth-Heinemann.

Chesneaux, J. (1979) *China: The People's Republic 1949–1976*, English translation by P. Auster and L. Davis. New York: Random House.

China Daily 19 April 2005 http://www.china.org.cn/english/culture/126301.htm

China Daily 22 November 2004 http://www.chinadaily.com.cn/english/doc/2004-11/22/content_393567.htm

China Publishing Yearbook (Zhongguo chuban nianjian) (1992). Beijing: Beijing Commercial Press.

China Statistical Yearbook (1996) New York: Praeger

China View 29 June (2004) 'Shaolin Temple applies for trademark registration in over 80 countries' http://news.xinhuanet.com/english/2004-06/29/content_1554164.htm

Christopherson, S. (2005) 'Divide and conquer: regional competition in a concentrated media industry', in Greg Elmer and Mike Gasher (eds), *Contracting out Hollywood: Runaway Productions and Foreign Location Shooting*. Lanham: Rowman & Littlefield.

Chun, Xiong (2006) 'Win in China', *Softpower (ruanshili)* 11: 28–33.

Cihai (Sea of words) (1989) Shanghai: Shanghai cihai chubanshe.

CIRAC & Cutler & Company (2004) *Research and Innovation Systems in the Production of Digital Content: Report for the National Office for the Information Economy*. Canberra: National Office for the Information Economy.

CITF Creative Industries Task Force (1998) http://www.culture.gov.uk/creative/creative_industries.html

CNNIC (2006) (China Internet Network Information Centre). Available online at http://www.cnnic.net.cn/en/index/0O/index.htm

Coe, N. and Johns, J. (2004) 'Beyond production clusters: towards a political economy of networks in the film and television industries', in Dominic Power and Allen J. Scott (eds), *Cultural Industries and the Production of Culture*. London: Routledge.

Cooke, P. and Morgan, K. (1994) 'The regional innovation system in Baden-Württemberg', *International Journal of Technology Management* 9 (3/4): 394–429.

Cowan, T. (2002) *Creative Destruction: How Globalization is Changing the World's Cultures*. Princeton NJ: Princeton University Press.

Cui Baoguo, Lu Jinzhu and Wang Xuhong (2005) 'Structural reform and transition: survey on China's media industry development 2004–2005' (gaizhi yu zhuanzhi 2004–2005 Zhongguo chuanmei chanye fazhan zong baogao), in Cui Baoguo (ed.), *Blue Book of China's Media*. Beijing: Social Sciences Academy Press.

Cunningham, S. (2006) *What Price a Creative Economy?* Sydney: Platform Working Papers.

Cunningham, S. and Sinclair J. (eds) (2001) *Floating Lives: the Media and Asian Diasporas*. Lanham MD: Rowman and Littlefield.

Curran, J. and Park, H.J. (2000) *De-Westernizing Media Studies*. London: Routledge.

Curtin, M. (2003) 'Media Capital: Towards the Study of Spatial Flows', *International Journal of Cultural Studies* 6 (2): 202–228.

Curtin, M. (2007) *Playing to the World's Biggest Audience: The Globalization of Chinese Film and TV*. Berkeley: University of California Press.

Curtin, P. D. (1984) *Cross-Cultural Trade in World History*. Cambridge: Cambridge University Press.

Dahlman C. and Aubert J-E. (eds) (2001) *China and the Knowledge Economy: Seizing the 21st Century*. Washington: WBI Development Studies.

DCMS (1998) Department of Culture, Media and Sport *Creative Industries Mapping Document*. DCMS: London.

de Bary, W. T. (1969) *Sources of Chinese Tradition*. New York: Columbia University Press.

De Toqueville, A. (1958) *Journeys to England and Ireland*. Edited by J.P. Mayer. London: Faber and Faber.

Deloitte Research (2005) *The World's Factory: China Enters the 21st Century*. Deloitte Consulting.

Denton, K. A. (ed.), (1996) *Modern Chinese Literary Thought: Writings on Literature 1893–1945*. Palo Alto CA: Stanford University Press.

Dicken, P. (2003) *Global Shift: Reshaping the Global Economic Map in the 21st Century*. Fourth Edition. London: Sage.

Doctoroff, T. (2005) *Billions: Selling to the New Chinese Consumer*. Basingstoke: Palgrave Macmillan.

Ding, X. L. (1994) *The Decline of Communism in China: Legitimacy Crisis, 1977–1989*. Cambridge: Cambridge University Press.

Donald, S. H. (2006) 'The Idea of Hong Kong, Structures of Attention in the City of Life', in Christoph Lindner (ed.), *Urban Space and Cityscapes*. London: Routledge.

Donald, S. H. and Benewick, R. (2005) *The State of China Atlas: Mapping the World's Fastest Growing Economy*. Sydney: UNSW Press.

Duan, Dong, and Deng Bin (2006) 'An exploration of Super Girl' (pandian chaoji nüsheng), in Zhang Xiaoming, Hu Huilin and Zhang Jiangang (eds), *The Blue Book of China's Culture*. Beijing: Social Sciences Academic Press.

Dunning, J. (ed.) (2000) *Regions, Globalization and the Knowledge-Based Economy*. Oxford: Oxford University Press.

EBD (2005) Ecology Bureau District, Chongqing: Chonqing Ecology Business District Publication.

ECR (2002) Economic Review Committee, Ministry of Trade and Industry See http://app.mti.gov.sg/default.asp?id=507#4

Edquist, C. (1997) *Systems of Innovation: Technologies Institutions and Organizations*. Washington: Pinter.

Einhorn, B. (2003) 'How Ningbo Bird Became a High-Flier', *Business Week Online*, 21 January. Available at: http://www.businesweek.com/technology/content/jan2003/tc20030121_7804.htm (accessed 6 June 2005).

Ellis, S. and Gadiesh, O. (2006) 'Outsmarting China's Start-arounds, *Far Eastern Economic Review* 169 (6): 5–10.

Elmer, G. and Gasher, M. (eds) (2005) *Contracting Out Hollywood: Runaway Productions and Foreign Location Shooting*. Lanham: Rowman & Littlefield.

Engardio, P. (2007) *Chindia: How China and India are Revolutionizing Global Business*. New York: McGraw-Hill.

Enright, M. (2006) 'Rethinking China's Competitiveness', *Far Eastern Economic Review* 169 (9): 16–20.

Ergazakis, K., Metaxiotis, K. and Psarras, J. (2004) 'Towards knowledge cities: Conceptual analysis and success stories', *Journal of Knowledge Management* 8 (5): 5–15.

Ergazakis K., Metaxiotis K. and Psarras J. (2006) 'An emerging pattern of successful knowledge cities' main features', in F. J. Carillo (ed.), *Knowledge Cities: Approaches, Experiences and Perspectives*. Burlington MA: Butterworth-Heinemann.

Ernst, D. (2006) 'The off-shoring of innovation', *Far Eastern Economic Review* 169 (4): 29–33.

Fan, Zhou (2006) 'Transcending the concept' (chaoyue gainian), ICCIE Magazine produced for the First Beijing International Cultural and Creative Industries Expo, Beijing, p. 2.

Farquhar, J. and Hevia, J. (1993) 'Culture and post-war American historiography of China', *Positions: East Asia Cultures Critiques* 1 (2): 486–525.

Feinstein, J. S. (2006) *The Nature of Creative Development*, Palo Alto: Stanford University Press.

Fishman, T. (2005) *China Inc. How the Rise of the Next Superpower Challenges America and the World*. New York: Scribner.

Fladmoe-Lindquist, K. (2000) 'International Franchising: a Network Approach to FDI', in Yair Aharoni and Lilach Nachum (eds), *Globalization of Services: Some Implications for Theory and Practice*. London: Routledge.

Flew, T. (2006) 'The new middle class meets the creative class: the Masters of Business Administration (MBA) and creative innovation in 21st century China', *International Journal of Cultural Studies* 9 (3): 419–429.

Florida, R. (1995) 'Towards the learning region', *Futures* 27 (5): 527–536.

Florida, R. (2002) *The Rise of the Creative Class and how it's Transforming Work, Leisure, Community and Everyday Life*. New York: Basic Books.

Frank, A. G. (1998) *Re-ORIENT: Global Economy in the Asian Age*. Berkeley: University of California Press.

Franke, S. and Verhagen, E. (eds) (2005) *Creativity and the City: How the Creative Economy is Changing the City*. Rotterdam: NAi Publishers.

Freeman, C. (1995) 'The National Innovations Systems in historical perspective', *Cambridge Journal of Economics* 19: 5–24.

Friedmann, J. (2002) *The Prospect of Cities*. Minneapolis: University of Minnesota Press.

Fu, Zhengqi (2002) 'The state, capital and restructuring in post-reform Shanghai', in John R. Logan (ed.), *The New Chinese City: Globalization and Market Reform*. London: Blackwell.

García Canclini, N. (1992) 'Cultural re-conversion' in George Yudice, Jean Framo and Juan Flores (eds), *On Edge: The Crisis of Contemporary Latin-American Culture*. Minneapolis: University of Minnesota Press.

Gardner, H. (1993) *Creating Minds: an Anatomy of Creativity Seen Through the Lives of Freud, Einstein, Picasso, Stravinsky, Eliot, Graham and Ghandi*. New York: Basic Books.

Gardner, H. (2004) *Changing Minds: The Art of Changing Our Own and Other People's Minds*. Boston: Harvard Business School Press.

Garnham, N. (2005) 'From cultural to creative industries: an analysis of the implications of the creative industries approach to arts and media policy making in the United Kingdom', *International Journal of Cultural Policy* 11 (1): 15–29.

Goldman, M. (1967) *Literary Dissent in Communist China*. Cambridge MA: Harvard University Press.

Goldsmith, B. and O'Regan, T. (2005) 'The policy environment of the contemporary film studio', in Greg Elmer and Mike Gasher (eds), *Contracting Out Hollywood: Runaway Productions and Foreign Location Shooting*. Lanham: Rowman and Littlefield.

Gong Yunbiao (2005) China's Ancient Arts Market (woguo gudai yishu shichang) http://www.todaygallery.com/Forum/ForumArticle.aspx?ForumID=63&ChannelId

Gordon, C. (1991) 'Government rationality: an introduction', in G. Burchell, C. Gordon and P. Miller, *The Foucault Effect: Studies in Governmentality*. London: Harvester Wheatsheaf.

Guinet, J. (2002) 'The knowledge-based economy: new trends and policy challenges', in B. Grewal, Lan Xue, P. Sheehan and F. Sun (eds), (2002) *China's Future in the Knowledge Economy: Engaging the New World*. Melbourne: Victoria University and Tsinghua University Press.

Guo Shangxin and Sheng Xingqing (1993) *A History of Chinese Culture*. Kaifeng: Henan University Publishing.

Guthrie, D. (1999) *Dragon in a Three-Piece Suit: the Emergence of Capitalism in China*. Princeton: Princeton University Press.

Hagel, J. III. and Brown J. S. (2006) 'Creation nets, harnessing the potential of open innovation', Working Paper April 2006 available at http://www.edgeperspectives.com

Hall, P. (1999) *Cities in Civilization: Culture, Innovation and the Urban Order*. London: Phoenix Giant.

Hansen, V. (2000) *The Open Empire: a History of China to 1600*. New York: Norton.

Hartley, J. (ed.) (2005) *The Creative Industries Reader*. London: Blackwell.

Havens, T. R. H. (1970) *Nishi Amane and Modern Japanese Thought*. Princeton: Princeton University Press.

He, Chuanqi (2004) 'Culture industry and modernisation in China', *The Second International Forum on China Cultural Industries Anthology*. Beijing: People's Daily Press.

He, Wenchao (2004) '718 gongchang: 798 yishu: yifen shehui shiyan de baogao' (718 factory, 798 art: a report on a social experiment), in Huang Rui (ed.), *Beijing 798: Reflections on Art, Architecture and Society in China* (Chinese language section).

Heilbroner, R. (1996) *Teachings from the Worldly Philosophy*. New York: W.W. Norton and Co.

Heise, U. K. (2002) 'Unnatural ecologies: the metaphor of the environment in media theory', *Configurations* 10 (1): 149–168.

Helm, L. (2001) 'Social communications innovation and destruction in Japan', in Lee McKnight, Paul M. Vaaler and Raul Katz (eds), *Creative Destruction: Business Survival Strategies in the Global Economy*. Cambridge MA: MIT Press.

Hesmondhalgh, D. (2007) *The Cultural Industries*. 2nd edn. London, Thousand Oaks and New Delhi: SAGE.

Higgs, P., Cunningham, S. and Pagan, J. (2007) *Australia's Creative Economy: Basic Evidence on Size, Growth, Income and Employment*. Brisbane: ARC Centre of Excellence for Creative Industries and Innovation. Available online at http://eprints.qut.edu.au/archive/000XXXX/

HKCI (2004) A Study on the Hong Kong Creativity Index, Interim Report. Centre for Cultural Policy Research. University of Hong Kong: The Hong Kong SAR Region Government.

Hobson, J. M. (2004) *The Eastern Origins of Western Civilisation*. Cambridge: Cambridge University Press.

Hodgson, G. (1999) *Economics and Utopia: Why the Learning Economy is not the End of History*. London: Routledge.

Holm, D. (1991) *Art and Ideology in Revolutionary China*. Oxford: Clarendon Press.

Hoskins, C., McFayden, S., Finn, A., Zhou Xiaojuan and Mitchell, D. (2003) 'International Joint Ventures for Television and Film Production: The Role of Cultural Distance and

Management Culture, in Ilan Alon (ed.), *Chinese Culture, Organizational Behavior, and International Business Management*. Westport, CT: Praeger.

Howkins, J. (2001) *The Creative Economy: How People Make Money from Ideas*. London: The Penguin Group.

Hu Anguang (2002) 'Knowledge and development: the new catch-up strategy', in B. Grewal, Lan Xue, P. Sheehan and F. Sun (eds), *China's Future in the Knowledge Economy: Engaging the New World*. Melbourne: Victoria University and Tsinghua University Press.

Hu Shuqing and Zhang Pinxing (eds) (1991) *Zhongguo wenhua shi (The History of Chinese Culture)*. Beijing: Zhongguo guangbo dianshi chubanshe.

Hui, D. (2006) 'From cultural to creative industries: Strategies for Chaoyang District, Beijing', *International Journal of Cultural Studies* 9 (3): 317–333.

ICCIE (2006) 'What are the creative industries', Jingbao Chupin, Magazine of the First Beijing International Cultural and Creative Industries Expo.

Jin, Liqun (2002) 'China: one year into the WTO process', address to the World Bank by China's Vice-minister Finance, 22 October 2002.

Jones, E. L. (2005) *Cultures Merging: A Historical and Economic Critique of Culture*. Princeton: Princeton University Press.

Kanamori, Toshiki and Zhao Zhijun (2004) *Private Sector Development in the People's Republic of China*, Asian Development Bank Institute, September 2004.

Ke, Huixin. (2003) 'China', in Chin Saik Yoon (ed.), *Digital Review of Asia Pacific*. Penang: Southbound Press.

Keane, M. (2004) 'Brave New World: Understanding China's Creative Vision', *International Journal of Cultural Policy* 10 (3): 265–279.

Keane, M. and Donald, S. H. (2002) 'Responses to crisis: convergence, content industries and media governance', in S. Donald, M. Keane, and Yin Hong, *Media in China: Consumption, Content, and Crisis*. London: RoutledgeCurzon.

Keane, M. and Spurgeon, C. (2005) 'Advertising Industry and culture in post-WTO China' *Media International Australia* 111: 104–117.

Keane, M., Fung, A. and Moran, A. (2007) *New Television, Globalisation and the East Asian Cultural Imagination*. Hong Kong: Hong Kong University Press.

Kelly, D. and He Baogang (1992) 'Emergent civil society and the intellectuals in China', in R. F. Miller (ed.), *The Development of Civil Society in Communist Systems*. Sydney: Allen and Unwin.

Kenney, M. (ed.) (2000) *Understanding Silicon Valley: The Anatomy of an Entrepreneurial Region*. Palo Alto: Stanford University Press.

Kong, L. (2005) 'The sociality of cultural industries: Hong Kong's cultural policy and film industry', *International Journal of Cultural Policy* 11 (1): 61–76.

Kong, L., Gibson, C., Khoo, L-M. and Semple, A-L. (2006) 'Knowledges of the creative economy: towards a relational geography of diffusion and adaptation in Asia', *Asia Pacific Viewpoint* 47 (2): 173–194.

Kong, Shuyu (2005) *Consuming Literature: Best Sellers and the Commercialization of Literary Production in Contemporary China*. Palo Alto: Stanford University Press.

Kraus, R. (2004) *The Party and the Arty: the New Politics of Culture*. Lanham, Boulder: Rowman and Littlefield.

Kynge, J. (2006) *China Shakes the World: the Rise of a Hungry Nation*. London: Weidenfeld and Nicolson.

Landes, D. (2006) 'Why Europe and the West? Why not China', *Journal of Economic Perspectives* 20 (2): 3–22.

Landry, C. (2000) *The Creative City: a Toolkit for Urban Innovators*. London: Earthscan Publications.

Landry, C. (2006) *The Art of City Making*. Sterling VA: Earthscan.

Landry, C. and Bianchini, F. (1995) *The Creative City*. London: Demos.

Leadbeater, C. and Wilsdon, J. (2007) *The Atlas of Ideas: How Asian Innovation Can Benefit Us All*. London: Demos.

Lechner, F. J. and Boli, J. (2005) *World Culture: Origins and Consequence*. London: Blackwell.

Lee, Dong-Hoo (2008) 'From the Margins to the Middle Kingdom: Korean TV Drama's Role in Linking Local and Transnational Production', in Ying Zhu, Michael Keane and Ruoyun Bai (eds), *TV drama in China: Unfolding Narratives of Tradition, Political Transformation and Cosmopolitan Identity*. Hong Kong: Hong Kong University Press (in press).

Lee, Leo Ou-fan and Nathan, A. (1985) 'The beginnings of mass culture: journalism and fiction in the late Ch'ing and beyond', in D. Johnson, A. Nathan and E. Rawski (eds), *Popular Culture in Late Imperial China*. Berkeley: University of California Press.

Li, Jianjun (1995) 'Zhongguo wentan de shichang qushi' (The market trend of China's literary world), *Xinxi Ribao* (*Information Daily*), 8 January.

Li, Lanqing (2004) *Education for 1.3 Billion*. Beijing: Foreign Language Teaching and Research, Pearson Education.

Li, Wuwei (2006) *Chuangyi chanye daolun* (*Introduction to Creative Industries*). Shanghai: Xuelin Publishing.

Li, Zhengfeng, Zeng Guoping, and Zhang Jingjing (2002) 'Innovation systems in China 1978 to 1998', in B. Grewal, Lan Xue, P. Sheehan and F. Sun (eds), *China's Future in the Knowledge Economy: Engaging the New World*. Melbourne: Victoria University and Tsinghua University Press.

Li, Zonggui (1988) *Zhongguo wenhua gailun* (*Introduction to Chinese Culture*). Guangzhou: Zhongshan daxue chubanshe.

Liao, Han-teng (2006) 'Towards creative datong: an alternative notion of creative industries for China', *International Journal of Cultural Studies* 9 (3): 395–406.

Lin, Mu (2004) 'Changes and consistency: China's media market after WTO entry', *Journal of Media Economics* 17 (3): 177–192.

Liu, Kang (1992) 'Subjectivity, Marxism and cultural theory in China', *Social Text* 31/32: 114–139.

Liu, L. H. (1995) *Literature, National Culture and Translated Modernity: China 1900–1937*, Palo Alto: Stanford University Press.

Liu, L. H. (2004) *The Clash of Empires: The Invention of China in Modern World Making*. Cambridge, MA: Harvard University Press.

Liu, Shifa (2004a) 'Implementing the creative century plan and promoting the creative China campaign', *The Second International Forum on China Cultural Industries Anthology*, Beijing: People's Daily Press.

Liu, Shifa (2004b) 'Bring about a creative century: take action to develop a Creative China', *China Culature Market* (*Zhongguo: wenhua sichang wang*) April 2004. http://www.ccm.gov.cn/netCultureChannel/main/lt-cyzg.html

Liu, Xielin and White, S. (2001) 'Comparing innovation systems: a framework and application to China's transitional context', *Research Policy* 30: 1091–1114.

Lu, Jin (1995) 'Wang Shuo hai "huo"' (Wang Shuo still 'hot'), *Tianjin ribao*, 11 March 1995.

Lundvall, B. (1992) *National Systems of Innovation: Towards a Theory of Innovation and Interactive Learning*. New York: Pinter Publishers.

Luo Liyuan and Zhao Mulan (2003) 'Knowledge industries in Beijing', in Bhajan Grewal, Lan Xue, Peter Sheehan and Fiona Sun (eds), *China's Future in the Knowledge Economy: Engaging the New World*. Melbourne: Victoria University and Tsinghua University Press.

McClatchie, C. (1973) *Classic of Change*. Taipei: Ch'eng Wen Publishing.

McDougall, B. S. and Louie, K. (1997) *The Literature of China in the Twentieth Century*. Gosford: Bushbooks.

McGregor, J. (2005) *One Billion Customers: Lessons Learnt from the Front Lines of Doing Business in China*. New York: The Free Press.

Malmberg, A. and Power, D. (2005) '(How) do (firms in) clusters create knowledge?', *Industry and Innovation* 12 (4): 409–431.

Mao, Zedong (1971) *Selected Readings from the Works of Mao Tse-tung*. Beijing: Foreign Languages Press.

Mao, Zedong (1977) *Selected Works of Mao Tse-tung*. Beijing: Foreign Languages Press.

Mar, P. C. M. and Richter, F-J. (2003) *China: Enabling a New Era of Changes*. Singapore: John Wiley & Sons.

Marks, R. B (2002) *The Origins of the Modern World: A Global and Ecological Narrative*. Lanham: Rowman and Littlefield.

Marshall, A. (1920) *Principles of Economics*, 8th edn. London: Macmillan and Co.

Maslow, Abraham. H. (1943) 'A theory of human motivation', *Psychological Review* 50: 370–396. Available from http://psychclassics.yorku.ca/Maslow/motivation.htm

Meisner, M. (1982) *Marxism, Maoism and Utopianism*. Madison: University of Wisconsin Press.

Miao, Qihao and Chen Chao (2003) 'Renewing knowledge of culture and cultural industries in the 21st century', in Ye Quyuan, Wang Yongzhang, and Chen Xin (eds), *A Review of China's Cultural Industries*, Shanghai: Shanghai People's University Publishing.

Miller, T., Govil, N., McMurria, J. and Maxwell, R. (2001) *Global Hollywood*. British Film Institute, London.

Minford, J. and Cha, L. (1994) *The Deer and the Cauldron: The adventures of a Chinese Trickster*, reprinted from *East Asian History* 5, Canberra: ANU.

Mok, Kin Wai P. (2006) 'In search of the market in China: the regional dimension of Hong Kong's creative industries', *International Journal of Cultural Studies* 9 (3): 333–347.

Mokyr, J. (2002) *The Gifts of Athena: Historical Origins of the Knowledge Economy*. Princeton: Princeton University Press.

Montgomery, L. and Keane, M. (2006) 'Learning to love the market: copyright, culture and China', in Pradip Thomas and Jan Servaes (eds), *Intellectual property Rights and Communication in Asia*. Delhi: Sage.

Moorhouse, F. (1985) 'The cultural delegate', in *Room Service*. Sydney: Penguin Books.

Morton, W. S. and Lewis, C. M. (2004) *China: Its History and Culture*. Fourth Edition. New York: McGraw-Hill Inc.

Naim, M. (1999) 'Fads and Fashions in Economic Reforms: Washington Consensus or Washington Confusion?' Working Draft of a Paper Prepared for the IMF Conference on Second Generation Reforms, Washington DC: Moses Naim, 26 October 1999. Available at http://www.imf.org/external/pubs/ft/seminar/1999/reforms/Naim.HTM. (accessed 12 September 2005).

National Bureau of Statistics (2005) Available online at http://www.stats.gov.cn/english/statisticaldata

Naisbilt, J. (1982) *Megatrends: Ten New Directions Transforming our Lives*. New York: Warner Books.

Nelson, R. R. (ed.) (1993) *National Innovation Systems: a Comparative Analysis*, New York: Oxford University Press.

Nelson, R. R. (2005) *Technology, Institutions, and Economic Growth*. Cambridge MA: Harvard Univeristy Press.

Nolan, P. (2004) *China at the Crossroads*. Cambridge: Polity.

North, D. C. (1981) *Structure and Change in Economic History*. New York: W. W. Norton and Co.

Oakes, T. (2005) 'Land of living fossils: scaling cultural prestige in China's periphery', in Jing Wang (ed.), *Locating China: Space, Place and Popular Culture*. London: Routledge.

Oakley, K. (2004) 'Not so cool Britannia: The role of creative industries in economic development', *International Journal of Cultural Studies* 7 (1): 67–77.

O'Connor, J. (2005) 'Creative exports: taking cultural industries to St. Petersburg', *International Journal of Cultural Policy* 11 (1): 45–60.

OECD (1990) *The Measurement of Scientific and Technological Activities: the Oslo Manual*. Paris: OECD.

OECD (1996) *The Knowledge-Based Economy*. Paris: OECD.

OECD (1998) 'Content as a new growth industry', *Directorate for Science, Technology and Industry, Committee for Information, Computer and Technology Policy*. Paris: OECD.

Ohame, Kenichi (2005) *The Next Global Stage: Challenges and Opportunities in Our Borderless World*. New York: Wharton School Publishing.

O'Mara, M. (2005) *Cities of Knowledge: Cold War Science and the Search for the Next Silicon Valley*. Princeton NJ: Princeton University Press.

Ozawa, T. (2003) 'Towards a theory of hegemon-led macro-clustering', in H. Peter Gray (ed.), *Extending the Eclectic Paradigm in International Business*. Cheltenham UK: Edward Elgar Press.

Ozawa, T., Castello, S. and Phillips, R. J. (2001) 'The Internet Revolution, the "McLuhan Stage" of Catch-up, and Institutional Reforms in Asia, *Journal of Economic Issues* 2: 289–298.

Peck, J. (2005) 'Struggling with the Creative Class', *International Journal of Urban and Regional Research* 29 (4): 740–770.

Piore M.J. and Sabel C.F. (1984) *The Second Industrial Divide: Possibilities for Prosperity*. New York: Basic Books.

Plattner, S. (2006) 'SoHo', paper presented to the Cultural Spaces Conference, Beijing, 798 Precinct, 19–21 October 2006.

Porter, M. (1990) *The Competitive Advantage of Nations*. New York: Free Press.

Porter, M. (1998) 'Clusters and the New Economics of Competition', *Harvard Business Review* Nov/Dec: 77–90.

Potts, Jason (2006) 'Four models of the creative industries' ARC Centre of Excellence in Creative Industries and Innovation QUT Working Paper No. 5.

Pratt, A. C. (2000) 'New media, the new economy and new spaces', *Geoforum* 31 (4): 425–436.

Pusey, J. (1983) *China and Charles Darwin*. Cambridge MA: Harvard University Press.

Ramo, J. C. (2004) *The Beijing Consensus*, London: The Foreign Policy Centre.

Rifkin, J. (2000) *The Age of Access: How the Shift from Ownership to Access is Transforming Work*. London: Penguin.

Rose, F. (2004) 'Hello, Ningbo', *Wired*, Issue 12.04, April. Available at: www.wired.com/wired/archive/12.04/ningbo_pr.html (accessed 6 June 2004).

Rosen, D. H. (2003) 'How China is eating Mexico's lunch', *The International Economy*, Spring, 22–25.

Ross, A. (2005) *Fast Boat to China: Corporate Flight and the Consequence of Free Trade – Lessons from Shanghai*. New York: Pantheon.

Ross, A. (2006) 'Nice work if you can get it: the mercurial rise of creative industries policy', *Work Organisation, Labour and Globalisation* Winter (2007) 1 (1): 13–30.

Rossiter, N. (2006) *Organized Networks Media Theory, Creative Labour, New Institutions*. Amsterdam: NAi Publishers.

Rostow, W. (1960/1990) *The Stages of Economic Growth: a Non-Communist Manifesto*. Cambridge: Cambridge University Press.

Sassen, S. (1991) *The Global City: New York, London, Tokyo*. Princeton NJ: Princeton University Press.

Saxenian, A-L. (2006) *The New Argonauts: Regional Advantage in a Global Economy*. Cambridge MA: Harvard University Press.

Schell, O. (1995) *Mandate of Heaven: A New Generation of Entrepreneurs, Dissidents, Bohemians and Technocrats Lays Claim to China's Future*. New York: Simon & Schuster.

Schumpeter, J. A. (1961) *The Theory of Economic Development*, originally published in German, English translation. New York: Oxford University Press.

Schwartz, B. (1996) *China and Other Matters*. Cambridge MA: Harvard University Press.

SCIC (2006) *2006 Shanghai Creative Industries Development Report*. Shanghai: Shanghai Scientific and Technological Publishing House.

Scott, A. J. (1986) 'Industrial organization and location: division of labour, the firm and spatial process. *Economic Geography* 62: 215–231.

Scott, A. J. (1988) *Metropolis: From the Division of Labour to Urban Form*. Ann Arbour: University of California Press.

Scott, A. J. (2004) 'The other Hollywood: the organizational and geographical bases of television-program production', *Media Culture and Society* 26 (2): 183–205.

Scott, A. J. (2006) 'Entrepreneurship, innovation and industrial development: geography and the creative field revisited', *Small Business Economics* 26 (1): 1–24.

Scott, R. (2006) 'Some areas of trans-cultural exchange' in Catherine Maudsley (ed.), *Art and Imitation in China*. Hong Kong: The Oriental Ceramic Society of Hong Kong Limited.

Seldon, M. (1979) *The People's Republic of China*. New York: Monthly Review Press.

Seoul Digital Media City (n.d.) *Development Direction*. Available at http://dmc.seoul.go.kr/index.jsp

Shanghai Creative Industries Clustering Parks (2005) Shanghai Economic Commission: Shanghai.

Shenkar, O. (2005) *The Chinese Century: The Rising Chinese Economy and Its Impact on the Global Economy, the Balance of Power and Your Job*. New Jersey: Wharton School Publishing.

Shils, E. (1996) 'Reflections on civil society and civility in the Chinese tradition', in Tu Wei-Ming (ed.), *Confucian Traditions in East Asian Modernity: Moral Education and Economic Culture in Japan and the Four Mini-Dragons*. Cambridge MA: Harvard University Press.

Shim Doobo (2006) 'Hybridity and the rise of Korean popular culture in Asia', *Media Culture & Society* 28 (1): 25–44.

Skinner, W. G. (1964) 'Marketing and social structure in rural China: part 1', *Journal of Asian Studies* 24 (1): 3–43.

Sofield, T. and Li Feng Mei Sarah (1998) 'Tourist development and cultural policies in China' *Annals of Tourism Research* 25 (2): 362–392.

Spence, J. D. (1974) *Emperor of China: Self-Portrait of K'ang-hsi*. New York: Vintage/ Ebury, a Division of Random House Group.

Stevenson-Yang, A. and DeWoskin K. (2005) 'China destroys the IP Paradigm', *Far Eastern Economic Review* 168 (3): 9–18.

SMH (2005) (*Sydney Morning Herald*) Mobile subscribers top 334m in China. See http://www.smh.com.au/news/Breaking/Mobile-subscribers-top-334m-in-China/2005/ 01/14/1105582683824.html

Storper, M. (1997) *The Regional World: Territorial Development in a Global Economy*. New York and London: Guilford Press.

Storper, M. (2000) 'Globalization and knowledge flows: an industrial geographer's perspective', in John Dunning (ed.), *Regions, Globalization and the Knowledge-Based Economy*. Oxford: Oxford University Press.

Storper, M. and Christopherson, S. (1987) 'Flexible specialization and regional industrial agglomerations: the case of the US motion-picture industry', *Annals of the Association of American Geographers* 77: 260–282.

Studwell, J. (2002) *The China Dream: The Elusive Quest for the Greatest Untapped Market on Earth*. London: Profile Books.

Studwell, J. (2004) 'MNC profits: dream, dream, dream ...', *China Economic Quarterly* 8 (4): 20–27.

Stross, R. (1990) 'The return of advertising in China: a survey of the ideological reversal', *The China Quarterly* 123: 485–502.

Su, Shaozhi (1993) *Marxism and Reform in China*. Nottingham: Russell Press.

Su, Xiaokang (1991) 'Dangdai Zhongguo de wenhua jinzhang' (The tension of contemporary Chinese culture), in Chen Kuide (ed.), *Zhongguo dalu dangdai wenhua bianjian 1978–89* (*Contemporary cultural debates in Mainland China 1978–89*). Taibei: Guiguan tushu gufen youxian gongsi.

Sum, Ngai-Ling (2002) 'Globalization and Hong Kong's entrepreneurial city strategies: contested visions and the remaking of city governance in post-crisis Hong Kong', in John R. Logan (ed.), *The New Chinese City: Globalization and Market Reform*. London: Blackwell.

Sunchime Cartoon Group Publicity Materials, Beijing.

Tang Yuankai (2005) 'Mega bucks in movie sets', *Beijng Review* **48** (46): 17 November 2005. Available online at http://www.bjreview.com.cn/EN/En-2005/05-46-e/bus-2.htm

Tang, Xiaobing (1996) *Global Space and the Nationalist Discourse of Modernity*. Palo Alto: Stanford University Press.

Tatsuno, S. (1990) *Created In Japan: From Imitators to World-Class Innovators*. New York: Harper and Row.

Teng, Ssu-yü and Fairbank, J. K. (1979) *China's Response to the West: a Documentary Survey*. Cambridge MA: Harvard University Press.

Toffler, A. (1981) *The Third Wave*. Toronto and New York: Bantam Books.

Törnqvist, G. (1983) 'Creativity and te renewal of regional life', in A Buttimer (ed.), *Creativity and Context: A Seminal Report* (Lund Series in Geography B. Human Geography, no. 50: 91–112. Lund: Gleerup.

Tylor, E. B. (1874) *Primitive Culture: Researches into the Development of Mythology, Philosophy, Religion, Language, Art and Custom*. Boston: Estes and Lauriat.

UNESCO (2005) *International Flows of Selected Cultural Goods and Services, 1994–2003*. Montreal, Quebec: UNESCO Institute for Statistics.

Veblen, T. B. (1919) *The Place of Science in Modern Civilization and Other Essays*. New York: Heubsch. Reprinted 1990 with a new introduction by Warren J. Samuels. New Brunswick: Transaction.

Vries, P. (2003) *Via Peking back to Manchester: the Industrial Revolution and China*. The Netherlands: Leiden University, CNWS Publications.

Wade, R. (1990) *Governing the Market: Economic Theory and the Role of Government in East Asian Internationalization*. Princeton: Princeton University Press.

Wall, D. and Yin Xiangshuo (1997) 'Technology development and export performance: is China a frog or a goose?', in Charles Feinstein, Christopher Howe (eds), *Chinese Technology Transfer in the 1990's: Current Experience, Historical Problems, and International Perspectives*. Cheltenham: Edgar Elgar Press.

Wang, Fengzhen (1992) 'Marxist literary criticism in China', in C. Nelson and L. Grossberg (eds), *Marxism and the Interpretation of Culture*. Chicago: University of Illinois Press.

Wang, Gungwu (1991) *The Chineseness of China: Selected Essays*. Oxford: Oxford University Press.

Wang, Hui (1995a) 'The fate of "Mr. Science" in China: the concept of science and its application in modern Chinese thought', *Positions: East Asia Cultures Critiques* 3 (1): 1–68.

Wang, Jing (1996) *High Culture Fever: Politics, Aesthetics and Ideology in Deng's China*. Berkeley: University of California Press.

Wang, Jing (2004) 'The global reach of a new discourse: how far can "creative industries" travel?' *International Journal of Cultural Studies* 7 (1): 9–19.

Wang, Jing (2005) 'Introduction: the politics and production of scales in China: how does geography matter to studies of local popular culture?', in Jing Wang (ed.), *Locating China: Space, Place and Popular Culture*. London and New York: Routledge.

Wang, Jing (2008) *Brand New China: Advertising, Media and Commerical Culture*. Cambridge, MA: Haward University Press.

Wang, Shaoguang (1995b) 'The politics of private time', in D. Davis *et al.* (eds), *Urban Spaces in Contemporary China: the Potential for Autonomy and Community in Post-Mao China*. Cambridge MA: Wilson Press.

Wang, Shujen (2003) *Framing Piracy: Globalization and Film Distribution in Greater China*. Lanham: Rowman and Littlefield.

Wang, Zhongyao (2002) 'Some preliminary investigations of the cultural markets of the Southern Song', *Business Economics and Management* (*shangye jingji and guanli*) 12: 53–56.

Watson, W. (1973) *The Genius of China*. London: Times Newspapers, Westersham Press Ltd.

Whitfield, S. (1999) *Life along the Silk Road*. London: John Murray Publishers.

Winseck, D. (2002) 'The WTO, emerging policy regimes, and the political economy of transnational communication', in M. Raboy (ed.), *Global Media Policy in the New Millennium*. Bedfordshire: University of Luton Press.

Woodside, A. (2006) *Lost Modernities: China, Vietnam, Korea and the Hazards of World History*. Cambridge MA: Harvard University Press.

World Bank (1993) *The East Asian Miracle: Economic Growth and Public Policy*. New York: Oxford University Press.

Wu, Qidi (2006) 'Creative industries and innovation in China', keynote speech at the International Creative Industries and Innovation Conference, Beijing, 5–7 July 2005, reprinted in *The International Journal of Cultural Studies* 9 (3): 263–266.

Wu, Weiping (2005) 'Dynamic cities and creative clusters', *World Bank Policy Research Working Paper 3509*, February 2005. Available online at http://econ.worldbank.org

Wu Xiaobo (2004) Interview with Michael Keane and Christina Spurgeon, World Trade Centre Hotel, Chaoyang District, 15 September 2004.

Xiong Zhongwu (ed.) (1992) *Dangdai Zhongguo liuxing yucidian* (*Contemporary Dictionary of Popular Words and Phrases*), Jilin: Jilin wenshi chubanshe.

Xu, Fangqi and Fangyi Xu (1997) 'Letter from China: a survey of creativity research', *Creativity and Innovation Management* 6 (4): 249–253.

Yang, Mayfair Mei-Hui (1996) *Gifts, Favors and Banquets: The Art of Social Relationships in China.* New York: Cornell University Press.

Ye Shuxian (ed.) (1987) *Shenhua yuanxing piping* (*Myth-archtype criticism*). Xian: Shanxi shifan daxue chubanshe.

2004 Yearbook of China's Publishing Industry (2004) See http://www1.cei.gov.cn/ce/doc/cenzq/200504151806.htm

Yi, Jixiong (2000) *Chuangxin lun* (*Innovation Theory*). Hefei: Anhui Arts Publishing.

Yúdice, G. (2003) *The Expediency of Culture: Uses of Culture in the Global Era.* Durham and London: Duke University Press.

Yue, A. (2006) 'The regional culture of new Asia: cultural governance and creative industries in Singapore', *International Journal of Cultural Policy* 12 (1): 17–33.

Yusuf, S. (2003) *Innovative East Asia: The Future of Growth.* New York: World Bank and Oxford University Press.

Zha, Jianying (1995) *China Pop: How Soap Operas, Tabloids, and Bestsellers are Transforming a Culture.* New York: The New Press.

Zhang Huaying (2005) 'Some thoughts on ancientg stringed instrument music' (guanyu guqin yinyue de sikao). See http://www.wenhuacn.com/article.asp?classid=77&articleid=3248

Zhang Xiaoming (1996) 'A summary of the forum on "A market economy and moral construction"', *Zhexue dongtai* (*Philosophical Trends*), translated by Fang Yinong, in *Social Sciences in China*, Winter: 93–97.

Zhang Xiaoming (2006) 'From institutions to industries: reform in cultural institutions in China, *International Journal of Cultural Studies* 9 (6): 297–306.

Zhang Xiaoming, Hu Hulin and Zhang Jiangang (2002) 'Embracing a new period of development of China's Cultural Industry', (yingjie Zhongguo wenhua chanye fazhande xin shidai), in Zhang Xiaming Hu Huilin and Zhang Jiangang (eds), *The Blue Book of China's Culture 2001–2002.* Beijing: Social Sciences Documentation Pulishing.

Zhang Xiaoming, Hu Huilin and Zhang Jiangang (2004) 'Only thorough reform can give fresh impetus to the rapid development of China's cultural industry', *The Blue Book of China's Culture 2004.* Beijing: Social Sciences Documentation Publishing.

Zhang, Yonghua (2006) 'China's efforts for international cooperation in copyright protection', in Pradip Ninan Thomas and Jan Servaes (eds), *Intellectual Property Rights and Communication in Asia: Conflicting Traditions.* New Delhi: Sage.

Zhao Yuzhong (2003) *The Concept of the Cultural Industry* (*wenhua shichang gailun*). Beijing: Zhongguo xiandai jingji chubanshe.

Zhong Yong and Qianting Wang (2006) 'Cannibalising the Chinese "Watching Mass": Documenting and analysing the evolution of Chinese terms of address from the "watching mass" to "snack food"', *Journal of International Communication* 12 (1): 23–36.

Zhou, Nan and Belk, R. (2004) 'Chinese Consumer Readings of Global and Local Advertising Appeals', *Journal of Advertising* 33 (3): 63–77.

Zhou, Yanping (2005) 'An analysis of the Sanchen Cartoon Company', in Zhang Xiaoming, Hu Huilin and Zhang Jiangang (eds), *The Blue Book of China's Culture 2005*. Beijing: Social Sciences Documentation Publishing.

Zhou Ziyan and Jiang Jiping (2006) *Chuangyi jingji xinlun* (*The New Theory of the Creative Economy: Chinese Blue Sea*). Beijing: New Star Press.

Zhu, Ying, Michael Keane and Ruoyun Bai (2008) *TV Drama in China: Unfolding Narratives of Tradition, Political Transformaion and Cosmopolitan Identity*. Hong Kong: HKU Press (in press).

Zukin, S. (1981) *Loft Living: Culture and Capital in Urban Change*. Baltimore: Johns Hopkins University Press (republished in paperback in 1989 by the Rutgers University Press).

Zukin, S. (1995) *The Culture of Cities*. Cambridge MA: Blackwell.

Index